The House of Representatives and Senate Explained

Congressional Procedure

A Practical Guide to the Legislative Process in the U.S. Congress

Richard A. Arenberg

Foreword by Alan S. Frumin

For more than 40 years, TheCapitol.Net and its predecessor, Congressional Quarterly Executive Conferences, have been training professionals from government, military, business, and NGOs on the dynamics and operations of the legislative and executive branches and how to work with them.

Our training and publications include congressional operations, legislative and budget process, communication and advocacy, media and public relations, testifying before Congress, research skills, legislative drafting, critical thinking and writing, and more.

Our publications and courses, written and taught by current Washington insiders who are all independent subject matter experts, show how Washington works.™ Our products and services can be found on our web site at <*www.TheCapitol.Net*>.

TheCapitol.Net is a nonpartisan firm.

Additional copies of *Congressional Procedure* can be ordered online: <*TCNBooks.com*>.

Design and production by Zaccarine Design, Inc., Chicago, IL, *zacdesign@mac.com*.
Ebook conversion by Paula Reichwald <*igossi.com*>.
Index by Enid L. Zafran <*IndexingPartners.com*>.

Library of Congress Control Number: 2018903177

Softcover	Hardcover	eBook Edition	FastSpring Edition
ISBN 10: 1587332825	ISBN 10: 158733299X	ISBN 10: 1587332833	ISBN 10: 1587332841
ISBN 13: 978-1-58733-282-1	ISBN 13: 978-1-58733-299-9	ISBN 13: 978-1-58733-283-8	ISBN 13: 978-1-58733-284-5

Dedication

For the love of my life, my wife of twenty years,
Linda (Baron) Arenberg.
Our first date was fifty-four years ago
and she's even more beautiful and loving today.

Table of Contents

Chapter 6

Resolving Differences
between the House and Senate 99

Chapter 7

The Congressional Budget
and Other Special Cases 113

Chapter 8
Additional Congressional
Responsibilities and Procedures

Chapter 9
Conclusion

About the Author

Richard A. Arenberg is Clarence Adams and Rachel Adams Visiting Professor of the Practice of Political Science and a Senior Fellow in International and Public Affairs at Brown University. He previously taught at Northeastern University and Suffolk University. He worked for Sens. Paul Tsongas (D-MA), Carl Levin (D-MI), and Majority Leader George Mitchell (D-ME) for thirty-four years. He served on the Senate Iran-Contra Committee in 1987.

Arenberg is co-author of the award-winning *Defending the Filibuster: Soul of the Senate,* named "Book of the Year in Political Science" by *Foreword Reviews* in 2012. A second edition was published in 2014. The U.S. Senate Historical Office published *Richard A. Arenberg: Oral History Interviews* in 2011.

He serves on the Board of Directors of Social Security Works and the Social Security Education Fund. He is an affiliate at the Taubman Center for American Politics & Policy. His work has appeared in *The New York Times*, *The Washington Post*, *The Providence Journal*, *Politico*, and *The Boston Globe*. He is a contributor at *Newsmax* and *The Hill*. Arenberg holds bachelor's and master's degrees from Boston University.

Acknowledgments

I worked in the Congress, mostly the Senate, for thirty-four years for three prominent members of the Senate of our era, George Mitchell, Carl Levin, and Paul Tsongas. I cannot find words adequate to express what I owe these three men. Each in his different way—and their styles in the Senate were different—taught me numerous life lessons.

From Paul Tsongas, I learned it's OK to be absolutely candid, to say what's on your mind. In the end, truth could still turn out to be good politics and people respect you for it.

From George Mitchell, I learned to take a step back from hard decisions to really weigh the arguments objectively and honestly. Hardest for me was learning to know when it's the right time to make a decision—when the issue has ripened.

And, from Carl Levin, I learned it is possible to be the toughest bulldog around, demanding answers to important questions, accountability, and the highest ethical standards, while still being a warm, loving human being.

I came to Washington with Paul Tsongas, filled with awe at the Congress; I never lost that sense of awe. On the very first day that we arrived in his new House office in 1975, then-Congressman Tsongas called me into his office. When the door was closed behind me, he impishly grinned, shrugged his shoulders, and asked, "Isn't this fun?" For the next thirty-four years, I never stopped asking myself Tsongas's question and every day the answer was, "Yes, this is!"

Each day as I arrived, I looked up at the great dome of the Capitol and was inspired by that symbol. The first glimpse of that dome, especially lighted at night, as you proceed up Pennsylvania Avenue toward the West Front, where every president from Reagan to Trump has taken the oath of office, never fails to stir a sense of patriotism and the desire to be a part of what goes on there. In *Mr. Smith Goes to Washington*, Jimmy Stewart's character, a newly appointed senator, innocent, idealistic, and naïve, but infused with a sense of patriotism, catches his first glimpse of the Capitol dome and cries out, "Look! Look! There it is!"

In the words of Winston Churchill, "We shape our buildings, thereafter they shape us." It was ultimately the people I met and worked with during my years on Capitol Hill that fuel my continuing faith in the resiliency of the Congress as the protector of our freedoms and the rule of law in the face of all evidence to the contrary.

I owe a debt of gratitude to Brown University, which has given me a better academic landing place than I could have hoped for. In my last years on the Senate staff, I thought often about what "life after the Senate" would be like for me.

"What," I thought, "does one do with decades of experience that is applicable in so few places?" Many of my colleagues "went downtown," meaning they became lobbyists. That wasn't for me. That is not why I came to Washington. I am a "true believer"; I came to get things done.

I began thinking if only some university would allow me to share my experience and insight with a classroom full of bright, engaged students wanting to do something in the world of public policy and politics, it would suit me perfectly. I had no idea if anyone would.

Then Professor Marion Orr, then the Director of the Taubman Center at Brown University, called. It was Thanksgiving of 2008. He asked, "Can you be here to teach a course in January?" I was not really yet ready to retire from the Senate. After all, Barack Obama had just been elected, and the Democrats in the Senate were about to have a filibuster-proof majority, something I had never experienced. But, Brown is Brown. I knew its reputation and I thought, "This is the perfect place for me."

When I was first making the decision to leave Washington, my academic friends said, "You don't really want to do this. You are used to being a 'big shot' on Capitol Hill. In academia, as an 'adjunct,' no one will respect you."

Nothing could turn out to be farther from the truth. I have benefited from the encouragement and wise advice of many colleagues at Brown. Never have I felt disrespected; to the contrary, I have seen that the practical experience I brought with me is valued by my colleagues and students.

I want to thank Marion Orr, who I have already mentioned, and Jim Morone, who first brought me into the Political Science Department, and the many Brown colleagues who have encouraged and supported me. However, I owe particular thanks to my friend, Political Science Department Chair Wendy Schiller, for her unfailing encouragement in my fledgling attempts to be an academic.

Since 2009, I have taught at Brown University in both the Political Science Department and at the Watson Institute for International and Public Affairs about the Congress, the presidency, campaigns and elections, political communication, and the political process. Here, too, I have found hope in the future of our democracy. I have interacted with many hundreds of bright and capable students, interested and engaged in public policy. It is often their enthusiasm for learning that drives me forward. A number are already working in positions on Capitol Hill or have sought elective office on their own. I am proud of this little "Arenberg caucus."

Being at Brown has given me the freedom to speak in my own voice. As a Senate staffer, one must always weigh the impact that one's own words might have on the senator for whom you work. Whatever you do, it is seen as a reflection on the senator. I miss the rough-and-tumble of Capitol Hill every single day, but I never regret the decision to come to Brown.

This book, like my first, *Defending the Filibuster: The Soul of the Senate*, that I wrote with former Senate parliamentarian Bob Dove, is a product of that freedom.

I am indebted to my support group of former "hill rats" who together cumulatively account for more than two centuries of congressional experience. They shared their special expertise to straighten me out when my writing veered off course or got it wrong.

This book could not have been written without the sage advice of the Senate Parliamentarian Emeritus, Alan Frumin. Alan and I served together in the Senate in very different capacities for more than three decades. His office as parliamentarian was always open to me for my eager questions about procedure and the rules of the Senate. As my long-time dear friend, he has graciously given of his time and expertise to scrub my books, many of my op-eds, and for a number of years has come to Providence to deliver guest lectures in my classes at Brown. On a number of occasions, we have shared the stage or appeared together on television programs and lectures. I am deeply grateful for his friendship and his willingness to improve my work writing about the Congress. No one knows the rules and precedents of the Senate better than Alan Frumin.

Donald Ritchie, Historian Emeritus of the United States Senate, also read and commented on each chapter as it was written. He has been unfailingly supportive and helps to strengthen my confidence that I have a credible historical perspective of the Senate. Don is a gifted oral historian and spent three days some years ago interviewing me for the Senate Historical Office's Oral History collection, an experience I treasure.

Always, it is Kaye Meier on whom I rely for the first reading of each chapter. She is a valued friend and former colleague whose smart edits and reliably upbeat assessments propelled this book forward. Kaye served as legislative director to Senator Barbara Boxer (D-CA) and senior counsel to Senator Carl Levin (D-MI).

Alex Harman served as the Obama Administration White House Liaison of the Department of Homeland Security, chief counsel to Senator Mazie Hirono (D-HI), chief of staff to Congressman Steven Horsford (D-NV), and general counsel to Senator Mark Udall (D-CO) (he also worked for Senators Bayh (D-IN), Kennedy (D-MA), and Reid (D-NV)). Alex, a friend and kindred spirit, gave freely of his time and I am indebted to him for his perceptive comments.

Joe Bryan served as Deputy Assistant Secretary of the Navy and as professional staff for the Senate Armed Services Committee, the Senate Select Committee on Intelligence, the Senate Permanent Subcommittee on Investigations, and as a legislative assistant to both Senator Carl Levin (D-MI) and Congressman John Lewis (D-GA). I hired Joe for Senator Levin's staff and could not have made a better choice. A friend for many years now, Joe brought a wealth of experience and perspective to his edits and advice.

My friends Elise Bean and Linda Gustitus were both enormously helpful and made numerous suggestions that strengthened the sections on congressional oversight and investigations, a subject on which Elise and Linda are nationally known experts. Both Elise and Linda served as staff director of the Senate Permanent Subcommittee on Investigations (Linda also was previously staff director of two other subcommittees). Currently, Elise and Linda are co-directors of the Levin Center at Wayne Law focused on improving public policy by strengthening in-depth, bipartisan oversight of public and private sector activities by the Congress and other legislative bodies. It was Linda Gustitus who first suggested I write this book.

Mark Cruz, a former graduate student of mine at Brown University, who is chief of staff to Congressman Todd Rokita (R-IN), made a number of useful suggestions regarding descriptions of procedures on the floor of the House of Representatives.

This is a better book for generous efforts of all of these people.

However, this book would never have been written but for the fact that Chug Roberts of TheCapitol.Net reached out to me and encouraged me to write it. Chug and Karen Hormuth, executive director of TheCapitol.Net, have been a pleasure to work with and very patient when my estimates of how long the manuscript might take proved too ambitious.

I am proud to be published by TheCapitol.Net, which has produced a long list of excellent publications about Congress. TheCapitol.Net also does an unparalleled job helping to educate congressional staff, federal employees, state and local officials, foreign delegations, college students, and many others who work with or around the Congress and need to be better informed about how it operates.

I love the Congress. Much of my adult life was dedicated to working with senators whom I admired greatly. I hope this book will impart some of that admiration and affection—and concern—to the reader.

Finally, I am especially grateful for the love and support that I receive from my family, especially my children, Josh, Georgina, Meg, and Ned and grandsons, Ethan, Owen, and Noah. And most important is the endless strength I derive, and enthusiasm I receive from my wife of twenty years, but soulmate of more than fifty years, Linda, to whom I have dedicated this book.

Foreword

Alan S. Frumin

Parliamentarian Emeritus, U.S. Senate

The confidence of the American people in our political institutions has suffered greatly in recent years, in no case more so than the Congress. According to the Gallup Poll, approval of the job Congress is doing remained at 20 percent or below for most of 2017 and 2018. Increasingly, the Congress seems incapable of successfully addressing the nation's most pressing problems.

Perhaps even worse, there appears to be a retreat occurring from the profoundly important role the Constitution gives Congress as a check and a balance on the executive branch. It appears that Congress is failing just when it is needed most.

James Madison, writing in *The Federalist* No. 47, declared, "The accumulation of all powers, legislative, executive, and judiciary, in the same hands, whether of one, a few, or many, and whether hereditary, self-appointed, or elective, may justly be pronounced the very definition of tyranny."

The expectation of the founders was that the division of power among the branches of government would restrain such tyranny. In *The Federalist* No. 51, Madison famously observed, "If men were angels, no government would be necessary. If angels were to govern men, neither external nor internal controls on government would be necessary." He thought, if any president went too far in exercising presidential power, the Congress, separately elected, would rise to the occasion to balance the excess.

I served the Senate as parliamentarian for almost nineteen years and as an assistant parliamentarian for another sixteen years. As a creature of the Senate, I, for many years, had confidence not only in the Senate's rules and precedents—which reflect the essential norms and culture of that institution—but in the Congress as a whole. Madison also stated, "In Republics, the great danger is that the majority may not sufficiently respect the rights of the minority." The Senate throughout its history has uniquely followed procedures that protect the minority. In practice, this is made possible by a critical intentional omission from the Standing Rules—a rule permitting a simple majority to impose a limitation on debate. This creates the possibility of unlimited debate, commonly known as a filibuster, which permits the minority, on occasion, to frustrate the agenda of the majority.

This unique aspect of the Senate works if and only if those on both the majority and the minority side behave responsibly. The minority, given the privilege of filibustering, should not abuse that privilege because the majority has the power to limit or even eliminate the filibuster by establishing precedents to that effect. They don't have to amend the rules to do that. The majority has the power to squash the minority. The minority has been given the privilege over the years by the majority to engage in filibusters. The balance can only be protected if both sides act with restraint.

In the House of Representatives, it is the majority that is overwhelmingly empowered. The majority clearly holds the reins. But, even that body works most effectively if that majority, led by the Speaker, acts with a modicum of restraint.

The hallmark of restraint in Congress is a respect for the rules and precedents of each chamber. Respect for each institution's rules requires that members restrain from abusing those rules and precedents even if it is possible and advantageous for one party to do so.

Much of the difficult struggle to respect, honor, and protect these rules is an "insiders'" game. When such questions reach the general public, they are too often twisted and unrecognizable. Such is the case in the battle to jettison the filibuster as undemocratic or unconstitutional. It is neither. It is an essential check on the abuses of the majority, both within the chamber and in the federal government more generally. The complexities of congressional rules and precedents are not only opaque to most Americans, but, unfortunately, they are mysterious even to many who work daily with the Congress, including some of those elected to serve within the House and Senate themselves. It is an admirable public service to shed light on those rules and precedents— to emphasize how they reflect the norms and culture of the Congress, and to explain why they are important to our democratic system of government.

Many are the members of Congress and their staff whose daily work involves the intricacies of congressional procedure; few are those who truly understand those rules of the legislative game; and fewer still are the small handful who can make these rules come to life for everybody from the curious high school student to the most senior senator or representative.

Richard Arenberg stands out in this select group. His first book, *Defending the Filibuster: The Soul of the Senate*, was a masterful defense of those Senate rules, precedents, and traditions that have helped to make the Senate great.

In this book, *Congressional Procedure: A Practical Guide to the Legislative Process in the U.S. Congress*, Arenberg helps the reader better understand the sometimes arcane rules, precedents, and norms of the House and Senate, and in doing so he demonstrates his understanding of—and deep affection for—the Congress. He describes it with clear-eyed appreciation for its strengths, but with criticism for short-sighted partisan expediency and abuse of the rules.

Arenberg begins *Congressional Procedure* with the observation in his Preface that "The Founders had high hopes for Congress." He promises to unpack the complexities of what Woodrow Wilson called "the dance of legislation."

By the time one reaches the Conclusion in Chapter 9 of this book, Arenberg has not only delivered on that promise, but has expertly weighed in on the misuse of procedures, traditions, and precedents. He points to the increasing tendencies by both parties in the Congress to opt for short-term partisan gain, often causing the other party, feeling victimized, to retaliate with whatever procedural tool is at hand. He calls this the weaponization of procedure.

Arenberg ends his book by linking Congress's current failures back to the fundamentals of democracy. He argues, as I would, that "Our democratic process operates on the assumption that both parties will come to the table and negotiate in good faith. Congress must negotiate, moderate, and compromise. In other words, 'legislate.'"

The implications of the current excessive partisanship and resulting abandonment of what the late John McCain and others have termed "the regular order" has—in Arenberg's words—led to "an erosion of courtesy, comity, and deliberation." This has undermined not only the Congress's ability to legislate effectively, but its ability to serve as a check and balance in our system, even now when the circumstances in Washington call urgently for a principled, bipartisan, effective Congress.

A strong, independent Congress is critically important in our experiment in democracy. An informed citizenry is the root of a strong Congress. In this volume, Richard Arenberg conquers the admirable task of informing the citizens about their Congress, and the vital role that it plays in protecting the democracy we all cherish.

Preface

The founders had high hopes for Congress. They created the institution in Article I of the new Constitution in 1789. The first section of that first article establishes the Congress and confers sweeping legislative powers: "All legislative Powers herein granted shall be vested in a Congress of the United States, which shall consist of a Senate and House of Representatives." The powers of Congress are so extensively laid out that Article I takes up more space in the Constitution than Articles II through VII combined.

The founders set up the elaborate system of checks and balances to assure that no one branch of government could dominate, but most of the framers fully expected the legislative branch to play the lead role. James Madison in *The Federalist* No. 51 wrote, "In republican government, the legislative authority necessarily predominates."

Yet, throughout our history, the American people have been skeptical of Congress, and the legislative body has suffered in the eyes of the American people. In *Following the Equator* (1897), Mark Twain wrote, "It could probably be shown by facts and figures that there is no distinctly native American criminal class except Congress." Former Congressman Mo Udall (D-AZ) loved to tell the tale of a constituent who wrote to him, "Of all the rats and snakes elected to represent the people and carry out their wishes, you rank head and shoulders beneath the lowest."

Congressional approval ratings have been reliably low since the beginning of public opinion polling in the United States in the 1940s, dipping as low as 9 percent approval in November 2013. With the exception of the nation's reaction in the wake of the September 11 attacks when the approval of Congress doubled virtually overnight to 84 percent, Americans have held the institution of Congress in low regard. The Gallup Poll historical average is about 33 percent.

Former Senate Majority Leader George Mitchell (D-ME) said that "The attitude of the public toward elected officials in American democracy has always been one of skepticism ..."

Legislative bodies in democracies typically suffer the same fate. Sir A. J. Herbert, a member of the British Parliament and a humorist, wrote a wonderful book, *The Point of Parliament*, in 1946 as a child's guide to Parliament. Although he was discussing the British Parliament and not the American Congress and there is lightheartedness to his descriptions, Herbert sheds light on the unpopularity of legislative bodies: "... I remind you that we have been fighting for freedom, which includes free speech and free parliaments. So you would expect to hear from time to time, a kindly reference to our own free Parliament and its members. But no. ... [M]embers of Parliament are known as 'politicians' and politicians, with the possible exception of journalists, are the lowest form of serpent life." (Sound familiar?)

George Mitchell cautioned, "It is a mistake to think of politics as something separate and apart from the rest of society. Politics are subject to the same influences. ... These influences of modern life—technology communications and changing standards in public life and the media—have led to a decline in public trust and confidence that is felt by all of our major institutions. ... Congress has been a particular recipient of current negative attitudes because it is so prominent, public, and focused on by the media."

The mainstream media is attracted to the drama and personalities of the partisan warfare on Capitol Hill. Much less coverage is focused on the understanding of the nitty-gritty of how Congress actually works.

For most American citizens and immigrants, Congress is a black box. They can see much of what goes in, and what comes out, but the process in the box is opaque.

This book will attempt to open that black box and examine the machinery in a way that is accurate but accessible. It seeks to educate the layman and average voters, but also hopefully to contribute to a fuller understanding of congressional procedure by students in the classroom and those who deal directly with the legislative branch, and perhaps even some within it.

Woodrow Wilson called lawmaking "the dance of legislation." He added, "It is not surprising ... that the enacting, revising, tinkering, repealing of laws should engross the attention and engage the entire energy of such a body as the Congress."[1]

Even members themselves, who often fail to use their leverage and power, simply because they do not know the rules, may benefit. Former Congressman John Dingell (D-MI), who served in Congress longer than any member, fifty-nine years, said, "I'll let you write the substance ... you let me write the procedure, and I'll screw you every time."

Procedures matter. The protector of stability, comity, and fair play in the House and the Senate is procedure.

---

1. Ronald J. Pestritto, ed, *Woodrow Wilson: The Essential Political Writings* (Lanham, MD, Lexington Books, 2005), 159.

Chapter 1 examines the relationship between the U.S. Constitution and the House and Senate. It discusses constitutional provisions that directly affect Congress. It continues with an examination of the rulemaking process in each chamber. It examines the qualifications for members of Congress, and contrasts the constituencies that individual members of each body represent.

The makeup, roles, and leadership of the House and Senate are compared and contrasted. Congressional committees and their place and power in the House and Senate are explored.

Chapter 2 begins with a discussion of why members submit legislation, explains the forms of legislation, and lays out the steps involved in drafting legislation. Bills, joint resolutions, concurrent resolutions, and simple House and Senate resolutions and their purposes are separately described. This chapter explains the roles and effects of sponsorship and cosponsorship of legislation and what happens when legislation is submitted. Also addressed is how the respective chambers refer legislation to committees for consideration, and, finally, the peculiarities of Senate Rule XIV. An important section that will reverberate through much of the book is the analysis of "regular order" and how members in both chambers circumvent procedure. Chapter 2 ends with a flowchart of the legislative process.

In Chapter 3, the work of congressional committees is examined in greater detail. First, the types of committees and their structures are described, including the establishment of subcommittees and how they relate to the full committees, particularly on the flow of legislation. The chapter focuses on the power of the chairs of committees, the importance of seniority, term limits, and the roles of ranking members of committees. Chapter 3 also attempts to demystify hearings, markups, and the amendment procedure in committee. It traces the process of shaping legislation through these stages and the reporting of legislation to the House and Senate floors, including the filing of committee reports.

The next two chapters follow the course of legislation through the respective chambers. Chapter 4 addresses some of the unique characteristics of the House, including the central and crucial role played by the Rules Committee and the special rules it reports. The scheduling, consideration, amending, and passage of legislation through the House is described in detail.

Both in Chapter 4 and in Chapter 5, an effort is made to unpack some of the more arcane elements of House and Senate floor action.

Chapter 5 is dedicated to the handling of legislation on the Senate floor. The absence of a mechanism like the House Rules Committee and the individual leverage available to members of the Senate along with more flexible rules, makes the Senate a very different body than the House. Intended by the framers to balance the often faster-moving House, the Senate's rules and precedents help to make it frequently the slower and more deliberative body. In Chapter 5, appropriate attention is paid to unique Senate characteristics like the filibuster, the nuclear option, holds, and the filling of the amendment tree.

When the House and Senate pass differing versions of legislation, the differences in legislative language must be resolved and the identical text passed by both chambers before it can be presented to the president for signature. Chapter 6 explains the various procedures for accomplishing this objective. At times, amendments will be traded back and forth between the chambers before a consensus is reached. That process, sometimes described as "ping-ponging," is detailed in this chapter.

For many years, the most common way of resolving differences in legislation between the Senate and the House was the formation of conference committees. The rules governing conferences are few and much can occur once legislation is in conference. Conference committees have become a less-used procedure in recent years. House and Senate leaders are more likely to rely upon amendments between the chambers or informal negotiations. The steps followed to convene a conference committee and alternative means of resolving differences between the chambers are closely examined in Chapter 6.

The budget process is addressed in Chapter 7. The 1974 Budget and Impoundment Control Act and the key role it has played since its adoption is explored. Especially noteworthy is the use of the optional budget reconciliation process, which has mushroomed beyond its original intent and become a major source of circumvention of the normal Senate rules. Also explained is the somewhat complex but crucial Byrd Rule, which prohibits the use of reconciliation for nonbudgetary provisions.

The appropriations and authorization procedures are also discussed in Chapter 7. Chapter 7 also explores other "expedited procedures" that limit debate in the Senate and therefore avoid the effect of the filibuster. A prime example is the War Powers Resolution.

Chapter 8 concludes the detail and analysis of congressional procedure with a number of processes that are not strictly legislative. Two categories are included. First, there are a number of constitutional responsibilities given to Congress that are described, including the Senate's obligation to provide advice and consent to the president on nominations, executive and judicial, and on ratification of treaties. Also, the procedures for amending the Constitution itself are illuminated. An old and interesting struggle between the president and the Congress that recently reached the Supreme Court centers on recess appointments authorized by the Constitution. This case is described and its significance analyzed.

Congress's oversight and investigatory powers are not explicitly listed in the Constitution, but they are implied by other congressional powers and are as old as Congress itself. Related to these powers are the legislative vetoes included in some legislation. These subjects are discussed in Chapter 8.

The role Congress plays in the counting of Electoral College ballots and the potential election of the president and vice president by Congress are explored. Congress has, under the Constitution, a critical role to play in establishing presidential succession and in the creation and operation of the federal courts. Also discussed are procedures under Article I, Section 5, for expelling a member of the House or Senate or denying a member-elect a seat in either body.

Finally, two Constitutional powers involve the impeachment and trial by the Congress of judges and executive branch officials, including the president. These powers and the importance of provisions in the Twenty-fifth Amendment involving temporary or permanent removal of the president from office are explained in Chapter 8.

The second category covered in Chapter 8 includes explanations of congressional procedures in the rules, including the important differences between recessing and adjourning of the Congress, how Senate morning business and House special orders are routinely used, and the implications of appeals of rulings of the chair.

The conclusion, Chapter 9, describes the way in which many of the procedures explained in this book are increasingly being used, and some would say abused, in both the House and the Senate.

Nineteenth century Prussian Prime Minister, Otto von Bismarck, famously warned, "If you like laws and sausages, you should never watch either one being made." Yet, democracy demands the constant vigilance of the citizenry. We must not turn away.

At the same time, in many ways, the high hopes with which the framers infused the Congress have been realized. Bismarck also said that "politics is the art of the possible." We are familiar with the many ways in which Congress has been dysfunctional, but in fundamental ways the Congress has proved both stable and resilient. We should remember that the central hopes around which the Constitution was built include the protection of liberty and the rule of law.

Senator George Mitchell (D-ME) points out that "the men who wrote the American Constitution had as their overriding objective the prevention of tyranny in America. They had lived under a British king; they did not want ever to have to live under an American king. They placed the highest value on individual liberty. In retrospect we can see they were brilliantly successful. As of 2018, we have had forty-five presidents (counting Grover Cleveland twice) and no kings. Americans enjoy a combination of personal freedom and shared material prosperity that is without parallel in the world, and arguably without parallel in human history. Therefore, who is to say that the institutions created by the Constitution don't work?"[2]

More than 200 years into the experiment, Congress continues to succeed at that.

A glossary of terms relating to Congress, its procedures, and related institutions follows the concluding chapter.

⟫⟫ *See also* related CRS Reports and links on **TCNCPAM.com**.

---

2. "Interview with Senator George Mitchell." Maine Policy Review 7.1 (1998): 22–29, https://digitalcommons.library.umaine.edu/mpr/vol7/iss1/3/.

Congressional Procedure

A Practical Guide to the Legislative Process in the U.S. Congress

Chapter 1
Congress and the Constitution

A. Introduction

The Constitutional Convention called together in Philadelphia in 1787 was merely expected to amend the Articles of Confederation to repair its defects arising principally from the weakness of the central government that it created. Among its inadequate provisions was the Congress it created, a weak and incompetent body beholden to the states for many of the essential functions of national government. But the Convention undertook to create a new Constitution.

The founders created a new Congress in the first Article of the Constitution. The bicameral institution they designed includes the House of Representatives and the Senate. Article I, Section 1 declares, "All legislative powers herein granted shall be vested in a Congress of the United States, which shall consist of a Senate and House of Representatives."

The founders had high hopes for Congress. They understood that a strong legislature is fundamental to a healthy democracy. At the same time, they feared a central government that was too powerful. To restrain that power they created a Constitution that divides power among the branches of the federal government (separation of powers) and between the federal government and the states (federalism).

They set up an elaborate system of checks and balances among the three branches of the federal government (executive, legislative, and judicial) to assure that no one co-equal branch could dominate.

Of course, the way Congress is organized and its procedures play a huge part in public-policy decisions and outcomes. The division of Congress into two chambers with differing structures was intended to create bodies with different roles. James Madison explained in *The Federalist* No. 51 that the legislature was itself divided, "into different branches; and to render them, by different modes of election and different principles of action, as little connected with each other as the nature of their common functions and their common dependence on the society will admit."

The design purposely created one chamber, the House, to be closer and more immediately responsive to the electorate, and another chamber, the Senate, to be more insulated from the winds of popular opinion. In the famous, probably apocryphal, story often used to illuminate this difference, George Washington explained the need for a Senate to Thomas Jefferson. Jefferson, who was in France during the deliberations of the Constitutional Convention, asked why a second body, an "upper body," was even necessary. Washington is said to have compared the Senate to a saucer, used in the polite society of the day to sip from in order to cool the hot tea poured from the cup.

The House of Representatives, the dispenser of "hot tea," is sometimes referred to as "the People's House." Given shorter terms of office (two years) and smaller and usually more homogenous constituencies than the Senate (six years), the House was expected to act more quickly in response to public opinion. The House has developed rules that provide the ability for a majority to respond in this way.

The Senate, Washington's "cooling saucer," by contrast is sometimes referred to as the "world's greatest deliberative body." James Madison referred to the Senate as a "necessary fence" against the "fickleness and passion" of the popular will and the members of the House of Representatives.

Like other checks and balances in the Constitution, the division of Congress into two separate and different chambers serves to protect against the concentration of power within Congress. The framers nonetheless expected that the legislative branch would prove to be the most powerful of the three branches. As Madison argued in the Federalist Papers, the legislative branch "necessarily predominates." To guard against concentration of legislative power, the founders created a system in which neither chamber is able to make laws alone.

≫ *See also* related CRS Reports and links on **TCNCPAM.com**.

B. Constitutional Provisions

The Constitution, in Article I, extensively lays out the powers of Congress. Central to the congressional role is the grant of "all legislative powers" and the "power of the purse." At the Constitutional Convention in 1787, Massachusetts delegate Elbridge Gerry (later James Madison's vice president) argued that the House of Representatives "was more immediately the representatives of the people, and it was a maxim that the people ought to hold the purse-strings."

Article I, Section 8 lists a number of specific powers, including in Clause 18 (Necessary and Proper clause) the power, "To make all laws which shall be necessary and proper for carrying into Execution the [other listed] Powers." This is often referred to as the "elastic clause" because it gives flexibility to Congress beyond the powers that are separately enumerated. An example of an early use of the elastic clause was the justification for the Louisiana Purchase in 1803, roughly doubling the size of the United States at the time. A strict reading of the Constitution would find no authorization for the purchase of foreign territory, but it was argued that the elastic clause allowed the action and the Senate ratified the treaty.

Among the enumerated powers are the power to lay and collect taxes and pay the debts (Clause 1), borrow money on credit (Clause 2), regulate commerce with foreign nations and among the states (Clause 3), create the courts below the Supreme Court (which is created in Article III) (Clause 9), raise and support an army (Clause 12) and navy (Clause 13), the power to declare war (Clause 11), and others.

Article I takes up more space in the Constitution than Articles II through VII combined. By comparison, the descriptions of presidential powers (Article II) and those of the courts (Article III) are less precisely stated.

Among the provisions of the Constitution affecting the Congress, several are of particular importance.

Article I, Section 2 stipulates two-year terms and sets the necessary qualifications for members of the House. Section 3 does the same for senators, creating six-year terms and the qualifications for senators (*see* Chapter 1E).

Article I, Section 7, Clause 1, commonly referred to as the "origination clause," states, "All Bills for raising Revenue shall originate in the House of Representatives; but the Senate may propose or concur with Amendments as on other Bills." The framers gave the "power of the purse," as Elbridge Gerry referred to it at the 1787 Constitutional Convention, to Congress, specifically to the House of Representatives.

Madison wrote in *The Federalist Papers*, No. 58, "The House of Representatives cannot only refuse, but they alone can propose, the supplies requisite for the support of the government … . This power over the purse may, in fact, be regarded as the most complete and effectual weapon with which any constitution can arm the immediate representatives of the people … ."

The House enforces this constitutional prerogative through the use of a process called the "blue slip." In the event that the Senate passes a revenue bill and sends it to the House, any member of the House may offer a resolution that the Senate bill violates the prerogatives of the House under the origination clause of the Constitution. Such resolutions are routinely adopted, often by voice vote, and the bill is returned to the Senate.

The blue slip takes its name from the fact that the message returning the bill to Senate is blue. This is, however, a bit of a misnomer since all messages from the House to the Senate are on blue paper.

The House has historically viewed "revenue bill" as encompassing tax and other revenue bills, as well as appropriations measures that spend government funds. The Senate interprets "revenue bill" more narrowly and contests whether appropriations bills are included. However, the blue slip process has rendered Senate objections in this regard relatively toothless.

Central to the independence of Congress are the protections provided by Article I, Section 6. Senators and representatives are not subject to arrest during sessions or when traveling to those sessions (with the exception of arrests for treason, felonies, or the breach of the peace). Further, the "speech and debate clause" prohibits questioning of members of Congress in any other place regarding what they say on the floor of the House or Senate.

Article I, Section 6 also stipulates that no member, while serving in Congress, may hold any other federal office. As a result, when senators or representatives are appointed to the cabinet, for example, they must resign their congressional office before taking the oath for their new position.

One additional noteworthy congressional power is granted in Article II. In Section 4, the Constitution provides that the president (vice president and other civil officers) may be removed from office "on impeachment for, and conviction of, treason, bribery, or other high crimes and misdemeanors." Earlier, in Article I, Section 2, it is the House of Representatives that has the "sole power of impeachment." Section 3 then grants the sole power to "try all impeachments" to the Senate. The Chief Justice of the United States presides over an impeachment trial of a president in the Senate, and a two-thirds vote of senators present is required for conviction and removal. The House has voted to impeach a president only twice: Andrew Jackson in 1868 and Bill Clinton in 1998. In both cases, the president was acquitted by the Senate. In 1974, Richard Nixon resigned the presidency in the face of what appeared to be certain impeachment by the House and subsequent conviction by the Senate.

The Constitution has been amended to provide additional power to the Congress. In 1967, the Twenty-fifth Amendment was ratified. In the event of a vacancy in the office of the vice president, it provides for the nomination by the president and confirmation by a majority vote in each chamber of Congress of an individual to fill that vacancy. The amendment also creates a procedure for the vice president to become acting president if the vice president and a majority of the cabinet declare the president unable to discharge his or her powers and duties. It further prescribes a process for resolving the matter if a president asserts, contrary to such a declaration, that he or she is capable of discharging those duties. Under these circumstances, the president would resume his or her powers and duties unless by a two-thirds vote of each chamber, Congress determines the president is unable to do so (*see* Chapter 8.H.).

Under Article V of the Constitution, Congress plays a central role in adopting amendments to the Constitution by a two-thirds vote of each chamber ratified by three-fourths of the state legislatures (*see* Chapter 8.Q.).

》》》 *See also* related CRS Reports and links on **TCNCPAM.com.**

C. Rules

Perhaps one of the most critical protections of congressional independence and power is Article I, Section 5 of the Constitution, which states in part, "Each House may determine the Rules of its Proceedings … ." Pursuant to this provision the House and the Senate have developed very different rules. Those rules have established the character of each chamber in ways that enhance their constitutional design.

The House of Representatives adopts its rules at the outset of every new term of Congress (every two years). These changes can be minimal from the previous Congress. When control of the House changes parties, the rules changes are more likely to be extensive. For example, in 1995, when House Republicans became the majority for the first time in forty years, newly elected Speaker Newt Gingrich (R-GA) led the Republican Conference to a major overhaul of the House rules.

The rules of the House are adopted by majority vote. The rules, precedents, procedure, customs, and mores of the House serve to protect the principle of majority rule.

The formal rules are set down in the *House Rules and Manual*, which contains the foundation for the parliamentary procedure followed by the House, including the adopted rules of the House, portions of *Jefferson's Manual*, the Constitution, relevant adopted resolutions, and House precedents, which are rulings made by the Speaker and other presiding officers.

The Senate Standing Rules, precedents, and practices are designed to protect legislative minorities and the rights of individual senators. The rules adopted by the first Senate provided for a previous question motion, however, the rule that permitted a senator to limit debate by moving the previous question, by simple majority vote, was dropped in 1806. The House of Representatives has a "previous question" rule: when the motion is made in the House, "I move the previous question," if agreed to, debate and further amendment is ended and the House moves to a vote on the matter before it. Most legislative bodies have such a motion in their rules.

Today we understand such motions as requiring an end to debate and an immediate vote on the pending matter. In the House of Representatives this motion to cut off debate requires only a simple majority vote.

The absence of such a rule in the Senate now permits what is commonly known as the filibuster. Filibusters characterized by extended debate and/or other dilatory tactics can be ended under Senate Rule XXII through a process called "cloture," requiring a supermajority of three-fifths of the senators duly chosen and sworn, sixty votes (with some exceptions) (*see* Chapter 5.H.). This has a broad range of implications because it requires the majority in many circumstances to consult or negotiate with the minority even in the routine workings of the Senate.

While the early Senate rules included a previous question motion, the evidence is that it served a different purpose. A scholarly essay by Johns Hopkins University Professor Joseph Cooper concludes that the previous question as it existed in the early Senate of 1789–1806 "was not designed to operate as a cloture mechanism … it was not in practice used as a cloture mechanism" and "it is even improbable that the Senate could have used the previous question for cloture."[1]

Unlike the House, where the rules can and frequently do change with each Congress, the Senate adopted its rules in 1789 and, although they have been amended and codified, the basic rules have been continuously in place. Because the Senate considers itself a "continuing body" it does not adopt its rules at the beginning of each Congress. This is based on the fact that only one-third of senators stand for election for each term of Congress (one-third of the senators are to be elected every two years "divided as equally as may be into three Classes." (Article I, Section 3, Clause 2.)). Since the remaining two-thirds are already "chosen and sworn" and since a quorum in the Senate, under the Constitution, is a majority, there is no period of time during which a quorum of the Senate does not exist.

In 1903, the Senator Henry Cabot Lodge (R-MA) described it best: "Administrations come and go, Houses assemble and disperse, senators change, but

---

1. Joseph Cooper, *Previous Question: Its Standing as Precedent for Cloture in Senate*, Senate Document No. 87-104, 87th Congress, 2nd Session (Washington: U.S. Government Printing Office, Volume 2, Serial 12445, 1962), 26.

the Senate is always there in the Capitol, and always organized, with an existence unbroken since 1789."

Even though Senate rules can be changed by a simple majority vote, the Senate rules that continue from one Congress to another do require a two-thirds majority of senators voting to end debate on any rules change.

》》》 *See also* related CRS Reports and links on **TCNCPAM.com**.

D. Congressional Terms

Each term of Congress lasts for a two-year period from January 3 of odd-numbered years. Terms are commonly divided into two sessions of Congress, although more are possible, either convened by the Congress or by the president calling Congress back into session (*see* **TermsofCongress.com**). The president, under Article II, Section 3, is granted the power to "on extraordinary Occasions, convene both Houses, or either of them." A session ends when the Congress adjourns "*sine die*," Latin meaning "without any day" set to reconvene.

When a Congress plans to reconvene a second session following the general election in November of even-numbered years, it does not adjourn *sine die*. The period after the election up to the *sine die* adjournment at the end of that second session is popularly referred to as a "lame-duck session."

The transition from the first session to the second session, at the end of the first calendar year of a given Congress, ends the consideration of nominations, but has no effect on the progress of legislative matters. However, when the Congress adjourns *sine die* at the end of the two-year term, all legislative matters die. Therefore, in order to advance any bill or resolution in the next Congress it must be reintroduced. An exception are treaties submitted to the Senate by the president for ratification, which carry over from one Congress to the next.

》》》 *See also* related CRS Reports and links on **TCNCPAM.com**.

E. Members of Congress

The Constitution stipulates in Article I, Section 2 that the House of Representatives must have at least one representative from each state. Further, it provides that members of the House serve two-year terms, must be at least twenty-five years old, have been an American citizen for at least seven years, and must reside in the state (although not necessarily the district) from which they are elected.

Article I, Section 3 states that each state is represented in the Senate by two senators, elected for six-year terms, who must be at least thirty years old, have been a citizen for at least nine years, and must also be a resident of the state from which they are elected.

Congressional elections occur every two years. Since members of the House serve two-year terms, all of the House of Representatives is elected in each congressional election. Elections for members of Congress held in the even years between presidential elections are called "midterm elections."

By contrast, senators serve six-year terms. The Constitution established a rotation in which one of three "classes" of senators is elected at each congressional election (*see* **SenateClasses.com**). This means that only one-third of the Senate stands for election every two years. Article I, Section 3 stipulated that senators would be "chosen" by individual state legislatures. The Seventeenth Amendment, ratified in 1913, changed the process and provided for direct election of senators in each state "by the people thereof."

The House currently consists of 435 members, a total set by law in 1913 and reaffirmed by the Permanent Apportionment Act of 1929 (2 U.S.C. § 2a). The District of Columbia is represented by a non-voting delegate. In addition, Guam, the Virgin Islands, American Samoa, and the Northern Mariana Islands each has one delegate. Puerto Rico is represented by a resident commissioner. These six representatives do not vote on final passage of matters on the House floor, but possess all other powers of members.

Members of the House represent districts drawn by their states, which are roughly proportional to population based on the census that the Constitution requires to be conducted every ten years. (In some states, district lines have been drawn to benefit the political party that controls the state legislature, a practice known as "gerrymandering.")

California, the nation's largest state, as measured in the 2010 census, is represented by fifty-three members of Congress, while Alaska, Delaware, Montana, North Dakota, South Dakota, Vermont, and Wyoming have only one representative.

There are one hundred senators, two from each state. This equality of state representation in the Senate was the product of the "Great Compromise" at the constitutional convention in 1787. Small states pressed for equal representation in Congress and the larger states sought proportional representation for both chambers of Congress. The compromise created one chamber based on each principle. As a result, Wyoming (2018 population of approximately 600,000 people) has the same representation in the Senate as California (2018 population of more than 39 million people).

Interestingly, that compromise was deemed so fundamental to the establishment of a federal government that it cannot be changed using the normal means of amending the Constitution. Article V states, "… no state, without its consent, shall be deprived of its equal suffrage in the Senate."

Members of the House and Senate may only be removed from office by a two-thirds vote of members voting, a quorum having been established, of the Senate (if a senator) or the House (if a representative). (The Constitution defines a quorum, in Article I, Section 5, "… a Majority of each [chamber] shall constitute a Quorum to do Business.") There is no recall provision allowing for removal of members of Congress by popular vote prior to regularly scheduled congressional elections.

》》》 *See also* related CRS Reports and links on **TCNCPAM.com.**

F. House of Representatives

The House of Representatives is a majoritarian body. This means that the House is ruled strictly, at most times, by majority vote.

Under the Constitution, Article I, Section 4 (as amended by the Twentieth Amendment), "The Congress shall assemble at least once in every Year." Under that provision the first meeting of each Congress, "shall begin at noon on the 3d day of January, unless they shall by law appoint a different day."

Members of the House serve two-year terms.

Vacancies in the House are filled by special elections (Article I, Section 2). There is no provision for appointment of members to the House.

Regarding leadership, Article I, Section 2 of the Constitution states, "The House of Representatives shall chuse their Speaker … ." This is done by majority vote of the whole body at the outset of each new Congress. Party caucuses nominate candidates and normally the election takes place between the candidates nominated by the Democratic and Republican caucuses respectively. On occasion the names of additional candidates are placed in nomination.

The Speaker, under existing law, is second in line of succession to the presidency behind the vice-president in the event of the death or disability of the president (*see* Chapter 8.P.).

House party leaders, the majority leader, the minority leader, the majority whip, the minority whip, and others are elected by majority vote of the respective party caucuses. At the beginning of each Congress, the leadership is elected on the first day (*see* **CongressLeaders.com**).

The Speaker is the presiding officer of the House. Speakers have, in the past, viewed themselves leader of the whole House, as well as a party leader, and have protected that distinction. Bob Michel (R-IL), who served as minority leader for fourteen years, from 1981 to 1995, but never became the Speaker, described the role of Speaker as, "… by history, tradition and rule the leader of the whole House, not the majority, not the minority, but the whole. The Speaker must drop the mantle of partisanship the day he assumes office."[2]

As the House has become more partisan, Speakers have been increasingly viewed predominately as party leaders. Michel, contrasting his comfortable relationship with Democratic Speakers Tip O'Neill (D-MA) and Tom Foley (D-WA) with the much more vitriolic leadership relationships of minority leaders with later Speakers like Newt Gingrich (R-GA), Nancy Pelosi (D-CA), John Boehner (R-OH), and Paul Ryan (R-WI), observed in 2008, "With Tom and Tip, ye gads, we got along. Sure, we had our doggone partisan differences; I expect that. You can't be namby-pamby about it. But when push came to shove, or during a real nitty-gritty situation, why, I always knew that I could talk with either one of them on a simply man-to-man basis and no holds barred. And that's a good feeling to have."[3]

By tradition, the Speaker normally does not cast a vote. When the Speaker votes, it underlines the importance of the measure in question.

The Speaker, as the presiding officer, under House rules has the power (sometimes delegated to other senior members of the majority) to recognize members to speak or make motions on the floor. This is important because it gives the Speaker greater control over debate and amendment on the floor. The Speaker refers legislation to committees of jurisdiction and names members of conference committees with the Senate. Conference committees are temporary joint committees appointed to resolve differences between the chambers on a measure passed by each (*see* Chapter 6.D.).

---

2. "Congress; Speaker O'Neill: Hardball or Hand Grenades?" *New York Times*, June 7, 1984, accessed March 5, 2018, http://www.nytimes.com/1984/06/07/us/congress-speaker-o-neill-hardball-or-hand-grenades.html.

3. "Robert Michel Dies at 93; House G.O.P. Leader Prized Conciliation," *New York Times*, February 17, 2017, accessed March 5, 2018, https://www.nytimes.com/2017/02/17/us/robert-michel-dies.html.

The Speaker is also afforded powers by the majority caucus, including a central role in the assignment of members to committees, particularly to the powerful Rules Committee. The Speaker, as a practical matter, controls what legislation is scheduled on the House floor.

The powers given to the Speaker are intended to assure that if he or she can marshal the votes of the majority caucus, the Speaker is able to largely control the legislative outcomes in the House. When sizeable factions oppose a Speaker in his or her own party, such control is in doubt. The Speaker's job is particularly challenging when the majority party's margin in the House is narrow, or when the majority is ideologically divided.

Neither the Speaker (nor the president *pro tempore* of the Senate) is required to be a member of Congress, although historically all have been.

The House majority leader is second in the line of party leadership. He or she works with the Speaker on the legislative agenda and plays a key role in persuading members of the caucus to follow the leadership.

The House minority leader heads the minority party and is the chief strategist in articulating the views of the minority party, frequently in opposition to the majority. He or she leads the minority's efforts to influence legislation. If the Speaker is able to keep the majority party in line, it can be difficult in the majoritarian House for the minority to have much effective input. However, there are times when the Speaker must rely upon members of the minority to pass legislation he or she considers critical. A recent example was a vote in 2014 to raise the debt ceiling and avoid a default on debts owed by the federal government. On that occasion, few members of the majority (twenty-eight) were willing to support Speaker John Boehner's (R-OH) position and virtually the entire minority voted to lift the debt ceiling.

Both parties elect a whip, third in the line of majority leadership and second among the minority leadership. The party whips lead a large whip organization on their respective sides of the aisle. The main role of the whips and their organizations is to provide a channel of communication between the leadership and rank-and-file members. This is important to keep leaders informed of the various views in the caucus, to assist in persuading rank-and-file members to support the party position, and to keep track of the likely vote count.

Others members of the House leadership include the chairs of the Democratic Caucus and the Republican Conference. These two organizations are primary vehicles for party communication of the respective party's message on policy and legislation. Also in the leadership are the chairs of the National Republican Congressional Committee (NRCC) and Democratic Congressional Campaign Committee (DCCC). These are the political arms of the congressional Republican and Democratic caucuses. They recruit candidates for House races across the country and raise and distribute campaign money to that party's candidates. (For a list of the current leadership, *see* **CongressLeaders.com**.)

>>> *See also* related CRS Reports and links on **TCNCPAM.com**.

G. Senate

The Senate is a very different body than the House. In addition to the longer terms and larger, more diverse constituencies, there are several factors that account for this difference. The most important are the twin pillars of the Senate, unlimited debate and unfettered amendment.

The Senate rules and precedents governing debate and the offering of amendments are fundamental to the protection of legislative minorities (*see* Chapter 5).

The right to debate, enforced primarily by the existence of the filibuster, means that much of the routine activity of the Senate requires unanimous consent (because the alternative is so time-consuming and burdensome). Much of the business in the Senate, both routine and consequential, is conducted through "unanimous consent agreements," often negotiated between the party leaders or their designees. The ability of a single senator to slow down or even prevent the Senate from doing business can make the Senate a very difficult body to lead; former Republican Majority Leader Howard Baker (R-TN) described it as "herding cats."

Increasingly the political polarization of the Senate and efforts by the minority to use procedure to obstruct the majority or by the majority to circumvent the minority have rendered these procedural rules more controversial.

James Madison wrote in "Notes of Debates in the Federal Convention of 1787" (June 26, 1787):

> In order to judge of the form to be given to [the Senate], it will be proper to take a view of the ends to be served by it. These were first to protect the people against their rulers: secondly to protect the people against the transient impressions into which they themselves might be led.

The founders' design for the Senate was contrary to legislative "efficiency." Sir A. J. Herbert, the British humorist and member of Parliament put it, "The second Chamber is an indispensable feature of any democratic constitution. For no one is always right the first time."

Senate vacancies are filled differently, depending on the respective state's election laws. In contrast to how House vacancies may be filled, most states permit temporary appointment of senators, usually until the next scheduled congressional election. Some states, however, require a special election (with or without provision for a temporary appointment until that special election).

Article I, Section 3 designates the vice president of the United States as President of the Senate, and stipulates that the vice president is to have no vote in the Senate except in the case of a tie. Section 3 also authorizes the selection of a president *pro tempore* to serve in the absence of the vice president.

The president *pro tempore* or his or her designee presides over the Senate when the vice president is not present. From the first Senate, senators have retained the important powers and kept the presiding officer of the body weak—the vice president comes from the Executive Branch and may not be of the same party as the Senate majority. Rulings by the presiding officer may be overturned in the Senate by majority vote. As a result, the president *pro tempore's* role is likewise relatively weak and largely honorific. The tradition in the Senate has been to elect the most senior member of the majority party as president *pro tempore*. This means that this officer, under current law behind only the vice president and the Speaker of the House in the line of succession to the presidency, can be more than eighty or ninety years old. (*See* **CongressLeaders.com**.)

The most powerful role in the Senate is accorded to the majority leader, who is elected by the caucus of the majority party. The Senate itself takes no action to ratify this decision made by the majority party. The majority leader is generally regarded as the "first among equals." He or she is given little in the way of formal powers. By precedent, the majority leader is given the "right of first recognition." This means that although the Senate rules require the presiding officer to recognize the senator who first seeks recognition, when the majority leader is among those seeking recognition, he or she will be recognized. This, along with the power to decide the Senate's agenda (even this, because of the Senate rules of debate, requires negotiation with the minority leader), are the principal tools the majority leader uses to "control" the Senate.

Notwithstanding the powers of the majority leader, little can be accomplished, even in the routine operation of the Senate, without negotiating with the minority leader. Former Majority Leader George Mitchell (D-ME) described this fact as creating "a near-permanent state of negotiation. With its checks and balances the Senate is a microcosm of the American system itself. … It's relatively easy to obstruct and prevent things from occurring. It's very difficult to gain enactment."

As a practical matter, the tools given to the Senate majority leader are much weaker than those wielded by the Speaker of the House.

Like the House, Senate leadership also includes party whips, formally titled assistant majority leader and assistant minority leader, but commonly referred to as majority or minority whip. Much like the whips in the House, these senators are charged with keeping track of votes in their respective caucuses and trying to persuade rank-and-file senators to support the caucus positions.

The leadership includes others such as officers of the Democratic Conference, the Democratic Policy and Communications Committee, the Democratic Senatorial Campaign Committee (DSCC), the Republican Conference, the Republican Policy Committee, and the National Republican Senatorial Committee (NRSC).

The number of senators serving in the leadership in the Senate has gradually increased over recent decades reflecting an effort by the parties to be more inclusive of factions and to assure that regional concerns are represented.

>>> *See also* related CRS Reports and links on **TCNCPAM.com**.

H. Congressional Committees

Committee chairmen wield considerable power in both the House and Senate. At times when power is less centralized in the House and Senate leadership, committee chairmen have even greater influence.

The more polarized the Congress the stronger the centralized leadership in both chambers, and concomitantly the role of committees and their chairs weakens somewhat. On occasion, major legislation is written and managed through the Speaker's office in the House or the majority leader's office in the Senate.

Nonetheless, much of the actual crafting of legislation occurs in committees in both the House and the Senate. For this reason, members, in order to influence legislation important to their constituencies, seek positions on the committees with jurisdiction over such legislation. For example, seats on the

House Committee on Agriculture are typically filled by many members representing rural districts.

Being assigned to committees with jurisdiction over issues important to their constituencies is even more important in the House where rank and file members have little opportunity to shape or amend legislation on the floor, as is more common in the Senate.

Committees hold hearings taking testimony from administration officials, outside experts, interested stakeholders, and sometimes other members of Congress.

Woodrow Wilson, a political science professor at Princeton before becoming president, wrote, "It is not far from the truth to say that Congress in session is Congress on public exhibition, whilst Congress in its committee rooms is Congress at work."

In the 115th Congress, there are twenty-one standing committees in the House (including the Permanent Select Committee on Intelligence), while the Senate has twenty committees, sixteen listed as standing committees. In addition, there are four joint committees that have members from both the Senate and the House, but do not have legislative jurisdiction. (*See* **Congress Leaders.com**.)

Members are appointed to the House committees by the respective Republican and Democratic Steering Committees. In the Senate the selection is made by the Republican Committee on Committees and the Democratic Steering and Outreach Committee. However, the party leadership in each chamber makes recommendations and these are generally adhered to. Once a nomination of a member to a committee is made, formal approval is granted first by the party caucuses and then the full House or Senate by the adoption of resolutions ratifying the choices made by each party. Normally, these approvals are virtually automatic.

The overall size of committees and the party ratios of seats on committees are negotiated between the party leaderships. In the Senate the expectation is that the ratio of committee seats assigned to members of the majority and minority parties, respectively, will reflect the party ratio in the entire Senate. In the House, the majority party has much greater control and therefore the ratio in the most important committees, especially the Rules Committee (which typically has two members of the majority for each member of the minority plus one extra majority member) and the Ways and Means Committee, are a supermajority in order to protect their control.

(*See* Chapter 3 for a more detailed discussion of committees and subcommittees).

>>> *See also* related CRS Reports and links on **TCNCPAM.com**.

I. Review Questions

>>> Why would the framers want one chamber to be comparatively less responsive to public opinion than the other?

>>> What are the principal tools for the majority leader to use to run the Senate?

>>> How are Senate vacancies filled? How does this differ from filling vacancies in the House of Representatives?

>>> What are the comparative sizes of the House and Senate?

>>> In the House, how do the voting rights of the delegate from the District of Columbia differ from that of representatives from congressional districts in the fifty states?

>>> Who draws congressional district lines?

>>> What is the process for removing a president under the Twenty-fifth Amendment to the Constitution?

>>> Were senators always directly elected by people? If not, when did it change?

>>> How is the Speaker of the House elected? How does this differ from other House leadership figures like the majority leader and the minority leader?

>>> Why is the "necessary and proper" language in Article I, Section 8 called the "elastic clause"? What is the significance of this language?

Chapter 2
Introduction of Legislation

A. Introduction

In Article I, Section 1, the Constitution places the power and responsibility to legislate in the hands of Congress. The Constitution created a bicameral Congress in which neither body is able to make laws alone. The founders designed the Congress with two distinctly different chambers and the histories of the House and Senate since 1787 have deepened those differences. At the same time, the difficulty of passing legislation and getting it to the president's desk has increased. Turning legislation into law requires steering legislation first through one chamber then the other and then resolving differences between them.

For legislation to become law, a bill must be passed by both the Senate and the House in exactly the same form; there cannot be the slightest difference in wording. Because House members are responsible to 435 separate constituencies and senators represent fifty different states, passing legislation requires consideration and balancing of numerous interests shaped by party considerations, local issues, regional concerns, outside organizations, and other political factors.

In recent Congresses, six to eight thousand bills were introduced in the House and three to four thousand bills in the Senate. Of these bills, the Senate passes less than 3 percent and the House an even lower percentage, below 2 percent. Overall, less than 3 percent of bills introduced in a Congress actually become enacted into law. (*See* "Resume of Congressional Activity" on the Senate web site.)

The process begins with the drafting and submission of bills, that is, legislative measures.

>>> *See also* related CRS Reports and links on **TCNCPAM.com**.

B. Why Submit Legislation?

If so little legislation filed by members of Congress passes either body (*see* Chapter 2.A.), let alone becomes law, why do members introduce so many bills?

Legislation is written and submitted for a range of reasons. Some bills are written to address a problem or issue in which the member has a particular interest or expertise. The author may chair a committee or subcommittee that has legislative jurisdiction over a matter. At other times, bills may be introduced merely to raise an issue, stimulate debate, or simply set down a marker for future action. Some legislation is filed over and over for a number of years before progress or enactment occurs. Legislators may file a broad bill in the hope that a portion may eventually be incorporated into other legislation. Often, legislation is offered simply to demonstrate to constituents or interested groups that a member is committed to action on a particular matter. This gives the member the opportunity to tell constituents and others, "I have filed legislation in the Senate to address that problem." Many of these bills never progress past the point of being referred to a committee.

Much legislation is filed both in the Senate and the House without the slightest expectation that it will become law. That said, the introduction of legislation can have a direct effect on executive branch actions. Intense interest in a matter demonstrated by an individual member can influence decisions even if the legislation goes nowhere. The military, for example, pays close attention to what pieces of legislation members, particularly those on the Armed Services Committee in the House or the Senate, are introducing.

Legislation referred to committees is in effect divided into three groups: bills that have no chance of being considered by the committee; bills that are not controversial and likely to be passed easily; and major bills that will require most of the committee's time. Most bills fall into the first category and are rarely the subject of committee hearings or formal consideration.

Both the Senate and the House permit the introduction of legislation "by request," such as a third-party request that the legislation be offered. This can be done by members of Congress whether or not they support the legislation submitted. This might be done by leadership when requested by the president, or by a committee or subcommittee chair when requested by a department or agency of the government within the jurisdiction of that particular committee. Individual members may also offer legislation requested by a constituent or an interest group. The designation "by request" is actually printed on the face of such legislation. This designation has no procedural effect on the consideration of that legislation.

Members sometimes introduce private bills that apply to one or several specific individuals. Most commonly, private bills are related to immigration or claims against the federal government. The House lists such bills on the Private Calendar. The Senate does not distinguish private bills from public bills in terms of the procedure for consideration. Most private bills introduced never receive consideration on the House or Senate floor. Those that do may require subsequent introduction in more than one Congress to reach enactment. However, the fact that most private bills do not become law does not mean they are without impact. For example, the introduction of a private bill, alone, can freeze immigration proceedings in some circumstances (*see* Chapter 4.E.).

In the first days of a new Congress, hundreds of pieces of legislation are introduced. Most of these are bills that were previously introduced and died at the end of a prior Congress when they were not enacted, since all legislation not otherwise disposed of dies at the end of a Congress, that is, at the end of the second session of a Congress. Legislation carries over between the *sessions* of a Congress if not enacted or disposed of, that is, from the first to the second session of a Congress. The 115th Congress met from January 3, 2017 through January 3, 2019, with the first session running from January 3, 2017 through January 3, 2018. (*See* Terms and Sessions of Congress at **Termsof Congress.com**.)

In most cases, for legislation to gain traction in the Congress, attract the attention of party or committee leadership, find its way to the floor of either chamber, survive and ultimately be enacted, its sponsors must build momentum outside of Congress among the public, influential leaders of special interest groups, businesses, labor unions, sometimes academics, and other stakeholders. The media frequently plays a role in focusing attention on particular problems and emerging solutions.

''' *See also* related CRS Reports and links on **TCNCPAM.com**.

C. Drafting Legislation

The first step in getting a law passed is drafting legislation. Anyone may write legislation, but only a representative in the House or a senator in the Senate may introduce a bill.

Most bills, however, are written by members of Congress. This is done with the assistance of staff in the member's office, committee staff, and legislative counsel.

A non-partisan legislative counsel office exists in both the House and the Senate. "Leg [pronounced "ledge"] counsel," as they are often called, are called upon to draft legislation on a confidential and nonpartisan basis. The policy objectives are defined by the member through his or her staff and often it is the legislative counsel who creates the legislative language to accomplish those objectives. This assistance is available to members for drafting bills, resolutions, and amendments.

The legislative counsel in the Senate is appointed by the president *pro tempore*. In the House, legislative counsel is appointed by the Speaker. Additional attorneys are hired by the legislative counsel in each chamber. These are career, nonpartisan positions. These attorneys specialize in particular issue areas and are frequently assigned to work with specific committees.

Less complex bills, resolutions, and amendments are sometimes drafted by House or Senate staff in the members' offices or by committee staff. On occasion legislative language is drafted and offered to members by outside groups, state legislatures, federal agencies, or even the president.

》》 *See also Legislative Drafter's Deskbook*, (**TCNLDD.com**) and related CRS Reports and links on **TCNCPAM.com**.

D. Forms of Legislation

There are four forms of legislation, each of which has a specific purpose. Which legislation is appropriate and is used depends on that purpose. These forms of legislation are the same in both chambers. Although legislative vehicles are frequently all referred to by the media and many others as a "bill," the legislative vehicle may be a bill (Chapter 2.E.), a joint resolution (Chapter 2.F.), a concurrent resolution (Chapter 2.G.), or a simple resolution (Chapter 2.H.). The Senate, in addition to legislative matters, also considers treaties (Chapter 8.D.) and presidential executive and judicial nominations (Chapter 8.B.).

》》 *See also* related CRS Reports and links on **TCNCPAM.com**.

E. Bills

Most legislation is drafted in the form of a bill. Bills can be narrowly drafted to address a discrete issue. Bills can also be extensive and address a multitude of issues affecting many Americans. Most bills, in both chambers, are referred to a committee with jurisdiction over the issue that the bill addresses.

A bill passed in the same form in both chambers and signed by the president becomes law. Article I, Section 7 of the Constitution also provides two additional ways for a bill to become law without the president's signature. If the president does not act to sign (or veto) a bill within ten days (calendar days not counting Sundays), it becomes law without the president's signature unless the Congress has adjourned during that period (referred to as the "pocket veto"). The second way for a bill to become law without the president's signature is if each house votes, with a two-thirds majority, to override the president's veto (Chapter 6.G.).

Bills are generally numbered in the order in which they are introduced, with the exception of a few that are reserved (*see* Chapter 2.J.), in each chamber: with an "H.R." designation in the House, (H.R. 1) and an "S." in the Senate (S. 1).

Among the purposes of bills are:

- authorize government activities (authorization bills) (*see* Chapter 7.G.)
- appropriate funds out of the federal treasury (appropriations bills) (*see* Chapter 7.H.)
- amend the tax code (tax bills)
- amend existing federal laws
- private bills

〉〉〉 *See also* related CRS Reports and links on **TCNCPAM.com**.

F. Joint Resolutions

A joint resolution is similar to a bill although usually more narrowly specific in scope, for example, used to correct an item in existing law or to create a national day honoring grandparents. Like a bill, all joint resolutions must be passed by both chambers. If the resolution is passed in identical form and signed by the president, or is allowed to become law without his signature or is passed over his veto, it becomes law. The exceptions are joint resolutions proposing amendments to the Constitution (Article V), which are not presented to the president for signature (*see* Chapter 8.R.). Unlike bills, resolutions may contain a number of "whereas" clauses that detail the rationale for the resolution.

Joint resolutions are also numbered in a similar fashion to bills. In the House, they are designated as "H.J. Res." (H.J. Res. 1). In the Senate, joint resolutions are assigned "S.J. Res." numbers (S.J. Res. 1).

Joint resolutions when used to propose amendments to the Constitution and passed with identical language by a two-thirds vote in each chamber are sent to the states rather than the president. Constitutional amendments then require ratification by three-fourths of the states within the period of time prescribed within the joint resolution in order to amend the Constitution.

Among the uses for joint resolutions are:

- continuing appropriations resolution (known as a "CR") (Chapter 7.H.)
- declaration of war (Chapter 7.N.)
- disapproval (or approval) of a presidential action or recommendation (for example, under the Congressional Review Act (Chapter 7.M.) or the War Powers Act (Chapter 7.N.))
- very specific purpose, such as establishing a national holiday

>>> *See also* related CRS Reports and links on **TCNCPAM.com**.

G. Concurrent Resolutions

Concurrent resolutions, in order to take force, must be adopted by both chambers with identical language. They do not go to the president and do not become law.

Concurrent resolutions are best described as an expression of the will of the Congress. In fact, some concurrent resolutions express the "sense of the Congress" on something; the resolution states "It is the sense of the Congress that ..." and lists one or more expressed opinions. Concurrent resolutions have been used to express Congress's views on a very broad range of matters over the years, probably most commonly in the foreign relations sphere. For example, both the House and Senate adopted a concurrent resolution in 2013 expressing the view of Congress that North Korea should respect the fundamental human rights of its citizens and abandon, dismantle its nuclear weapons program, and end its nuclear and missile proliferation.

Although concurrent resolutions do not carry the force of law, they are frequently viewed as influential and important. Resolutions provide the opportunity for members to show support or opposition to a policy without the need to pass a law. Government agencies, states, and foreign governments pay attention to what the Congress is expressing on issues of importance to them.

Concurrent resolutions are also used to take joint administrative actions. They are not binding except on the Congress itself, which is subject to change by a later Congress. The most prominent concurrent resolution is the congressional budget resolution under the Budget and Impoundment Control Act of 1974 (*see* Chapter 7).

Under the Constitution, Article I, Section 5, neither chamber can adjourn for more than three days without the approval of the other house. This approval is granted by means of a concurrent resolution either for adjournment *sine die* (Latin for "without any day") or other adjournments lengthier than the three-day limit.

Among the purposes for which concurrent resolutions are used are:
- congressional budget resolution
- adjournment of Congress
- corrections of enrolled measures
- creation of joint committees
- providing for a joint meeting or session of Congress
- sense of Congress on some matter

Concurrent resolutions, like bills and joint resolutions, are assigned a number as they are submitted and designated as "S.Con.Res." (S.Con.Res. 14) or "H.Con.Res" (H.Con.Res. 14).

》》》 *See also* related CRS Reports and links on **TCNCPAM.com**.

H. Simple Resolutions

Simple resolutions may be adopted by either the Senate or the House. They are similar to concurrent resolutions in that they do not become law. They require adoption in only one chamber and are binding only on that chamber.

They are numbered sequentially and separately like bills, joint resolutions, and concurrent resolutions. They are designed as "H.Res." in the House (H.Res. 14) and "S.Res." in the Senate (S.Res. 14).

Both the House and the Senate adopt "sense of the House" or "sense of the Senate" resolutions respectively to express the opinion of that body.

Simple resolutions are also used in each chamber to change the rules. In the House this requires only a simple majority vote. In the Senate, although the rules may be changed by a simple majority, ending debate on that rules change, in the event of a filibuster, may require a two-thirds vote of all senators voting provided a quorum of fifty-one senators or more is established. This makes it extremely difficult to adopt a controversial rules change.

In the House, simple resolutions reported by the Rules Committee play a crucial role and are an important tool for majority control (and the Speaker's power) in that chamber. For most major legislation, it is the Rules Committee that decides if and how a measure will be considered on the House floor.

Before most major bills come to the House floor for consideration (many bills are considered under suspension of the rules, *see* Chapter 4.F.), the Rules

Committee reports a special rule in the form of a simple resolution to govern floor debate. The Rules Committee through a special rule determines whether any amendments are in order and if so, how many, and sometimes which specific amendments are in order. The special rule also sets the time for debate and when the vote will occur and under what specific rules. A vote on that special rule in the form of a simple resolution occurs on the House floor prior to the legislation itself being considered. On the extremely rare occasions when a rule is defeated, it is a major embarrassment for the majority leadership (*see* Chapter 4.D.).

Some of the uses of a simple resolution include:

- changes to chamber rules
- administration of the chamber
- resolution of election contests
- election of House or Senate officers
- election of committee members
- sense of the House or Senate on some matter
- in the House, special rules from the Rules Committee

》》 *See also* related CRS Reports and links on **TCNCPAM.com**.

I. Sponsorship and Cosponsorship

The representative or senator introducing the legislation is known as the sponsor. Other members may wish to be closely identified with the introduction of a particular bill and sign on as cosponsors. Legislation can have numerous cosponsors.

Cosponsors who sign onto a bill prior to its introduction are often referred to informally as "original cosponsors." This status is sometimes cited by members to indicate more involvement (and may reflect a role in the actual drafting) than those cosponsors who join after a bill is introduced.

Frequently, sponsors and other key proponents of legislation send a letter referred to as a "Dear Colleague Letter" to other members explaining the purposes of the bill or resolution and seeking additional cosponsors. This practice is more common in the House because it is an efficient way to communicate a bill's intent to a large number of House members, but it is not unusual in the Senate. However, because the Senate is a much smaller body, it is easier to seek the support of potential cosponsors directly. A bill's sponsor may also encourage supportive organizations and lobbyists outside of Congress to encourage other members to cosponsor. Dear Colleague Letters are also used by members to communicate with all other members for many purposes beyond seeking cosponsorship.

>>> *See also* related CRS Reports and links on **TCNCPAM.com**.

J. Submitting Legislation

The formal submission of legislation in the House begins by a Member of Congress dropping a copy of the bill or resolution signed by the sponsor into the "hopper," which is an actual mahogany wooden box located on the House floor affixed to the side of the clerk's desk on the rostrum. (*See* "View of the Speaker's Dais and Well of the House" and "View of the Speaker's Dais, Floor of the House, and Galleries.")

In the Senate, bills and resolutions are submitted by bringing a signed copy to the parliamentarian at the rostrum. The parliamentarian is seated at the front of the chamber just below the presiding officer. Alternatively, the senator may submit the amendment by introducing the bill or resolution from the Senate floor. In the latter case, once the measure is introduced the presiding officer will state, "the bill will be received and appropriately referred." (*See* "View of the Senate Rostrum, or Presiding Officer's Dais.")

Once the bill is submitted, it is assigned a number by the bill clerk reflecting the order in which bills were submitted in that particular Congress. In the House, the number will be preceded by "H.R." (H.R. 56) indicating it is a House-originated piece of legislation. A bill introduced in the Senate will have an "S." designation preceding the number (S. 56).

It has become customary for the majority leadership in each chamber to reserve the first several bill numbers, generally ten, for legislation reflecting the party's major policy objectives. Similarly, the next ten are often reserved for use by the minority leadership. Members are able to reserve particular numbers that may have symbolic value. Another reason to reserve a number is to retain the number for a particular bill previously introduced in preceding Congresses to make it easier for others to recognize and remember, which may help in the effort to build momentum from one Congress to the next.

Identical bills may be introduced in both chambers.

>>> *See also* related CRS Reports and links on **TCNCPAM.com**.

(*Continued on page 32*)

View of the Speaker's Dais and Well of the House

The Speaker or Speaker pro tempore sits on the uppermost level of the dais, and the mace is on the pedestal to the Speaker's right if the House is meeting as the House. If the House is meeting as the Committee of the Whole House on the State of the Union, the chairman of the Committee of the Whole occupies this level, and the mace is placed on a lower pedestal. If Congress is conducting a joint session or meeting, the vice president is seated on this level with the Speaker, a second chair having been added.

One might also see one of the parliamentarians to the Speaker's or chairman's right, advising on parliamentary statements or rulings. A time clerk stands on the presiding officer's left.

The reading clerk as well as several other clerks occupy the middle level. The reading clerk is regularly directed by the Speaker or the chairman of the Committee of the Whole to read measures or amendments or provide other information to the membership, which he does from the lectern on this level.

Members may speak from the well of the House, using the Democratic lectern on the Speaker's right or the Republican lectern on the Speaker's left. The official reporters of debate use the table and chairs.

Illustration by Marilyn Gates-Davis. Copyright ©2005 by TheCapitol.Net

View of the Speaker's Dais, Floor of the House, and Galleries

While the view of the Speaker's dais on the previous page identifies some of the occupants of the dais, this illustration gives a better indication of the size of the dais. On the lowest level of the dais nearest to the viewer are seats occupied by the bill clerk, who is responsible for the "hopper" in which House members place bills and resolutions for introduction.

This illustration also shows in the lower right one of the four committee or party tables from which members may address the House, in addition to the lecterns they may use in the well of the House. Each party has two tables on its side of the center aisle of the House.

The door to the Speaker's left and another out of view to the Speaker's right provide access to the Speaker's Lobby. (The party cloakrooms are in the back of the chamber, out of view in this illustration.)

Immediately above the Speaker's dais is the press gallery. In the walls above the press gallery are the display panels where members' names and votes appear when a vote is taken by electronic device. One of the voting stations is shown at the bottom center-left of the illustration.

Also on the gallery level, to the Speaker's left, one can also see some of the seats that are used for specific guests such as family members and for other visitors and tourists. Visitor seating surrounds the House chamber on the gallery level.

Illustration by Marilyn Gates-Davis. Copyright ©2005 by TheCapitol.Net

View of the Senate Rostrum,
or Presiding Officer's Dais

The presiding officer of the Senate—the vice president, the president pro tempore, or a designee of the president pro tempore—alone occupies the upper of the two levels of the Senate rostrum.

On the lower level of the rostrum, the journal clerk sits. That person reads bills and amendments and other information as directed by the presiding officer. The journal clerk also calls the roll on votes and quorum calls. The parliamentarian also sits on this level and advises the presiding officer on parliamentary statements and rulings.

The two tables in front of the rostrum are controlled by the parties, the one to the presiding officer's right by the Democrats and the one to the presiding officer's left by the Republicans.

In the foreground, the aisle desk on the presiding officer's right is occupied by the Democratic leader of the Senate and may be used by the Democratic floor manager of legislative or executive business being considered by the Senate. The aisle desk on the presiding officer's left is occupied by the Republican leader of the Senate and may be used by the Republican floor manager of legislative or executive business.

Doors to the presiding officer's left and right lead to the Senate Lobby. Immediately above the presiding officer and outside of this view is the press gallery. Visitor galleries surround the Senate chamber on the same level as the press gallery.

Illustration by Marilyn Gates-Davis. Copyright ©2005 by TheCapitol.Net

K. Introductory Statements

In both chambers, legislation can be introduced without any accompanying statement by a bill's sponsor. In the House there is usually no statement of introduction. In the Senate, it is common for a senator to submit a statement of introduction to appear in the Congressional Record. On occasion, senators will deliver that statement on the Senate floor at the time the bill is introduced.

Members in both chambers typically issue press releases announcing the introduction of legislation and for significant legislation may hold news conferences or other events.

»» *See also* related CRS Reports and links on **TCNCPAM.com.**

L. Referral to Committee

In both chambers, once introduced most bills are referred to the appropriate standing committee with jurisdiction over the subject of the legislation. Similar to an original bill, legislation passed by one chamber is messaged to the other body and is referred to a committee. Rules (principally Rule XXV in the Senate and Rule X in the House) and precedents have established jurisdictions for each chamber's committees. In some cases, the jurisdiction is affected by agreements made between committees. Such agreements are generally in writing in the form of a memorandum of understanding between the committees involved, and the memorandum is subsequently placed in the Congressional Record. However, for the Senate parliamentarian to act pursuant to any such inter-committee agreement, a unanimous consent agreement would be necessary to formalize such an agreement in the Senate.

Legislative jurisdictions are vigorously defended by both Senate and House committees. Challenges are usually worked out between committee chairs and may lead to written agreements and unanimous consent agreements. On occasion jurisdictional battles spill onto the floor.

The determination of which committee a particular piece of legislation will be referred to is made by the Speaker in the House of Representatives, and in the Senate the presiding officer makes the decision pursuant to Senate Rule XVII and Rule XXV. In both chambers, the judgment is made by the respective parliamentarian and reliably followed by the presiding officer.

Most referral decisions are comparatively routine. Legislation affecting taxes, for example, is referred to the Ways and Means Committee in the House and to the Finance Committee in the Senate. A bill raising the salaries of members of the armed services would be referred to the Armed Services Committee in the chamber where the bill was introduced.

In some cases overlapping jurisdictions or the complexities of the bill itself make the committee referral decision difficult, and occasionally controversial. Disputes are generally resolved informally and sometimes result in a unanimous consent agreement.

The success or failure of a bill or resolution at the committee stage can depend greatly on its committee referral. Some committees might be more amenable to a particular proposal than others. Sometimes the fate of a measure can hinge on who chairs the committee.

As a result, in some cases bills are written with the committee referral in mind and specific language may be used to influence the referral decision. The parliamentarian may identify for sponsors the specific factors considered in order to determine jurisdiction and the parliamentarian may assist staff in making the appropriate and best arguments to steer a bill to a specific committee.

When legislation impacts matters in the jurisdiction of several committees, a bill or resolution may be referred to more than one standing committee. This occurs more commonly in the House than in the Senate, where it almost always requires unanimous consent, and is therefore quite rare.

In the House, multiple referrals of several types are sometimes made. One committee is designated as the "lead" committee by the Speaker. Committees may also receive a "sequential" or "split" referral from the Speaker. A sequential referral refers to a circumstance in which a second committee considers the measure after it is reported by the lead committee. A split referral involves designating different segments of the bill to the two committees. The Speaker may impose a time limit on committees receiving such multiple referrals.

In the Senate the parliamentarian normally determines which committee's jurisdiction "predominates" and the legislation in question is referred to that committee in the name of the presiding officer. One common exception is the Intelligence Authorization bill, which is reported by the Senate Select Committee on Intelligence each year. The Senate Armed Service Committee seeks and is granted sequential referral of this bill. This is because many of the personnel decisions and much of the funding provided for intelligence activities relate to parts of the Department of Defense.

>>> *See also* related CRS Reports and links on **TCNCPAM.com**.

M. Senate Rule XIV

Any senator may, and the majority leader frequently does, make use of Senate Rule XIV. Under the rule, any senator wanting to circumvent the normal referral of a bill or joint resolution to a standing committee can take steps that result in the legislation bypassing referral to a committee and being placed directly on the Senate Calendar of Business on the next legislative day (*see* Chapter 5).

Senate Rule XIV requires that every bill or resolution submitted be read twice before being referred to committee. A third reading is required just prior to the vote on final passage of legislation. Rule XIV stipulates after the first two readings of a bill or resolution "if objection be made to further proceeding thereon, be placed on the Calendar." Since such an objection may be lodged by any senator, all senators have the procedural ability to circumvent the committee referral process and have the legislation placed directly onto the Senate's calendar, meaning that it is available for consideration on the Senate floor. This process takes two legislative days: the day on which the measure is first introduced and read twice, followed by an adjournment of the Senate, and the next convening of the Senate. In the Senate "legislative days" end upon adjournment of the Senate. Therefore, legislative days may take multiple calendar days.

However, getting legislation to the Senate's calendar by no means assures that it will be considered on the floor.

By Senate tradition and precedent, only the majority leader decides which matters will be scheduled for floor consideration. Therefore, as a practical matter, using Rule XIV as a strategy to bring a bill to the Senate floor without committee consideration is only available to the majority leader. It has been a powerful tool for the majority leader to expedite certain major legislation, to consolidate the work of several committees in one bill, or on occasion, to avoid the referral of the bill to a particular committee where the chair might have views different from those of the leadership.

As the Senate in recent years has become more polarized along party and ideological lines, the leadership in the Senate has become more centralized. As a result, recent Congresses have seen tools like Rule XIV, and other procedural rules and traditions like the filibuster, holds on legislation and nominations, the filling of the amendment tree (*see* Chapter 5.K.), the blue slip in the Judiciary Committee, and the reconciliation process in the Budget Act, increasingly used to circumvent the normal procedure of the Senate.

>>> *See also* related CRS Reports and links on **TCNCPAM.com**.

N. Regular Order

In both chambers, some members have spoken out against the growing trend toward use of the rules to bypass what is commonly called "the regular order." Much of what is meant by members of Congress when they refer to regular order is the normal legislative procedures set out in this chapter and Chapter 3. Such procedures would include the referral of legislation introduced to the committees of jurisdiction, availability of proposed legislation to the public, the conduct of hearings in committee, debate and consideration of amendments in committee markups, and potentially the reporting of legislation to the House or Senate floor for debate and amendment in the respective chambers.

Since the 1990s the regular order has not been respected on some pieces of major legislation. Bills crafted in the Speaker's office or the Senate majority leader's office have been brought directly to the floor through the Speaker's control of the House Rules Committee or the use of Rule XIV in the Senate.

The abandonment of regular order can be best illustrated with respect to the appropriations process. Congressional decisions about the expenditure of public funds—appropriations—normally require that the Appropriations Committee report twelve separate appropriations bills that fund the various departments and agencies of government. The inability of Congress to pass the necessary twelve appropriations bills as required by the end of the fiscal year on September 30 to avoid the shutdown of the federal government has led to the reliance on short-term joint resolutions known as "continuing resolutions" or huge "omnibus appropriations bills" (*see* Chapter 7.H.). Omnibus bills lump multiple appropriations measures together, sometimes with other extraneous legislation. These omnibus bills are sometimes sent directly to the House and Senate floors and passed, frequently with only minimal time for members to review their contents. If an omnibus only includes a few bills, maybe three or four, it is referred to by some as a "minibus."

In July, 2017, the late Senator John McCain (R-AZ), in a speech with virtually all senators present on the floor, urged his Senate colleagues to "… return to regular order. We've been spinning our wheels on too many important issues because we keep trying to find a way to win without help from across the aisle. That's an approach that's been employed by both sides, mandating legislation from the top down, without any support from the other side, with all the parliamentary maneuvers that requires."

O. Legislative Process Flowchart

(See **TCNLPF.com***)*

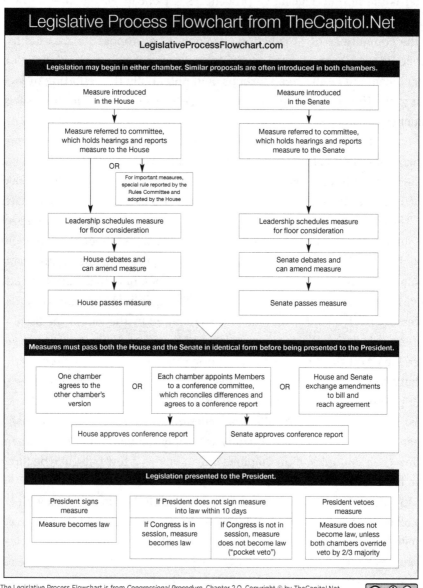

It should be pointed out that this popular use of the term "regular order" could confuse some observers of the Senate because the term does have a technical parliamentary meaning in that body. It technically refers to returning to an amendment or measure set aside for another amendment or measure by unanimous consent, upon "a call for the regular order."

》》》 *See also* related CRS Reports and links on **TCNCPAM.com.**

O. Legislative Process Flowchart

(*See* previous page and **TCNLPF.com.**)

P. Review Questions

》》》 As a member of Congress, what factors might cause you to submit legislation?

》》》 What if you have no idea how to draft legislation to carry out your solution to a particular problem?

》》》 Why might a private bill even be fair?

》》》 What are the forms of legislation and what is the usage of each?

》》》 Why might the sponsor of a bill prefer referral to one committee over another? What can the sponsor do about it?

》》》 Some people argue that Senate Rule XIV has been abused in recent years. Why could frequent use of that rule to circumvent committees be considered an abuse?

》》》 What is "regular order" and why does it matter, if it does?

》》》 Why would a member write a "Dear Colleague" letter?

》》》 Who makes the judgment as to which committee a bill will be referred?

》》》 Who must pass a sense of the Congress resolution for it to take effect? Why might it be important?

Chapter 3
Committees

A. Introduction

Much of the real work of Congress occurs in the committees. When each chamber of Congress follows its routine procedures, sometimes referred to as "the regular order" (Chapter 2.N.), the vast majority of issues regarding any piece of proposed law are addressed at the committee stage of the legislative process. Pursuant to these routine procedures, it is in congressional committees that legislation is evaluated, debated, amended, shaped, and, for most bills and resolutions, discarded.

It is through their committee assignments (Chapter 1.H.) that most members of Congress get involved in and have an opportunity to impact the drafting, consideration, and adoption or rejection of legislation. Many seek assignment to particular committees because of existing expertise that they bring with them to Congress. Others use their positions on committees to develop specialized expertise. It is also common for members of Congress to seek assignments to committees with jurisdiction over issues that are important to their constituents. For example, a member from a congressional district with a major army base might seek a position on the House Armed Services Committee and a senator from a state with major agricultural interests might want to serve on the Senate Agriculture Committee.

Committee assignments are especially important in the House and of less importance in the Senate. With 435 members, in order to have any appreciable impact, rank-and-file House members must develop areas of specialization. Committee assignments give members a few issues on which they may have the opportunity to play a significant role. By contrast, senators serve on a larger number of committees and subcommittees. In the 115th Congress, the average senator served on nearly fourteen committees and subcommittees. For members of the House, the average was a little more than five.[1]

There are thousands of bills introduced in each Congress (*see* Chapter 2.A.). One of the first tasks of a committee in either chamber is to decide which of the hundreds of bills referred to them are to be actually considered. Bills and resolutions generally fall into three categories; first, those with no chance of passage, which will not be considered by the committee; second, those that are not controversial, will take little of the committee's time and energy, and

---

1. "Vital Statistics on Congress: Data on the U.S. Congress, Updated September 2017," Brookings Institution, September 7, 2017, accessed March 7, 2018, https://www.brookings.edu/wp-content/uploads/2017/01/vitalstats_ch4_full.pdf.

that can likely be expedited; and third, major legislation on which the committee will focus.

Normally, there is no requirement in the House or Senate rules that a committee to which legislation is referred actually take up that measure. However, there are exceptions, such as "fast-track" procedures on some matters. For example, the Congressional Budget and Impoundment Control Act of 1974 (P.L. 93-344, 88 Stat. 297, 2 U.S.C. §§ 601–688), establishes special procedures to expedite consideration of the concurrent budget resolution that is required to be adopted each year (although some years, Congress fails to meet this obligation). Included in the law is a requirement that the Senate Budget Committee, for example, report the measure by April 1 (*see* Chapter 7.B.). However, the deadlines dictated by the Act are frequently not met and there is no enforcement mechanism.

When a committee decides to take up a major bill, the decision is made primarily by the chair. Committee chairs have wide discretion in setting the committee's agenda. Frequently chairs will work with the leadership in their chamber on bills of major interest to the majority party. Chairs also must be mindful of the need to assemble a majority of the votes in the committee in order to report a bill to the floor. This typically results in their consulting with other committee members, certainly members in the majority, but often with members in the minority as well, at least in the Senate, where a bipartisan bill is far more likely to overcome the obstacle of the legislative filibuster (Chapter 5.H.).

⟫⟫ *See also* related CRS Reports and links on **TCNCPAM.com**.

B. Committees and Subcommittees

There are three types of committees in each chamber.

Standing committees in the Senate and House are permanent and have a defined legislative jurisdiction under Senate Rule XXV or House Rule X, respectively. In the Senate, there are sixteen standing committees: Agriculture, Nutrition, and Forestry; Appropriations; Armed Services; Banking, Housing, and Urban Affairs; Budget; Commerce, Science, and Transportation; Energy and Natural Resources; Environment and Public Works; Finance; Foreign Relations; Health, Education, Labor and Pensions; Homeland Security and Governmental Affairs; Judiciary; Rules and Administration; Small Business and Entrepreneurship; and Veterans' Affairs. (*See* "Congressional Leadership and Committees" **CongressLeaders.com** .)

In the 115th Congress, the House has twenty standing committees: Agriculture; Appropriations; Armed Services; Budget; Education and the Workforce; Energy and Commerce; Ethics; Financial Services; Foreign Affairs; Homeland Security; House Administration; Judiciary; Natural Resources; Oversight and Governmental Reform; Rules; Science, Space and Technology; Small Business; Transportation and Infrastructure; Veterans' Affairs; and Ways and Means.

The second type of committee is variously called a select committee, special committee, or other. They are sometimes temporary and have a specific mandate. Some have legislative authority, some do not. The Senate has four such committees: Indian Affairs (became a permanent committee in 1984); Ethics; Intelligence; and Aging. The Senate Indian Affairs and Intelligence Committees have legislative jurisdiction, the Senate Select Committee on Ethics and the Special Committee on Aging do not. In the House, the most notable is the Permanent Select Committee on Intelligence, which has legislative jurisdiction.

The third type of committee is a *joint* congressional committee. Joint committees have members from each chamber. Established by law or concurrent resolution, joint committees have legislative information-gathering and congressional administrative roles. Unlike standing committees or some select committees, joint committees have no legislative jurisdiction. There are currently four such committees: the Joint Committee on Taxation, the Joint Economic Committee, the Joint Committee on the Library, and the Joint Committee on Printing.

Each congressional committee creates its own rules consistent with guidelines contained in the rules of the House or Senate. Senate Rule XXVI establishes specific requirements for committees, including that the committee rules are "not inconsistent with the Rules of the Senate." Similarly, House Rule XI states that committee rules "may not be inconsistent with the Rules of the House." House Rule XI also states that the rules of the House "are the rules of its committees and subcommittees so far as applicable."

Committee rules include things like how investigative subpoenas may be authorized and issued, what authority resides with subcommittees, and so forth. As such, a committee's rules help determine the amount of influence that the chair, the minority, and individual members have over committee business.

Funding for committees is mostly provided in the Legislative Branch Appropriations bill each year. The distribution of those funds is controlled by biennial House and Senate resolutions, respectively.

With respect to funding, in the House Rule X stipulates only that the minority party be "treated fairly" (House Rule X, 6.(d)). The Speaker has, in recent Congresses, encouraged committee chairs to provide the minority with one-third of the funding.

Senate Rules establish no standard for the disbursement of committee funds to the majority and minority. In recent Congresses, the majority and minority leaders of the Senate have agreed to a funding formula, ratified by the adoption of a Senate Resolution, based on the party division in the Senate, with additional funds allocated to the majority for the committee's administrative costs. In addition, the agreement has included the caveat that the minority cannot receive less than 40 percent of the full committee funding.

Because the Senate rules protect the minority, fairness is policed by the minority party's potential ability to filibuster the funding resolution. The power of the filibuster in this respect was particularly on display at the outset of the 107th Congress. The 2000 election had resulted in a fifty-fifty split of Republicans and Democrats in the Senate. With the deciding vote of Republican Vice President Dick Cheney, the Republicans became the majority party in the 107th Congress. The minority, led by then-Minority Leader Tom Daschle (D-SD), threatened to filibuster unless a "power sharing agreement" could be reached. Such an agreement was negotiated between Daschle and then-Majority Leader Trent Lott (R-MS). Among its provisions was that committee seats would be equally divided between members of each party on all committees and that committee budgets would be evenly split.

Individual committees have developed differing staffing arrangements. Staff positions are divided between the majority and minority parties. In some committees, the chair and ranking minority member of the full committee retain tight control over the staffing of the majority and minority staff, respectively. In other committees, other members (subcommittee chairs in particular) may participate in the naming of committee staff, particularly those assigned to work with the subcommittees. For example, on the Senate Armed Services Committee all staff decisions are traditionally made by the chair and the ranking minority member. Conversely, on the Homeland Security and Governmental Affairs Committee, subcommittee chairs hire their own staffs.

At least some staff changes are made when a new chair takes over the gavel of a committee. If control of the chamber switches parties, the impact on committee staffing is much greater.

Subcommittees are created by the committees as a means of dividing the workload and as a way of providing leadership roles (subcommittee chairs) for a broader range of members. The use of subcommittees grew after 1946 when the committee system was reorganized and the number of standing committees in each chamber was reduced.

Subcommittee assignments are made by each committee from among its members. In the 115th Congress, there were ninety-two subcommittees in the House and sixty-eight in the Senate. These numbers change from Congress to Congress. Senate Rule XXV, 4. places restrictions on the number of subcommittees on which senators may serve, although these restrictions are often waived by unanimous consent or by resolution.

The role played by subcommittees differs depending on what they are tasked to do by the full committee. The scope of subcommittee activities can range from holding the initial hearings on a policy or legislative idea to marking-up and reporting bills to the full committee for its consideration.

An example of committees in which the subcommittees play a critical legislative role are the House and Senate Appropriations Subcommittees (*see* Chapter 7.H.). Each of the twelve subcommittees in each body's Appropriations Committee is responsible for one of the twelve appropriations bills required to fund the government each year. These subcommittees hold extensive hearings on the appropriations bill for which they have jurisdiction and then subsequently mark up that bill. The choices made by the subcommittees are influential. It is not uncommon for the full House or Senate Appropriations Committee to mark up and report an appropriations measure prepared for it by a subcommittee without making substantial changes.

On some committees, the major work and consideration of legislation is retained at the full committee level. Several committees conduct hearings in the subcommittee and then mark up bills (that is, consider amendments) in the full committee.

The power and independence of a subcommittee depends in large part on the latitude provided to subcommittee chairs within a committee to select and supervise subcommittee staff and the budget for that staff. The degree of control in the hiring, firing, and supervision of subcommittee staff by the full committee chair differs greatly from committee to committee.

When a bill is referred to a committee, if the committee decides to act, that bill is sometimes held at the full committee level for legislative action. Most commonly, however, bills are referred to the appropriate subcommittee of jurisdiction where hearings will take place. At the conclusion of the hearings, the subcommittee may act on the measure, for example, mark up the bill and report it to the full committee. In some instances, following hearings, a measure may be returned to the full committee for debate and amendment. Whatever action is taken by the subcommittee, the committee chair may decide to repeat the step in the full committee or the committee may just act to report the subcommittee's product to the House or Senate floor.

>>> *See also* related CRS Reports and links on **TCNCPAM.com.**

C. Committee Chairs

Congressional committee chairs are very powerful. During periods when the centralized leadership of the House or Senate is weak, the role of committee chairs is even more powerful.

The majority member who has served on the committee for the longest time is frequently named as the chair. This is known as the "seniority system." For much of congressional history, the seniority system was nearly iron-clad.

However, in recent decades, Speakers and the respective steering committees in the House have increasingly exercised their power and named a chair who is not the senior-most member of the majority on the committee. This has been more true of the House Republicans than the Democrats.

By contrast, in the Senate, the decisions by the two parties in choosing chairs and ranking minority members of the various committees are ratified by a vote of the Senate on the so-called committee organizing resolutions. The Senate has largely continued to follow the seniority system for selection of chairs, with rare exceptions. However, in the 1970s both parties decided that seniority should not dictate the choice of committee chairs. In 1995, the Senate Republicans changed their rules to permit Republican members of the committee to vote for the chair without regard to seniority.

One of the most prominent seniority fights in the Senate occurred in 1987 for the chair of the influential Foreign Relations Committee. The sitting chair for the previous two years, Senator Richard Lugar (R-IN), was challenged by Senator Jesse Helms (R-NC), who was the senior-most member of the committee. Since the Democrats had gained control of the Senate in the 1986 elections, the Lugar-Helms battle was actually for the ranking minority member post on the committee. The drama was heightened by the fact that Lugar was a prominent moderate Republican and Helms was arguably the most conservative member of the Republican Conference. The Foreign Relations Committee Republicans backed Lugar for the post, but the full Republican Conference named Helms, who was senior. As a result, seniority won out and Helms assumed the chair. The outcome was evidence of the continued strength of the seniority system in the Senate.

Another titanic committee leadership battle took place in the House in 2008. In that case, the challenge was to Congressman John Dingell (D-MI), who had served as the top Democrat on the powerful House Energy and Commerce Committee for twenty-eight years. The challenger was himself a major figure in the House, Congressman Henry Waxman (D-CA). In this case, the weaker hold of seniority in the House was evident when the Democratic Caucus selected Waxman.

Nonetheless, seniority remains a major factor in the House. For example, in 2014, in the battle for ranking member of the same Energy and Commerce Committee when Waxman retired, the third-most senior Democratic contender, Representative Frank Pallone (D-NJ) defeated Representative Anna Eshoo (D-CA) in an intense contest. Pallone, citing his seniority, won the battle in the full caucus even after the Democratic Steering and Policy Committee had chosen Eshoo.

Because committee chairs exercise considerable discretion over committee action, contests for committee leadership can have high stakes. The chair presides over hearings, markups, and other committee meetings. The chair largely determines the committee agenda and controls most of the committee's staff and funding. In addition, the chair controls the referral of bills and resolutions to the subcommittees. Presidents, department heads, lobbyists, and colleagues in Congress know that within the legislative jurisdiction of his or her committee, the chair is often the most important member who must be persuaded. While the opposition of a committee chair to a bill may be overcome, it is exceedingly difficult.

The ranking member leads the minority party on the committee and may or may not be widely consulted by the chair depending on the rules, the political climate, and their personal relationship. The ranking member controls a portion of the budget and names minority witnesses for hearings.

Especially in the Senate, some chairs and ranking members forge a close working relationship. Therefore, some Senate committees have a reputation for bipartisanship.

There are limits on the number of chair or ranking minority positions a member may hold on committees and subcommittees. Senate Rule XXV and both parties in the House impose these limitations (Senate Rule XXV, House party rules).

Senate Rule XXV divides Senate committees into three categories designated "A," "B," and "C." These are ranked by their relative importance with "A" committees being the highest. These classifications are used to impose limitations on the number of assignments a senator may have in each. For example, senators are limited to membership on two class A committees. These include most of the standing committees and the Select Committee on Intelligence. Waivers from these limitations are common.

The most coveted committee assignments are to the so-called "Super A" committees. Senators may only sit on one such committee. The Democrats consider the Appropriations Committee, the Finance Committee, and the Armed Services Committee to be "Super A" committees. The Republicans include a fourth "Super A," the Foreign Relations Committee. The limitation on "Super A" committee assignments for any senator is sometimes also waived.

In 1995, House Republicans, under Speaker Newt Gingrich (R-GA), adopted term limits for committee chairs. In the House, Republicans may serve as chair or ranking minority member of a committee or subcommittee for no more than three consecutive terms, six years, with time spent as chair and as ranking minority member counting toward the limit. In 1995, Senate Republicans also imposed term limits of six years as chair of a standing committee. However, a senator may serve a separate six years as ranking member of the same Senate committee.

The argument made for term limits is that a chair with fresh ideas is desirable. Also, long-term chairs may appear too close to the government agencies and outside interests that have a stake in their committee. However, the counterargument is that chairs develop expertise over time and that it takes a number of years at the head of a committee to develop that knowledge and expertise.

Neither House nor Senate Democrats impose term limits on committee or subcommittee chairs. Many observers believe this gives Democratic committee chairs an advantage because of the power and expertise accrued over time.

》》》 *See also* related CRS Reports and links on **TCNCPAM.com**.

D. Hearings in Committees

Normally, the first step of committee consideration of legislation, once the chair (sometimes with consultation) has decided to take up a matter, is a public hearing. Hearings may also be held to gather the information necessary for the committee to draft its own legislation.

In both chambers, committee hearings must be open to the public unless the committee, in open session, votes to close the hearing. The most common reason for closed hearings is to protect classified national security material and testimony. For example, many of the hearings held by the House and Senate Intelligence Committees are closed. Hearings are also sometimes closed for other reasons, such as taking witness testimony in an investigation. The public release of transcripts or information obtained in closed sessions requires a majority vote of the committee.

A witness may testify either individually or as a member of a panel. At times, a committee may require that a witness testify under oath. Witnesses may include executive branch officials, representatives of the private sector, or public-interest organizations, academics, and sometimes members of Congress who are not on the committee.

Committees generally require witnesses to file an advance written statement and limit their oral testimony to a brief summary. (For more details, *see Testifying Before Congress*, by William LaForge.)

Subsequent to the oral statements by witnesses, and sometimes opening statements by members of the committee, committee members question the witnesses. In the House, rules of all committees require a five-minute limit for the first rounds of questions to witnesses. In the Senate, some, for example, the Senate Banking Committee, but not all committees have established a five-minute rule. Time limits on questions are often set by the chair frequently in consultation with the ranking member. The chair can decide to allow additional rounds of questioning.

Members of the committee may also ask witnesses to respond to questions in writing at a later time. Members are also able to submit questions for the record (QFRs), which are written questions submitted for the hearing record that require written responses from witnesses before the committee. The chair will often permit the record to remain open for additional material to be submitted.

Committee hearings are sometimes sparsely attended by members of the committee. Since members serve on multiple committees and subcommittees, often there are time conflicts that members must juggle, even more so in the Senate.

The average senator in the 115th Congress serves on nearly fourteen committees and subcommittees. Of these, nearly four are full committee assignments. The average member of the House serves on more than five, including an average of about two full committees. Of course, other events in members' schedules compete for their time.

Senate Rule XXVI authorizes committees to establish a quorum of as little as one-third to conduct routine committee business. Senate committee rules vary, but quorum requirements to hear testimony can be as few as one member. House Rule XI requires at least two members for a committee to take testimony. Even if committee members are not able to attend hearings, the member's staff will often be present in order to brief the member should he or she arrive late, or to report at a later time.

In addition to legislative hearings, committees regularly hold oversight hearings as part of Congress's constitutional responsibility to assess how well programs are being carried out by the executive branch, confirmation hearings to question and evaluate presidential executive or judicial nominees, and sometimes investigative hearings focused on matters within the committee's jurisdiction that may involve scandal, wrongdoing, or criminal behavior (*see* Chapter 8). Witnesses at investigative hearings may also be required to testify or provide written materials under subpoena.

Although most hearings are held in Washington, on occasion committees will hold field hearings, generally in locations related to the subject of the hearing or the home state or district of a committee member.

>>> *See also Testifying Before Congress* (**TCNTBC.com**) and related CRS Reports and links on **TCNCPAM.com**.

E. Markups

A committee or subcommittee may decide to hold a business meeting to take action on a measure after the hearings have concluded. Major legislation can require many hearings. For example, in 2009, the House held seventy-nine hearings on the Affordable Care Act (Obamacare) (P.L. 111-148). The Senate Health, Education, Labor and Pensions Committee held seventy-nine hearings on that same bill and the Senate Finance Committee another fifty-three.

One purpose of a business meeting is to debate and amend a measure. This is referred to as a "markup" session.

Like the rules for public hearings, both the House and Senate require that markups be open to the public unless the committee by majority vote in open session closes the markup.

A quorum of at least one-third of the committee members is required under the rules of both chambers in order to hold a markup session. Some committees establish a higher number. The vote to report the legislation requires a quorum of a majority of the committee.

Some committees in the Senate permit their members to vote by "proxy" during a markup. The proxy is a signed piece of paper stating the member's intent with respect to votes to be held in a markup session they are unable to attend. On occasion such proxies may be open-ended and allow the chair or another committee member to cast the proxy vote for the absent senator. Sometimes a senator's staff will have been supplied with proxies for expected votes. The staffer may provide them to the chair as appropriate. Proxy voting is not permitted in the House.

The chair of the committee or subcommittee will likely decide what version of a piece of legislation will be used as the base text for the committee to mark up. This is referred to as the "chair's mark." The selection of a particular base text is an important power for the chair and can significantly influence the final product.

Provisions in the chair's mark may only be changed or deleted by majority vote during the markup process, a clear advantage for the chair. The chair's mark may be legislation that was introduced and referred to the committee or an entirely new alternative measure.

In some committees, where the subcommittee has marked up a bill and reported it to the full committee, that bill will be the vehicle for amendment. In such cases, the reported text is often printed or offered by the chair as a substitute for the original measure that was referred to the committee. The chair may also introduce an entirely new bill incorporating the subcommittee's changes, and that measure is then referred back to the committee and used as the markup vehicle.

At the outset of the markup, the chair of most committees usually permits opening statements. The chair is first to speak, followed by the ranking committee member. The remainder of committee members present are then recognized, alternating between parties.

》》》 *See also Testifying Before Congress* (**TCNTBC.com**) and related CRS Reports and links on **TCNCPAM.com**.

F. Amendment Procedure

The amendment procedure in committee markups generally follows the same rules as on the floor of the chamber (*see* Chapter 4 and Chapter 5). Committees modify some rules, but these modifications cannot be inconsistent with the rules of the chamber. In the Senate, the floor amendment process is largely governed by practices and precedents.

Bills and resolutions in committee may be amended in two degrees. That is, an amendment to the language and an amendment to that amendment is in order. In the House, amendments must be germane, that is pertain to the same subject as the legislation or amendment to which they are offered.

Like amendments on the floor, amendments in the committee may add new language, delete specific language from the bill, or both delete and replace language. At the end of the process the committee reports the legislation, with any amendments adopted by the committee, to the floor.

House committees generally consider a bill section by section. When all amendments to one section have been considered, that section is closed to further amendment and the committee moves on to the next section. The chair may decide to allow amendment to any provision in the bill and this may be accomplished by unanimous consent. If a full substitute amendment is offered (only permitted at the beginning or end of the markup), that measure itself is open to amendment at any point.

Measures are usually open to amendment at any point in Senate committees. Germaneness is not required; however, an amendment reported by a committee containing any significant matter outside of the committee's legislative jurisdiction is subject to a point of order should it be adopted in committee and the legislation be considered on the Senate floor.

When an amendment is offered, it is read and copies are distributed. By unanimous consent, the committee sometimes dispenses with the reading of the amendment.

In the House, debate on amendments offered in committee is generally limited under a five-minute rule. By contrast, similar to debate in the Senate chamber, Senate committee rules permit extended debate. Some committees have adopted rules that can curtail a filibuster of an amendment in committee.

Amendments in committee are adopted or rejected by majority vote. Votes are conducted by voice vote or roll call. The chair on a voice vote will ask those voting in the affirmative to say "aye" and those opposed to say "nay." The chair judges which side prevailed. During a roll call, a clerk reads the names of members of the committee and records the individual votes in the committee record. In the House, votes may also be by division, where the votes of individual members are counted, but not recorded by name.

Members may first offer an amendment that is highly controversial and expected to be rejected, and then decide to withdraw the amendment before the vote is taken. This permits the member's amendment to be discussed without establishing a defeat in committee.

When all sections of the measure have been considered by a House committee, the "previous question" is moved. This is the parliamentary procedure that ends debate. If the previous question is adopted, it brings the measure to a final committee vote. This motion is not subject to debate.

A motion to end or limit debate is also in order, in the House. While the previous question motion would preclude any further amendment, closing or limiting debate would not end the committee amendment process, but any further amendment must be decided without debate.

The Senate no longer has a motion for the previous question in its rules. Although such a motion was in the original Standing Rules of the Senate in 1789, the Senate dropped that motion when it recodified its rules in 1806 (*see* Chapter 1.C.).

It is important to note that amendments offered by committee members and adopted by the committee, in general, do not actually change the text of the markup legislation. Such amendments are reported to the House or Senate floor accompanying the measure. The committee is merely recommending these adopted amendments to the full House or Senate. When that chamber considers the legislation, those committee amendments will be adopted or rejected prior to further consideration of the bill or resolution. In the Senate, such committee amendments are automatically pending and must be disposed of before floor amendments are in order.

>>> *See also* related CRS Reports and links on **TCNCPAM.com**.

G. Reporting Legislation to the Floor

At the end of the markup process, a motion is made to report the measure favorably to the House or Senate. A committee may also report a measure unfavorably or without recommendation. Legislation reported unfavorably or without recommendation by a committee is rare. This may occur if there is a statutory requirement to report a bill or if the committee believes that the full House or Senate should have the opportunity to work its will on a measure even though it's not supported by the committee.

In both the House and the Senate, a majority of committee members voting, with a quorum present, is needed to approve a measure and to report it to the chamber floor. Under House and Senate rules, a majority of the committee is necessary to establish the quorum. Some Senate committees permit voting by proxy on the motion to report a measure under Senate Rule XXVI. However, under Senate rules, committees cannot permit proxies to affect the outcome of the vote to report the measure, meaning that a member's proxy will be recorded as long as it is not necessary to approve or defeat the measure. However, under consistent interpretations of the Senate's rules, if a committee permits proxies on the vote to report a measure only negative proxies count. Proxies also cannot be used to establish the necessary quorum to report a bill or resolution.

Committees report a bill to the full House or Senate with amendments or incorporate those amendments in an amendment in the nature of a substitute. The chair may also decide to have the committee introduce an original bill known as a "clean bill" in the House or referred to as an "original bill" in the Senate. This is a new bill, with a new number, reflecting all of the actions taken by the committee during markup. If many changes were made to the legislation during markup, the reporting of an original bill may facilitate floor action by avoiding separate consideration of each committee-adopted amendment.

As noted above, the committees in either chamber are not required to take any action on bills or resolutions referred to them and the majority of bills and resolutions are not acted upon. Therefore, if a committee does not report a bill or a resolution referred to it, the bill or resolution cannot be considered on the floor in the normal course of events. As discussed in Chapter 4, in the Senate it is possible to offer such legislation as an amendment on the floor. However, both chambers have rules providing a means of bringing a measure to the floor that has not been reported by a committee.

Under Senate rules, a motion to discharge a bill from a committee can be made by any senator, but, absent unanimous consent, consideration of such a motion is almost impossible. If a discharge motion is agreed to (majority vote, but subject to filibuster), the measure is removed from the committee and placed on the Senate's Calendar of Business. Such motions in the Senate are rare, and are frowned upon by the majority leadership.

Senate Rule XIV permits any senator (usually the majority leader) to circumvent the normal referral of a measure to committee and allows that measure to be placed on the Senate Calendar of Business (*see* Chapter 2.M.).

In the House, under Rule XV, any member may file a discharge petition with the Clerk of the House once the committee has had a measure for more than thirty days.

A discharge petition must reference only one measure, not multiple pieces of legislation. While discharge petitions are sometimes threatened by the minority, success requires the petition be signed by a majority of the House (normally 218 members) and therefore is exceedingly rare. Once the necessary signatures appear on a discharge petition, a motion to discharge is placed on the House's Discharge Calendar. Any member who signed the petition is eligible under the rules to offer the motion on the floor, although such motions are restricted to a "discharge day," which occurs only on the second and fourth Monday of each month. If a majority votes for the motion when it is brought up on discharge day, the measure is brought to the floor. Since the House is a majoritarian body, a successful discharge petition is considered a rebuke to the Speaker, the majority leadership, and the powerful Rules Committee. Members of the majority are expected to follow the leadership on procedural votes.

A successful use of a discharge petition in the House is very rare. The last discharge motion approved was for the Bipartisan Campaign Reform Act (P.L. 107-155), known as "McCain-Feingold," in 2002.

》》》 *See also* related CRS Reports and links on **TCNCPAM.com**.

H. Committee Reports

A committee report is a document drafted by a committee that explains a piece of legislation and amendments adopted by the committee. The report often makes arguments for why the full chamber should accept the committee's recommendation on the legislation.

House Rule XIII requires committees to file a committee report. In the Senate, the filing of a committee report is at the discretion of the committee (Senate Rule XXVI).

A committee report is written by the majority of the committee. It reflects their views. Members in opposition to the reported bill or resolution may choose to file minority views. At times, supplemental or additional views can also be included. Supplemental or additional views are typically filed by committee members who agree with the majority or the minority, but perhaps on different or additional grounds. These may be filed by individual or groups of committee members to amplify issues addressed by the bill.

Committee reports can be very important and can influence the debate and decisions in the full chamber. Committee reports are also important because they may be used by executive branch agencies and others to more fully understand the legislation. Federal courts at times turn to committee reports and floor debate to understand the "intent of Congress" when they find the text of the statute unclear.

It may take a considerable period of time from the point at which a measure is reported to the House or Senate to when the decision is made by the House or Senate leadership to call it up for floor consideration. Many factors can influence that decision, including timelines for expiring authorization legislation, appropriations deadlines, politics, and public opinion, how much time is available on the floor, a pending recess or any number of other considerations. Committee chairs regularly lobby floor leaders for the timely consideration of bills or resolutions their committees have reported; their competitors for floor time, other committee chairs, may be lobbying for their bills at the same time.

Legislation reported to the House floor is placed either on the Union Calendar for bills that raise or spend funds or the House Calendar used for other measures. In the Senate, the legislation is placed on the Legislative Calendar (Senate Calendar of Business).

》》 *See also* related CRS Reports and links on **TCNCPAM.com**.

I. Review Questions

》》 How does a select committee differ from a standing committee?

》》 Why might a federal court be interested in a committee report?

》》 What is a discharge petition in the House and why would a member file one?

》》 What are the quorums necessary in the House and Senate, respectively, to begin marking up a bill in the committee? Are those quorums the same in order to report a bill to the House or Senate floor?

>>> If an amendment to an amendment is pending in a committee markup, is it then in order to offer an amendment to that amendment? If not, why not?

>>> Is it true that committee hearings in the House must be open to the public, but the Senate has no such rule, it is at the discretion of the chair? Why might a committee hearing be closed?

>>> What is the importance of the previous question motion? Does this motion have the same effect in the Senate as the House?

>>> Why might a member of a committee file a supplemental report as opposed to a minority report?

>>> Why would a bill reported to the House be placed on the Union Calendar?

>>> As a committee staffer advising the chair on the scheduling of a hearing regarding crop insurance, why might you recommend a field hearing? Would it matter whether it was a House or Senate committee?

Chapter 4
House Floor

A. Introduction

While much of the laborious work on legislation is done during the committee process in the House, it is on the floor of the House where that work bears fruit or fails.

Whether or not legislation successfully navigates the House floor depends heavily on the Speaker, the House majority leadership, and the Rules Committee. Success or failure is also influenced by policy considerations, political context and the merits of the bill itself.

Article I, Section 5 of the Constitution provides the House the power to write its own rules, including the parliamentary rules under which measures are considered in the House. House rules are adopted by majority vote at the outset of each new Congress, often with slight alterations. In some Congresses, sweeping changes to the rules may occur, especially when the speakership changes parties, such as when Newt Gingrich (R-GA) became Speaker in 1995 (*see* Chapter 1.C.), when the Republican party assumed the House majority for the first time in forty years.

Understanding the differences in legislative procedures between the highly structured House of Representatives (described in this chapter) and the less predictable Senate (Chapter 5) is central to an appreciation of lawmaking on Capitol Hill.

It bears emphasizing that the House is a majoritarian body. This means that it is governed by majority vote. Thus, the Speaker, elected by a majority of the House, wields great potential power. This power, as it is applied to legislation, is largely executed through the House Rules Committee.

The power of the Speaker depends in part on his or her ability to hold the majority together or forge a new temporary one as a coalition with the minority, which can be difficult for the Speaker.

In the 113th Congress, Speaker John Boehner (R-OH) lost reliable control of the House Republican Conference. On some major legislation, most notably passage of a continuing resolution to avoid a government shutdown, Speaker Boehner was required to work with the minority leader, Nancy Pelosi (D-CA), to get the votes to pass legislation he believed was necessary and critical. In October 2013, the government had been shut down for sixteen days when Congress could not agree on appropriations for the new fiscal year. With public disapproval of the shutdown rising, Boehner was able to get compromise legislation through the House to reopen the government. To accomplish this, he needed to work with the Democrats. Eighty-seven Republicans supported the bill, while all 198 Democrats in the House voted to end the shutdown. However, Boehner's working with the minority, in this instance and others, exacerbated his already difficult relationship with the conservative segment of his majority party in the House, and he decided to step down as Speaker.

Normally, the Speaker, working with the rest of the majority leadership and the committee chairs, retains firm control over the legislative process in the House. Speakers often adhere to the so-called "Hastert Rule." The Hastert Rule holds that the Speaker will only bring a bill to the House floor for a vote if a majority of the majority supports it. Although not a formal rule of either the House or the party conference, this practice associated with former Republican Speaker Dennis Hastert (1999–2007) (R-IL) has been followed by Republican Speakers after him. Later Speakers, like Boehner, however, have at times been forced to abandon it.

Among the most powerful House Speakers was Thomas Brackett Reed, a Republican from Maine, who was elected Speaker in 1889, and who was the architect of an array of parliamentary changes, referred to by many historians as the "Reed Rules." These changes, coupled with his chairmanship of the Rules Committee even as he served as Speaker, made him one of the most powerful Speakers in the House's history and the first of the "modern" Speakers.

Reed was noted for his acerbic wit. A member of the House, identifying with Senator Henry Clay, declared to Reed that he would "rather be right than be president." Reed fired back, "The gentleman need not be disturbed, he never will be either."

The iron-fisted Reed characterized the relationship between the majority and the minority in the House, capturing the spirit that many contemporary observers would recognize, "The right of the minority is to draw its salaries, and its function is to make a quorum." On another occasion he declared, "The best system is to have one party govern and the other party watch … ."

When it comes to controlling the floor in the Senate, the Senate majority leader faces a far greater challenge (*see* Chapter 6).

>>> *See also* related CRS Reports and links on **TCNCPAM.com**.

B. Scheduling of Legislation

Measures reported to the House from a committee are placed on a calendar. There are two main calendars on which bills and resolutions reported from committees are placed in the House: the Union Calendar and the House Calendar. There are a total of four calendars in the House, the other two being the Private Calendar and the Discharge Calendar.

All bills that spend funds or those that raise revenues are placed on the Union Calendar. Other reported legislation is placed on the House Calendar with the exception of private bills, which are targeted to affect an individual or group of individuals. For example, some private bills affect an individual's immigration status. Private relief measures are listed on the Private Calendar.

The Discharge Calendar is reserved for motions to discharge committees. Such motions are placed on the Discharge Calendar when a discharge petition has received the necessary number of signatures, which is a majority of the total membership of the House, normally 218 (*see* Chapter 3.G.).

The Speaker, majority leader, and other members of the majority leadership decide if and when legislation listed on any of the House calendars should receive floor consideration. Such decisions must be consistent with House Rules, which affect the priority of certain bills and the particular days when a measure can normally be considered. Even when a measure is listed on one of these calendars, there is no guarantee that it will reach the House floor.

House leadership working with the Rules Committee also has control over how a measure is considered. Speakers make certain that the ratio of majority to minority members with seats on the Rules Committee is heavily weighted to the majority, almost always at least a two-to-one advantage over the minority. The Speaker also tries to ensure that members appointed to serve on the Rules Committee are loyal to the leadership. The House Rules Committee (Chapter 4.C.) is sometimes referred to as "the Speaker's committee."

Much of the power wielded by modern Speakers and the majority leadership grows out of their control of scheduling in the House. A Speaker must consider and balance numerous competing factors in making scheduling decisions. Pressures influencing the Speaker's decisions include the opinions and desires of the committee chairs, the views of his or her caucus (including factions within that caucus), the administration (particularly if the president is of the same party), outside interest groups, public opinion, and the Senate.

⟫⟫ *See also* related CRS Reports and links on **TCNCPAM.com.**

C. House Rules Committee

In many ways, the Rules Committee is the most powerful committee in the House. It functions as the strong right arm of the Speaker because of its role in the scheduling of major legislation and dictating the process by which legislation is considered in the House. Recent Speakers have retained tight control over the Rules Committee. Generally the ratio of majority to minority members on the Rules Committee is greater than other committees. Since the late 1970s, the ratio has been two-to-one plus an additional one. For members, it is prestigious to sit on the Rules Committee, which exercises considerable power over favorable or unfavorable amendments.

When legislation comes to the House floor under regular order, House Rule XVII provides for one hour of debate equally divided between the parties. However, to more tightly control proceedings on the floor, the leadership usually prefers that the Rules Committee issue a "special" rule. A special rule takes the form of a simple House resolution (H.Res. ###) that the Rules Committee reports to the House. Such a resolution requires a majority vote of the House for adoption. If the resolution is adopted, it determines what amendments, if any, will be in order and how much debate will be permitted before a vote on passage.

When a House committee reports legislation, its chair contacts the leadership seeking a hearing before the Rules Committee and a special rule. The chair of the Rules Committee typically holds a hearing only after the leadership has decided to schedule consideration of a measure on the House floor. The chair, usually in consultation with the leadership, decides when that hearing will be held.

Legislation can be held up in the Rules Committee without a hearing for a considerable period, even indefinitely, in order to kill it. For example, during the Civil Rights Era in the 1950s and early 1960s, the Rules Committee's chair (from 1955 until 1967), Howard Smith (D-VA), known as Judge Smith, was able to hold civil rights legislation that he vehemently opposed in the House Rules Committee, even after Speaker Sam Rayburn (D-TX) added members loyal to him to the committee seeking to move the legislation.

The Rules Committee may also block or delay a bill or resolution because the Speaker does not want his or her caucus to have to take responsibility for a vote on an unpopular measure.

The Rules Committee, following instruction by the Speaker, exercises jurisdiction over the order of business in the House. For most major legislation, it is the Rules Committee that determines if and how a measure will be considered on the floor. It will hold a hearing and take member testimony focused exclusively on the bill or resolution proposed as well as potential amendments.

Rules Committee hearings are similar to hearings held by other committees, however, only members of the House are generally invited to testify. The chair of the committee reporting the measure under consideration by the Rules Committee testifies before the committee. The author of the bill or resolution may also testify, so may other members seeking to get support for a particular amendment to be made in order under the special rule.

When the hearing is concluded, the Rules Committee will decide whether to grant a special rule for consideration of the measure. If they decide to grant a special rule, the committee will mark up and report the rule, technically a simple House resolution, often written in consultation with the majority leadership, that provides for consideration of the measure taken from the Union Calendar or the House Calendar.

》》》 *See also* related CRS Reports and links on **TCNCPAM.com**.

D. Special Rules

In order to maintain tight control over the proceedings on the House floor during consideration of major legislation, the Speaker may request that a special rule be created by the House Rules Committee, which provides a structured process for the consideration (debate and amendment) of a specific piece of legislation.

A "special rule" has that title because, for the purposes of the measure under consideration, the special rule supersedes the general rules of the House. This special rule is a privileged matter on the House floor. "Privileged" means that it is business that has priority over the regular order of business as defined under House Rule XIV.

In reality, the House rarely, if ever, follows this order of business. The legislative business of the House is overwhelmingly conducted by unanimous consent or as privileged matters and most often by suspension of the rules (*see* Chapter 4.F.).

Special rules frequently dictate how a measure can be debated. Special rules typically provide for a fixed period of general debate on the House floor and may also stipulate if any debate will be in order on amendments and, if so, how much time will be allotted.

Also, the special rule can determine what types of amendments and how many amendments, if any, can be offered to a measure on the floor. They may also waive all potential points of order against the bill.

If the special rule permits amendments on the floor without restriction, it is known as an "open rule." Under House Rule XVI, all amendments must be germane, that is, must relate to the same subject as the bill under consideration. For much of the House's history, open rules were common. As the House has become more polarized on partisan and ideological lines, open rules have become less popular with House leadership. This is because open rules can give rise to time-consuming and unpredictable debate and results. The tighter control of special rules can also prevent the minority from offering amendments that the majority wishes not to consider.

If the rule prevents floor amendments entirely, it is known as a "closed rule." Some rules, known as "modified closed rules" or "modified open rules," provide a limitation on amendments. The distinction between the two types of modified rules hinges on how restrictive the limitations are on floor amendments and therefore tends to be subjective. A modified open rule may limit amendments to those printed in advance in the *Congressional Record* or place an overall limit on submission and debate of amendments, or both. Modified closed rules limit amendments to specific amendments identified in the special rule.

Special rules are debated on the House floor under House Rule XVII that limits debate to no more than one hour. The time is controlled by the majority, but customarily half of the time is yielded to the minority for debate.

≫ *See also* related CRS Reports and links on **TCNCPAM.com**.

E. Privileged Business

Bills or resolutions that under the House Rules can interrupt the regular order of business to be taken up, debated, and voted on, are referred to as privileged.

Matters privileged in the House include special rules from the Rules Committee, appropriation bills, budget resolutions and reconciliation bills, conference reports, and reports from the House Ethics Committee.

Privileged business also includes legislation listed on certain calendars like the Private Calendar and the Discharge Calendar, which are privileged on certain dedicated days.

In the case of the Private Calendar, bills may be considered on the first and third Tuesdays of each month (House Rule XV). However, these bills can be recommitted or sent back to committee if objected to by two or more members.

Private relief bills typically involve individual immigration and naturalization matters or individual claims against the government. Private bills are placed on the calendar when reported by a committee, most commonly the Judiciary Committee.

Private bills are called up in the order that they are reported by committee and listed on the Private Calendar. They are considered in the Committee of the Whole (*see* Chapter 3.G.) with no general debate, but members may speak for five minutes.

There may be objections to bills on the Private Calendar. Because few members have the resources or time to study all private bills, each party appoints three members to a committee of "official objectors" to review bills. Usually, bills that raise a concern are "passed over without prejudice." This permits them to be revised by their sponsors in an effort to meet these concerns.

Motions to discharge (*see* Chapter 3.G.) may be called up on the House floor as a privileged matter by any member who signed the discharge petition. This may be done only on the second and fourth Monday of each month.

》》》 *See also* related CRS Reports and links on **TCNCPAM.com**.

F. Motion to Suspend the Rules

Most legislation considered by the House is done so by suspending the rules (House Rule XV). These are bills and resolutions that are not controversial and are supported by a large majority of the members. Passage of a measure under suspension of the rules requires at least a two-thirds vote of members voting, a quorum being present.

The Speaker may recognize a member to move to "suspend the rules and pass" a particular measure. This may occur only on Monday, Tuesday, or Wednesday of each week, unless by unanimous consent. The motion on occasion will stipulate "suspend the rules and pass *with an amendment*." If so, no separate vote on the specified amendment will occur on the House floor.

When the House considers a bill under suspension of the rules, amendments to the measure are not in order. Also, debate is limited (usually to forty minutes). No points of order can lie against the measure. If a recorded vote (two-thirds required) is not requested, these noncontroversial bills can often be passed by voice vote.

》》》 *See also* related CRS Reports and links on **TCNCPAM.com**.

G. Debate

When the leadership wishes to take up major legislation on the House floor (except for some privileged matters and matters taken up under suspension of the rules) the process generally begins by calling up a special rule that has been reported from the Rules Committee. The special rule determines what the conditions for debate and amendment on floor will be.

Special rules must be approved by the House (*see* Chapter 4.D.). They are generally debated on the floor with a one-hour limit, are adopted by majority vote, and are almost always passed by the House. Special rules are rarely rejected. One exception was the defeat of the rule to take up President Clinton's 1994 crime bill even though Democrats controlled the House. Even if the Speaker lacks a majority of the votes and is forced to withdraw the special rule, it is a defeat for the Speaker and the majority leadership.

If the special rule is adopted, the House usually convenes "the Committee of the Whole House on the State of the Union." The Committee of the Whole, as it is commonly called, is made up of all the members of the House. It is, in effect, the House of Representatives in a different parliamentary form. The House resolves itself into the Committee of the Whole either by the action of a special rule or by unanimous consent. A quorum of one-hundred members is required to do business in the Committee of the Whole. It is within the Committee of the Whole that the bill or resolution will be debated and amendments, if any, considered.

When the House resolves itself into a Committee of the Whole, the Speaker or Speaker *pro tempore* (the Speaker's designee to preside in his or her absence) steps down and appoints a chair to preside over the Committee of the Whole. The member who presides over the Committee of the Whole is addressed as either "Mr. or Madam Chairman or Chairwoman," and not as "Mr. or Madam Speaker."

The practice of using a committee composed of all of its members to give the House a way of considering controversial and often complex legislation dates from the early days of the House of Representatives.

As a symbol of this change from the House to the Committee of the Whole, the "mace" is moved. The mace is a 46-inch-long staff of ebony and silver that signifies the dignity and authority of the House, adopted by the first House in 1789. Historically it has been used by the House Sergeant at Arms to reestablish order in the House by parading it in front of offending members. Reportedly, it was last used for that purpose during World War I. (*See* "The Mace.")

The Mace

The mace is the symbol of authority of the House of Representatives. The following physical description of the mace appears with other information about the mace on the web site of the clerk of the House:

The mace is 46 inches high and consists of 13 thin ebony rods representing the original 13 states of the union. The rods are bound together by four crossing ribbons of silver, pinned together and held at the bottom and at the top by silver bands. The bands are decorated with floral borders and a repoussé design. The name "Wm. Adams/Manufacturer/New York/1841." is engraved in the cartouche, located in the front center of the bottom band. This shaft is topped by a silver globe 4-1/2 inches in diameter and engraved with the seven continents, the names of the oceans, lines of longitude, and the major lines of latitude. The Western Hemisphere faces the front. The globe is encircled with a silver rim marked with the degrees of latitude, on which is perched an engraved solid silver eagle with a wingspan of 15 inches. The total weight of the mace is 10 pounds.

The mace is placed on a pedestal (on the rostrum beside the Speaker on his or her right) whenever the House of Representatives is meeting. When the House is meeting as the Committee of the Whole, the mace is moved to a lower-level pedestal. A viewer watching the chamber on C-SPAN can easily find the mace on left side of the screen and tell by its height whether it is the House of Representatives or the Committee of the Whole that is meeting at the time.

》》》 *See also* related CRS Reports and links on **TCNCPAM.com**.

H. Amendment on the House Floor

In the Committee of the Whole, as on the floor of the House itself, amendments must be germane. That is, an amendment must be relevant to the bill or amendment to which it is offered and it must fall within the legislative jurisdiction of the committee that reported it. The House germaneness rule is complicated and many precedents have arisen from its interpretation and application on the House floor. If a point of order is raised that an amendment is not germane, it is usually necessary for the parliamentarian to provide advice to the Speaker or the chair of the Committee of the Whole on the proper ruling. The parliamentarian's advice is almost always followed.

If the special rule (*see* Chapter 4.D.) is adopted and does not provide otherwise, legislation is usually open for amendment "by section." A section is the basic unit of organization of a bill. Sections may be further broken down into subsections, paragraphs, subparagraphs, clauses, and subclauses. In the most complex bills, sections are organized into "titles."

If the special rule adopted is an open rule, any germane amendment that complies with House rules and the Budget Act (*see* Chapter 7.B.) may be offered.

A special rule that permits amendments, but provides for a time limitation on amendments, is referred to as a modified open rule. If the Rules Committee provides for the offering of a specific amendment or specific list of amendments and prohibits other amendments, the special rule is referred to as a modified closed rule.

Under a closed rule, no amendments are in order.

Amendments, even if otherwise in order, may be constrained by the absence of room on what is called the "amendment tree." The amendment tree is a diagrammatic depiction of the types of amendments and the numbers of amendments permitted to be pending in the House at any given time and parliamentary situation (the Senate has its own amendment trees, *see* Chapter 5.K.). The tree also makes clear the order in which various types of amendments can be offered, and if offered, in what order votes would occur.

The text of the bill underlies the amendment tree. An amendment to that base bill is called a "first degree" amendment. This amendment is subject to being amended by a "perfecting" amendment (an amendment that simply alters the language, but does not completely replace it) or a substitute, considered as being in the "second degree." A substitute amendment that would replace the entire text of the base bill is also in order and would also be considered a first degree amendment. The substitute is, in turn, subject to a perfecting second degree amendment.

If offered, four such amendments constitute the full amendment tree. If all four are pending, they are voted upon in the following order: (1) the second

Basic House Amendment Tree

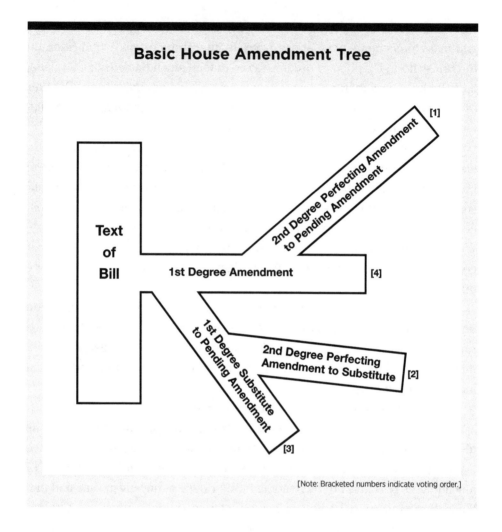

[Note: Bracketed numbers indicate voting order.]

degree amendment to the amendment to the bill text would be voted upon first; (2) the perfecting amendment in the second degree to the substitute amendment would be voted next; (3) the substitute amendment, as amended if amended, would be third; and finally, (4) the amendment that was offered to the base bill is voted.

As amendments (depicted as branches on the tree) are disposed of, that branch is again open for an amendment of that type. However, an amendment may not amend language that has already been amended. (*See* "Basic House Amendment Tree.")

≫ *See also* related CRS Reports and links on **TCNCPAM.com.**

I. Voting

House members have smaller personal legislative staffs than do senators. Generally, their personal legislative staffers are less specialized than those on a senator's personal staff. As a result, it can be more difficult for individual House members to prepare for every specific vote on the House floor and, as a result, many House members rely on their party leadership to advise them on their votes.

Members of the whip organization for each party are usually stationed near the doors entering the House chamber. They try to make the leadership position clear to members coming to the floor to vote. However, with the improvements in electronic communication, it is now easier for personal staff members to keep their members updated on leadership guidance on votes and other matters.

Recorded votes by individual members in the House are displayed on a lighted scoreboard on the wall above the visitors' gallery, clearly visible from the floor. Members are able to quickly check the votes cast by others of their party in their state delegation, their committee chair, or others whose votes may provide guidance. In this way, if a member is inclined to vote in a certain way, but finds unexpected discordance with others they typically vote with, they are prompted to seek clarification before actually casting their vote.

There is a tale about the (then-twelve) members of the Massachusetts House delegation in 1975. One member of that delegation, Congresswoman Margaret Heckler (R-MA) (later Secretary of Health and Human Services under President Reagan), became notorious among her colleagues for voting late in roll calls and relying too heavily on the cues from her colleagues' votes. On one occasion, they chose a minor bill and all cast a nay vote for a bill they favored. Heckler came into the chamber, looked up at the electronic vote tally board and voted nay. Seconds before the time for the roll call ran out, her eleven colleagues instantly switched their votes to yea, leaving her stranded. Presumably she was more careful after that.

There are four methods for counting votes on the floor of the House. Votes may be conducted by voice vote, yeas and nays, division (or standing) vote, or record vote. Voice votes, division votes, and recorded votes are also available options in the Committee of the Whole.

When voice votes are taken, members shout out yea and nay votes and the presiding officer judges which position has more votes. Once the voice vote is taken, any member may demand a vote by division. When the vote is determined by division, first those voting yea are asked to stand and then those voting nay are asked to stand. The presiding officer counts and announces the result of the vote. Individual votes are not recorded, just the totals.

Both yeas and nays and record votes are taken by electronic device: members place their voting card into a slot in one of many voting stations on the floor and press a button to indicate a yea or nay vote or present. If a yeas and nays vote is taken, any member may object on the ground that a quorum is not present. Under those circumstances, the electronic vote will determine both the outcome of the vote and the establishment of a quorum. A "record vote" is taken when requested if one-fifth of a quorum in the House (forty-four members), or one-fourth of a quorum in the Committee of the Whole (twenty-five members), rise in support of the request. The individual votes of members are displayed on the electronic scoreboard in the House chamber. Normally, the minimum time for a record vote, yeas and nays, or quorum call, is fifteen minutes in both the House and the Committee of the Whole. However, the Speaker or presiding officer may allow voting to take additional time. The House Rules also provide for a reduction to a minimum of five minutes, at the Speaker's discretion (or chairman of the Committee of the Whole), when votes occur in sequence.

The special rule reported by the Rules Committee may stipulate the way in which amendments are voted on in order to gain a parliamentary advantage.

For example, a special rule may provide for a way to vote on several alternative amendments to the same language in the bill. An example is the so-called "king of the hill" rule. Under this structure several amendments are permitted and the rule stipulates a specific order in which the amendments will be considered. Each amendment is voted on. If more than one alternative achieves a majority vote, the last one to be approved becomes the king of the hill. That is, the bill is amended by that last successful amendment. Such special rules are sometimes referred to as "designer rules."

An alternative inspired by the king of the hill procedure is the so-called "queen of the hill." Under this process, several alternative amendments for the same language are made in order, similar to the king of the hill procedure. Unlike the king of the hill, however, if more than one amendment receives a majority vote, the surviving amendment is not the last one, but the amendment that received the most votes.

The special rule for consideration of a measure on some occasions contains a "self-executing rule." Under this procedure, the majority vote on the special rule not only adopts that rule, but the House by that very action is "deemed" to have passed a measure or adopted an amendment to a measure. This is typically used by the leadership to avoid a separate vote on a matter that might be uncomfortable for some in the majority caucus, like an unpopular increase in the debt ceiling.

From 1979, until its repeal in 2011, the House actually had a standing rule (former House Rule XXVIII), known as the "Gephardt rule" (named after former Democratic leader Richard Gephardt (D-MO)) that functioned in the same way. It provided for a self-executing House joint resolution to automatically lift the debt ceiling upon passage by the House of the congressional budget resolution. This served the purpose of protecting members of the House from having to vote to increase the statutory debt limitation, a vote often unpopular with constituents.

When the Committee of the Whole has completed its work on a bill, typically the special rule provides that the Committee of the Whole automatically rises and reports that bill with a recommendation back to the House. The Speaker returns to the chair and is handed the gavel by the chair of the Committee of the Whole.

》》》 *See also* related CRS Reports and links on **TCNCPAM.com**.

J. Motion to Recommit

The minority party in the House has the right to offer a motion to recommit a matter to the committee of jurisdiction.

A motion to recommit may be made "with instructions." Ten minutes of debate are in order. This motion is generally voted down by the majority once made, but it does give the minority the ability to get a procedural vote, framed in the way that they would like, in order to force the majority to vote on a proposition on which they may prefer to not be recorded.

If no instructions are included, the motion is nondebatable and a successful motion to recommit kills the bill.

》》》 *See also* related CRS Reports and links on **TCNCPAM.com**.

K. Final Passage

Once the Committee of the Whole has reported the bill back to the full House, the Speaker declares that under the special rule the previous question is ordered. That is the motion that brings debate on the matter to its final votes. Thereafter, no debate is in order and no amendments not adopted in the Committee of the Whole are in order. Separate votes may occur in the House on amendments adopted by the Committee of the Whole if demanded by a member, unless prohibited under the special rule.

On rare occasions, the House may reject controversial amendments that were adopted in the Committee of the Whole.

When all amendments are disposed of, the measure is read for the third time (by title). After that reading and prior to any vote on passage, the motion to recommit is in order, usually offered by a member of the minority.

The passage of the measure is determined by majority vote in the House.

》》》 *See also* related CRS Reports and links on **TCNCPAM.com**.

L. Review Questions

》》》 What is a private bill and how is it considered on the floor?

》》》 Why might the minority offer a motion to recommit even if they know it will not be successful?

》》》 How does a modified open rule differ from a modified closed rule?

》》》 In the House, what is meant by "privileged matters"?

》》》 Compare and contrast a king of the hill vote and a queen of the hill vote.

》》》 What is the required vote to pass a bill called up from the Suspension Calendar?

》》》 Who makes up the Committee of the Whole?

》》》 What are the methods for counting votes on the floor of the House? If the presiding officer determines the nays have prevailed on a voice vote, what is the recourse for a member who disagrees?

》》》 What is an amendment tree? What potential "branches" exist in the House?

》》》 What is the significance of the mace? Where is it located?

Chapter 5
Senate Floor

A. Introduction

James Madison, before the U.S. Senate had even taken shape, recorded his own words in his *Notes of Debates in the Federal Convention of 1787*. On June 7, 1787, Madison rose to argue that "The use of the Senate is to consist in its proceeding with more coolness, with more system, and with more wisdom, than the popular branch."

The Senate, unlike the House of Representatives, was designed as a continuing body. Because of this the rules of the Senate have rarely changed since 1789. Senate rules have remained continuously in place for the most part. The House rules, which are adopted and potentially changed every two years, favor the organized majority. By contrast, over its history the Senate's rules and the precedents interpreting those rules have steadfastly protected the legislative minority and championed the independence of the individual senator.

These differences reflect the founders' design for the Senate to stand as Madison's "necessary fence," against the dangers of overzealous majorities. Madison in *The Federalist* No. 63 wrote that "history informs us of no long-lived republic which had not a senate."

In 1793, Founder John Adams, the nation's second president, but the Senate's first president (Adams was vice president from 1789–1797) wrote in a letter to John Stockdale, May 12, 1793, "Mankind will in time discover that unbridled Majorities, are as tyrannical and cruel as unlimited Despots."

In many ways, Adams's quote captures the spirit of the Senate. From the outset, the rules, precedents, and practices of the Senate were shaped to protect the privileges of the individual senator to debate and amend legislation and to guard against overzealous majorities. This is reflected in the Senate's DNA.

Even Thomas Jefferson, in a letter to James Madison dated December 20, 1787, expressed concern: "The instability of our laws is really an immense evil. I think it would be well to provide in our constitutions that there shall always be a twelve-month between the ingrossing a bill and passing it: that it should then be offered to it's passage without changing a word: and that if circumstances should be thought to require a speedier passage, it should take two thirds of both houses instead of a bare majority."

The twin pillars of the Senate's unique rules are unlimited debate and unfettered amendments, as these ensure that the minority can almost always have some influence on legislative outcomes. This has often made the Senate the cradle of compromise. In the Senate, debate is largely unlimited and, in most circumstances, every senator has the right to offer nongermane amendments.

As former Majority Leader Robert Byrd (D-WV) once said, the Senate is, "the last bastion of minority rights, where a minority can be heard, where a minority can stand on its feet, one individual if necessary, and speak until he falls into the dust."

Beneath the rules of the Senate is its bedrock constitutional principle: equal representation of the states. The Constitution, Article I, Section 3, provides for two senators from each state, with each senator casting one vote, and Article V qualifies the ability to amend the Constitution by guaranteeing that "no state without its consent, shall be deprived of its equal suffrage in the Senate."

Originally, senators were elected by their state legislatures. However, since 1913, when the Seventeenth Amendment to the Constitution was ratified, senators have been directly elected by the voters of their state.

The length of the six-year term of office, the diversity of statewide constituencies, and the protections of senators' privileges in rules and procedures of the Senate lie at the root of the fierce independence and formidable individual influence of each member of the Senate. Former Senate Majority Leader George Mitchell (D-ME) often referred to the Senate as "a collection of independent contractors."

Discussing the course of legislation through consideration on the House floor, former Speaker Thomas Brackett Reed said, "The best system is to have one party govern and the other party watch … ." The journey of legislation through the Senate is quite different. Former Majority Leader Howard Baker (R-TN), referring to the difficulties majority leaders face in steering legislation through the Senate where much can occur only by unanimous consent, called it "herding cats."

Supreme Court Justice Louis Brandeis wrote, "The greatest dangers to liberty lurk in insidious encroachment by men of zeal, well-meaning, but without understanding." The Senate has historically been the one place in our government where legislative minorities are protected, with rules, precedents, and practices to check overzealous majorities.

This chapter explores the procedures on the Senate floor guided by those rules, precedents, and practices, including how legislation is scheduled, debated, amended, and enacted. It attempts to shed light on the sometimes complex maze of holds, filibusters, "amendment trees," and "legislative days."

》》》 *See also* related CRS Reports and links on **TCNCPAM.com.**

B. Scheduling of Legislation

In the Senate, by precedent and tradition, the majority leader sets the agenda and decides which matters to call up for consideration on the Senate floor. The majority leader's powers derive from the precedent that he or she has the privilege of prior recognition. This means that if the majority leader is seeking recognition, the presiding officer will always recognize him or her first.

Matters available for consideration are listed on the Legislative Calendar (Senate Calendar of Business) or the Executive Calendar (*see* Chapter 5.C.). The majority leader brings a matter to the Senate floor, from the calendar, by taking one of two different actions. The majority leader either moves to proceed to consider a matter or requests unanimous consent to take up the matter. In most instances, the motion to proceed to a legislative matter is debatable and therefore subject to a filibuster.

Consideration of legislation on the Senate floor is generally more flexible than the House. Although the Senate has a set of formal standing rules and precedents that are often arcane and difficult to navigate, they are frequently set aside by unanimous consent. However, although the Senate's flexibility is often used to circumvent its formal rules, consideration of legislation on the Senate floor is sometimes complicated by unlimited debate and numerous and sometimes non-germane amendments.

Individual senators, including those in the minority, wield considerable independent power and often their scheduling needs will be accommodated by the leadership. However, because unanimous consent is frequently required in order to move forward expeditiously, and a single objection can prevent such an agreement, the majority leader is often forced to consult with the minority leader. This occurs on an ongoing basis, often at the floor staff level. The leadership may negotiate any manner of scheduling and consideration.

Agreements are usually captured in unanimous consent agreements, sometimes called "time agreements" (*see* Chapter 5.E.). These are generally worked out between the majority and minority leaders and detail how the Senate will proceed. At times, these negotiations are lengthy and involve numerous senators. These agreements between the two leaders are then formalized by the unanimous consent of the entire Senate, when no objection is heard to the proposed agreement (in other words, none of the hundred Senators verbally disapproves of an agreement; it is approved in the absence of an objection).

Unlike the House, all bills and resolutions are placed on one calendar, called the "Calendar of General Orders," which is published daily in a pamphlet called the "Calendar of Business." The form the measure takes (bill, joint resolution, concurrent resolution, or simple resolution) does not affect the order in which it might be called up.

>>> *See also* related CRS Reports and links on **TCNCPAM.com**.

C. Senate Calendars

There are two calendars[1] in the Senate that are printed in separate pamphlet form each day the Senate is in session. These are the "Calendar of Business," which is frequently referred to simply as "the Senate calendar," and the "Executive Calendar," which contains all treaties, nominations and related measures.

Senate Rule VIII provides for a daily call of the "Calendar of Bills and Resolutions" understood to be that section of the pamphlet titled "Calendar of Business" labeled the "Calendar of General Orders." Rule VII makes a call of that calendar mandatory on Mondays. These are among the many provisions of the Senate rules regarding routine procedures that are regularly circumvented by unanimous consent agreements put forward by the majority leader or his or her designee. This is done because following the arcane Senate rules precisely, particularly at the outset of every daily Senate session, is difficult and time-consuming.

The Calendar of General Orders lists every bill and joint resolution reported by the Senate committees and any measures that were directly sent to the calendar by a senator pursuant to Rule XIV (*see* Chapter 2.M.). Measures are listed based in the order in which they were placed on the Calendar of General Orders.

The Executive Calendar lists all nominations and treaties available for floor action. In addition to its legislative responsibilities, the Constitution, in

---

1. The labeling of the Senate legislative calendar and its sub-calendars can be confusing. A call of the calendar under Senate Rules VII and VIII means the calendar of "General Orders," what Rule VII simply calls "the calendar," and what Rule VIII calls the "Calendar of Bills and Resolutions." The pamphlet titled "Calendar of Business" has as its primary component the Calendar of General Orders, but also contains a calendar of resolutions and motions that have gone "over, under the rule," as well as a calendar of bills and joint resolutions read the first time, motions for reconsideration, and a list of measures in conference.

Article II, Section 2, confers on the Senate the power to confirm major presidential nominees (*see* Chapter 8.B.), that is, all judicial nominees and nominees to many executive branch offices (promotions of military officers also are confirmed). The Senate is also charged with the power to ratify treaties (*see* Chapter 8.D.) (by two-thirds of senators present, a quorum having been established).

The Senate proceeds to measures listed on the Senate calendars, either by unanimous consent to take up the measure or by a motion to proceed to it. Obviously, because unanimous consent requires the cooperation of all senators, a single senator can block the Senate from proceeding to the measure.

A motion to proceed to a measure may be made by any senator. However, by Senate tradition it is the majority leader who holds that privilege. Legislation that has been on the calendar for one legislative day (*see* Chapter 5.J.) is eligible to be brought up by a simple majority vote on a motion to proceed. However, a motion to proceed is generally debatable in the Senate, therefore debate is unlimited. Should a motion to proceed be filibustered, pursuant to Rule XXII, a supermajority (sixty votes) would be required to invoke cloture and overcome the filibuster.

Historically, filibusters on the motion to proceed were rare. Most senators saw the simple decision to take up a matter for debate and amendment as a routine step in the legislative process. However, as a consequence of increasing partisan polarization in the Senate, the minority party in recent Congresses has often sought to block motions to proceed to major legislative items that they oppose, or simply to delay proceedings, on the theory that all delay is good because it reduces the amount of legislation the majority party will be able to enact in any given session.

By precedent, a motion to proceed to a matter on the Executive Calendar (nominations or treaties) is not debatable.

It is the majority leader who makes the decision to seek a unanimous consent agreement and the leader or his or her designee makes the motion and waits for the presiding officer to declare that there are no objections when it is made. Alternatively a vote could occur, but is generally not necessary.

》》》 *See also* related CRS Reports and links on **TCNCPAM.com**.

D. Holds

When the Senate majority leader intends to ask unanimous consent to take up a matter, advance notice is usually given to all senators. The principal way the majority leader's intent is communicated is by use of a "hotline," originally a telephone line connected to each office. Hotline messages are now sent via email through the party cloakrooms. Hotline messages are usually addressed immediately. This notice provides the opportunity for senators to object to the consideration of a matter (legislation or nominations or treaties, for example).

If a senator has an objection, this is communicated to the leadership staff of the senator's party. An objection implies that unanimous consent will not be granted, and further that extended debate would likely occur if the majority leader were to move to proceed to the matter.

It is not uncommon for senators to object in response to hotline requests. The threatened objections are referred to as "holds." Holds are rooted in the traditions of senatorial courtesy and do not appear anywhere in the Senate rules.

By Senate tradition, the majority leader shows deference to these holds. Senators are supposed to notify their respective leadership of holds in writing. As a practical matter, many such notifications are conveyed orally.

Some holds are actually anonymous. Leadership has traditionally honored the requests for anonymity. In recent years, however, efforts have been made to end the practice of these "secret holds." In 2007, senators were required to place a "notice of intent to object" in the *Congressional Record* within six days of Senate session. In 2011, that period was tightened to two days. Those efforts have not been effective, as cooperation among two or more senators intent on holding a matter could extend the time indefinitely by rotating their holds, each taking the hold off before triggering the requirement and the other entering their hold at the same time.

Some holds take the form of a request to be consulted by the leadership before any action is taken on a measure.

A measure "clears" if no member of the Senate indicates their intention to object. The majority leader will likely then take up the proposed action. If the proposed action is to "take up and pass" a bill or resolution by unanimous consent, the majority leader or his or her designee will usually include that measure in a stack of measures and motions called up at the end of the day. This is commonly referred to as "wrap-up." If the proposed action is to move to proceed to a matter on the calendar, the majority leader, once it has cleared, knows he or she can schedule that measure with confidence that, at the time it is offered, the motion to proceed will be agreed to by unanimous consent.

It is ironic that successive majority leaders have complained about the excessive use of holds when it is the majority leader who may, at any time, refuse to honor a hold.

 See also related CRS Reports and links on **TCNCPAM.com.**

E. Unanimous Consent Agreements (Time Agreements)

Most major pieces of legislation are considered in the Senate under unanimous consent agreements, frequently referred to as "time agreements." These agreements may limit general debate and debate on amendments and may limit the number of amendments to be considered. At times, the agreement may even specify a time certain for the vote on passage.

If a senator objects to a request for unanimous consent to proceed to a measure, the majority leader may engage in negotiations with all interested parties. The majority leader may decide, however, that it will be too difficult and time-consuming for the Senate to overcome objections. In such cases, the majority leader may choose to abandon plans to consider that measure at that time.

The majority leader may also use an alternative way to proceed to the measure, called a motion to proceed. Most often a motion to proceed to consideration of legislation on the calendar is made after an objection has been made to unanimous consent to take the matter up. The motion to proceed raises its own difficulties as it is debatable in most circumstances, making it subject to unlimited debate. Ending debate and precluding a filibuster, therefore, may require a cloture vote (a three-fifths vote of the senators duly chosen and sworn (sixty votes)). Even if cloture is adopted on a motion to proceed, there can be up to thirty hours of consideration before a vote occurs on that motion to proceed. And this is simply to proceed to consider the legislation—not pass it. Only after the motion to proceed is adopted can the Senate begin to debate and amend the bill or resolution.

Negotiations to reach a time agreement on debate on a bill or resolution can be extensive and involve many senators. As a result, whether the decision is to use unanimous consent as the method to call up the legislation or risk a motion to proceed, individual senators have leverage to have their substantive concerns and scheduling needs considered. This gives senators far more procedural autonomy and influence than members of the House.

Although it is frequently noted that Senate tradition and precedents put the majority leader in charge of the agenda, as a practical matter the majority leader can rarely act to take up any controversial measure without consultation with and cooperation from the minority leader.

》》》 *See also* related CRS Reports and links on **TCNCPAM.com**.

F. Consideration on the Senate Floor

When legislation successfully reaches the Senate floor by unanimous consent, a debatable motion to proceed, or by adoption of a nondebatable motion to proceed under expedited procedures like those established by the 1974 Congressional Budget and Impoundment Control Act (*see* Chapter 7.B. and Chapter 7.L.), the floor managers of the measure are usually the chair and the ranking minority member of the committee that reported the legislation. The adoption of a bill or resolution by the Senate often requires the relevant committee chair, the principal floor manager, to work closely and cooperatively with the ranking minority member of the committee. Of course, there are occasions when this relationship is strained. For example, there are times when the majority has the votes necessary to enact the measure without minority input and thus might not be in a compromising mood. At other times, this occurs because the majority chooses to do so or because the minority refuses to cooperate, though it is often unclear which is which.

A prominent example where relationships broke down was the passage in 2010 of the Affordable Care Act (the major component of the two laws referred to as "Obamacare"). Sixty Democratic senators voted both for cloture to end debate and then for passage. No Republicans supported the bill.

Upon proceeding to a measure, the floor debate customarily begins with opening statements by the floor managers although, under the rules (Senate Rules VII, VIII, XV, XVI, and XXII) the legislation is subject to amendment as soon as it is called up before the Senate. If the legislation reaches the floor under a unanimous consent agreement or pursuant to expedited procedures provided by law, amendments may be controlled and limited by the provisions of the agreement or the law.

》》》 *See also* related CRS Reports and links on **TCNCPAM.com**.

G. Quorum Calls

A common feature of debate on the Senate floor is frequent quorum calls, some of which carry on for long periods, even hours. The roll is called at a very slow pace. The slow pace is to prevent completing the entire roll without a quorum having presented itself. Under the rules (Senate Rules XII, XX, and XXII), should a quorum call reveal the lack of a quorum, the Senate would then be required either to produce a quorum, or to adjourn. These slow-motion quorum calls are a way for the Senate leadership to conduct negotiations with other senators. Such negotiations can be complex and protracted at times. If successful, the outcome is often a unanimous consent agreement breaking a deadlock.

When a quorum call becomes a serious effort to bring enough senators to the Senate floor to establish a quorum, it is known as a "live quorum." Senators are notified that a vote is in progress to produce a quorum, and they usually proceed to the Senate floor to be recorded on that vote. Article I, Section 5 of the Constitution provides that each body can "compel the attendance of absent members … ." In 1798, the Senate adopted a rule enforcing senators' attendance. When the majority leader seeks to ensure a quorum, Senate Rule VI provides that "a majority of the Senators present may direct the Sergeant at Arms to request, and, when necessary, to compel the attendance of the absent Senators." A motion to instruct the sergeant-at-arms to compel the attendance of absent senators is made and a vote is held, the purpose of which is to produce a quorum making the motion to compel moot.

On one occasion in 1988, during an all-night filibuster of a campaign finance reform bill, Majority Leader Robert Byrd (D-WV), with a Republican minority attempting to deny him a quorum, made a motion to instruct the Senate sergeant-at-arms to arrest absent senators in order bring them to the chamber to establish a quorum. The Senate voted 45 to 3 to authorize the arrests. Article 1, Section 5, Clause 1 of the Constitution provides that "a smaller number (than the Senate quorum of a majority of senators) may be authorized to compel the attendance of absent senators." Senator Bob Packwood (R-OR) was carried into the Senate chamber to help establish the quorum. The Senate sergeant-at-arms had located Senator Packwood hiding out in his office, had the door removed from its hinges and the senator brought to the chamber.

》》》 *See also* related CRS Reports and links on **TCNCPAM.com**.

H. Filibuster

The Constitution provides each chamber with the right to establish and revise its own rules. Article I, Section 5, Clause 2 states, "Each house may determine the rules of its proceedings." In the case of the Senate, the most prominent characteristic created by the rules of its proceedings has come to be called the filibuster.

Senate Rule XIX states: "… the Presiding Officer shall recognize the Senator who shall first address him" and that "… no Senator shall interrupt another Senator in debate without his consent." This rule combined with the absence in the Senate rules of a "previous question motion," a motion to end debate and vote on the matter before the body, assures that each senator has the privilege of unlimited debate and that the minority has leverage.

The only ways in which Senate debate can be constrained are: when the Senate invokes cloture; by unanimous consent; by adopting a motion to table (which defeats the question); or when the Senate is operating under expedited procedures (contained in laws like the 1974 Budget Act). Rule XIX also states that "… no Senator shall speak more than twice upon any one question in debate on the same legislative day without leave of the Senate." This is the so-called "two-speech rule." The two-speech rule has not proven to be an effective way to break a filibuster because the "any one question" has been interpreted in such a way that a senator who makes a motion or offers an amendment is then able to make two speeches on those matters.

As a result, a senator or group of senators may delay action on an amendment or the legislation itself, or block them entirely. Any matter subject to unlimited debate under the Senate rules may be filibustered.

During debate on a matter before the Senate, if a senator simply yields to another senator, the chair may rule that the floor has been relinquished. However, a senator may yield to another colleague for a question, but the yielding senator still controls the floor. In practice, this is sometimes used as a way for colleagues to assist a senator who is intent on holding the floor for an extended period of debate. The colleague asks the speaking senator if he or she would "yield for a question." Frequently, the words "without losing your right to the floor" are added just to be sure. What follows are often long, meandering questions designed to use time and relieve the filibustering senator.

Since the rules do not provide a means, aside from cloture, to bring the matter to a vote, the filibuster can be effective even with no one holding the floor. This can make reaching a vote on a particular amendment (except to table it, which defeats it) or passage itself potentially extremely difficult or impossible.

Cloture, under Senate Rule XXII, requires a vote of three-fifths of senators duly chosen and sworn to end debate, sixty votes when the Senate has its full one hundred members.

The process to "invoke cloture" originates with a "cloture motion" signed by at least sixteen senators. The cloture vote automatically occurs, under Senate Rule XXII, one hour after the Senate has convened on the second calendar day on which the Senate is in session after the cloture motion is made. A quorum call precedes the vote on cloture. The quorum call is frequently dispensed with by unanimous consent, and it is not uncommon for the Senate, by unanimous consent, to set a more convenient time for the cloture vote.

Even when cloture is invoked, Rule XXII provides an additional thirty hours of consideration, which includes time consumed in debate, quorum calls, and roll call votes. In the polarized atmosphere of recent years, those on the losing side on cloture votes have insisted on the use of the full thirty hours, mostly for delay and obstruction.

Amendments after cloture is invoked must be germane. At times, this may be the majority leader's main objective in acquiring early cloture on a measure.

All senators know that any amendment or legislation proposed in the Senate may require that supermajority of sixty votes. Therefore, senators usually begin immediately searching for a cosponsor for their proposal from the other side of the aisle. This fosters negotiation, compromise, and moderation—in other words, legislating.

Critics of the filibuster point to the increase in its use in recent years, arguing that it has become largely a means of obstructionism by the minority, claiming that its use has shifted the control of the Senate from its majority to its minority party.

The right to filibuster has been increasingly used by both parties in recent years. The use of the filibuster for much of its history was based on senators' restraint in its use. Senators understood that overuse could endanger the existence of the filibuster and they sought to protect this valued privilege by not overusing it.

However, use of the filibuster has increased as the minority party has increased its use and the use of other procedural rules, including the filling of the amendment tree (*see* Chapter 5.J.), the use of Senate Rule XIV to circumvent committees (*see* Chapter 2M.), the circumvention of normal Senate rules by the use of the reconciliation process under the Budget Act (*see* Chapter 7.D.), the use of the nuclear option to distort the interpretation of the rules (*see* Chapter 5.H.), and others like the increased use of holds in the Senate (*see* Chapter 5.D.).

It is difficult to attempt to count filibusters, because it is not always clear that a filibuster is occurring. Usually it is the cloture votes that are counted; however, cloture votes can occur when there is no filibuster. The majority leader may use a cloture vote to preclude the possibility of a filibuster or to exclude nongermane amendments. Also, the existence of a filibuster needn't always lead to a cloture vote. Sometimes a compromise is reached or one side gives up. Nonetheless, the best approximation of the increase in filibusters is to look at the increase in cloture votes, and, while not exact, it shows that the use of the filibuster has increased.

The cloture rule was adopted by the Senate in 1917. Prior to that time, from 1806, when the previous question motion was dropped, there was no way to end debate until all senators were ready to vote. Even prior to 1806, the previous question motion was not used to cut off debate (*see* Chapter 1.C.). From 1917 through 1970, a total of only forty-nine cloture votes were held. Beginning in 1971, this began to change. In the 92nd and 93rd Congresses (1971–1974), fifty-one cloture votes were held. Beginning in 1991, no single Congress (two-year period) has seen fewer than forty-six cloture votes.

Defenders of the filibuster[2] argue that the solution to excessive partisanship and the deterioration in the bipartisan comity of the Senate is not to rewrite Senate rules. They say that eliminating the filibuster, in fact, would worsen the polarization. They point to the role of the filibuster as a protection of minority rights and a force for consensus building.

There are two exceptions to the sixty-vote requirement in the Senate's rules and precedents regarding cloture. First, when the Senate is considering a change to its Standing Rules, cloture can only be invoked by a two-thirds vote, a quorum being present. This requirement makes changes in the Senate rules extremely difficult to accomplish because ending debate requires sixty-seven votes if all senators are voting.

Second, cloture ending debate on the confirmation of executive branch or

---

2. The author is co-author of *Defending the Filibuster: The Soul of the Senate*, 2nd Edition, 2014.

judicial nominations requires only a simple majority vote, under precedents established in 2013 by Senate Democrats and in 2017 by Senate Republicans using the "nuclear option" (*see* Chapter 5.I.). The simple majority threshold is frequently misunderstood to mean fifty-one affirmative votes (or fifty votes plus the deciding vote of the vice president). Actually, as the Senate parliamentarian has interpreted the 2013 and 2017 precedents, cloture could be invoked by a plurality of the Senate, provided a quorum is present. In theory, this could be as few as twenty-six votes required to invoke cloture on confirmation of a nomination.

》》 *See also* related CRS Reports and links on **TCNCPAM.com.**

I. The Nuclear Option

In November of 2013, Senate Majority Leader Harry Reid (D-NV) executed a parliamentary maneuver labeled the "nuclear option." This was accomplished by raising a point of order that "the votes on cloture under Rule XXII for all nominations other than for the Supreme Court of the United States is by majority vote." The President *pro tempore* of the Senate, Senator Patrick Leahy (D-VT) declared, pursuant to the advice of the parliamentarian, "Under the rules, the point of order is not sustained." The Democratic majority then overturned the Leahy ruling on a nondebatable motion to appeal. Ironically, Senator Leahy himself voted to overturn his own ruling. In this way, Senate Democrats created a precedent that the words of Senate Rule XXII that ending debate requires a vote of "three-fifths of the Senators duly chosen and sworn" would now be interpreted to mean a simple majority. Nominations to the Supreme Court were excluded and the required sixty-vote supermajority remained in force for such nominations. Senate Republicans changed it in 2017 so that Supreme Court nominations can be approved by a simple majority.

One danger of weakening the filibuster rules to permit Senate majorities of a president's party to place judges on the courts without input from the minority is the risk of permanent partisan politicization of the federal courts, including the Supreme Court.

As Nelson Mandela said, "Where you stand depends on where you sit." Majority parties in the Senate, of both parties, have typically been impatient with the filibuster and wanted to see it reformed, while the minority parties have fought for the privileges of unlimited debate and unfettered amendments protected by the filibuster.

Beyond the impact of the nuclear option on the nomination process, those who defend the filibuster are concerned that the precedent could be used again in the future to eliminate the filibuster for legislative matters.

In 2010, just a few months before his death, Senator Robert Byrd (D-WV) wrote: "If the rules are abused, and Senators exhaust the patience of their colleagues, such actions can invite draconian measures. But those measures themselves can, in the long run, be as detrimental to the role of the institution and to the rights of the American people as the abuse of the rules."

For more than 200 years, since the removal from the Standing Rules of any reference to the previous question, the Senate has defended the privilege accorded to individual senators to speak without limit.

In April 2017, a bipartisan group of sixty-one senators sent a letter to the Senate's leadership expressing opposition to "… any effort to curtail the existing rights and prerogatives of Senators to engage in full, robust, and extended debate … ."

In March 1949, then-Senator Lyndon Johnson (D-TX), declared: "If I should have the opportunity to send into the countries behind the iron curtain one freedom and only one, I know what my choice would be. I would send to those nations the right of unlimited debate in their legislative chambers. Peter the Great did not have a Senate with unlimited debate, with power over the purse, when he enslaved hundreds of thousands of men in the building of Saint Petersburg. If we now, in haste and irritation, shut off this freedom, we shall be cutting off the most vital safeguard which minorities possess against the tyranny of momentary majorities."

〉〉〉 *See also* related CRS Reports and links on **TCNCPAM.com**.

J. Amendment on the Senate Floor and in Committee

A bill or resolution that reaches the Senate floor is normally subject to amendment by both individual senators and by the committee that reported the bill or resolution with amendments.

Committee amendments take priority. When a committee amendment is pending, it is subject to further amendment, but while committee amendments are under consideration no other amendments are in order, except to language addressed by that committee amendment.

If the committee reported a total substitute for the text of the measure, the total substitute is voted on last because, if adopted, it would preclude further amendment. This is because amendments are not in order to portions of the measure previously amended, unless the new amendment takes a "bigger bite." That is, when an amendment is offered that encompasses a portion of the measure that has been previously amended, but seeks to amend more of the measure, it is in order.

Committee amendments are often adopted by the Senate by unanimous consent. Consent may also be given to consider the committee amendments as original text. This means that further amendment to parts of the measure, or all of it if a committee total substitute was adopted, would be considered in the first degree (*see* Chapter 5.I.).

The number of amendments, whether amendments are required to be germane, and even which specific amendments may be the only ones in order, can be the subject of a unanimous consent agreement governing debate and amendment on a particular measure.

Absent a unanimous consent agreement or cloture, debate on amendments is not limited. The amendment need not be germane (strictly related by subject matter) to the bill. Nongermane amendments are often referred to as "riders." Also, nongermane amendments adopted in the Senate can raise significant problems with the House as the House requires amendments to be germane. When conferees meet (*see* Chapter 6) to work out the differences between House-passed and Senate-passed versions of a bill, the House often insists that nongermane provisions be dropped by the Senate, which can be a sticking point for reaching agreement.

There are exceptions under Senate rules (Senate Rules XVI and XXII) and the Congressional Budget and Impoundment Act (Section 305(b)), where germaneness is required, for example, appropriations bills, measures under the Budget Act, and after cloture has been invoked by the Senate. On occasion, a germaneness requirement may be imposed by unanimous consent. When germaneness is required in the Senate, precedents impose a stricter standard than in the House.

Amendments are either in the "first degree," meaning it changes the text of the measure before the Senate, or in the "second degree," meaning it amends the text of the first degree amendment. No third degree amendment is in order.

A "perfecting amendment" if adopted changes the text of the measure to which it is offered. "Substitute amendments" by definition replace all available text with new language.

After adoption of an amendment, a senator invariably moves to "reconsider the vote." This motion to reconsider is normally routinely made by a senator from the prevailing side or one who did not vote and immediately tabled, thus killing the possibility of a revote on the matter. If the motion to reconsider were to be adopted, the Senate would vote again on the original matter.

In the Senate, different amendment trees are possible based on the form of the initial amendment offered and pending. One tree is designed for "motions to strike and insert," another for "a motion to insert," third for a "motion to strike," and a fourth for a motion to strike all the text of a measure and insert completely new text, which is a complete substitute for a measure.

》》》 *See also* related CRS Reports and links on **TCNCPAM.com**.

K. Filling the Amendment Tree

The Senate amendment tree is considerably more complex than in the House (*see* Chapter 4.H.). Under the most complex scenario, which only occurs under limited circumstances and if all of the amendments are offered in a particular order, there could be as many as eleven amendments pending in the Senate at the same time. Highly complex trees are rare. Amendments are added to the tree in the order they are offered and they are voted upon in the reverse order of their submission.

However, the practice of purposely filling the amendment tree by the majority leader has become more frequent in recent years.

Like the House amendment tree, the Senate amendment tree is a diagrammatic depiction of the types of amendments and the numbers of amendments permitted to be simultaneously pending in the Senate at any given time and parliamentary situation. Four charts printed in the published precedents and practices compiled in *Riddick's Senate Procedure* depict possible trees in the Senate (the most recent edition was prepared and edited in 1992 by former Senate parliamentarians Floyd Riddick and Alan Frumin, S. Doc. 101-28), and are reproduced on the following pages. (*See* "Senate Amendment to Insert," "Senate Amendment to Strike," "Senate Amendment to Strike and Insert (Substitute for Section of a Bill," and "Senate Amendment to Strike and Insert (Substitute for Bill.")

As in the House, amendments, even if otherwise in order, may be constrained by the absence of room on the amendment tree. Also, the tree indicates the order that amendments, if offered, are voted on.

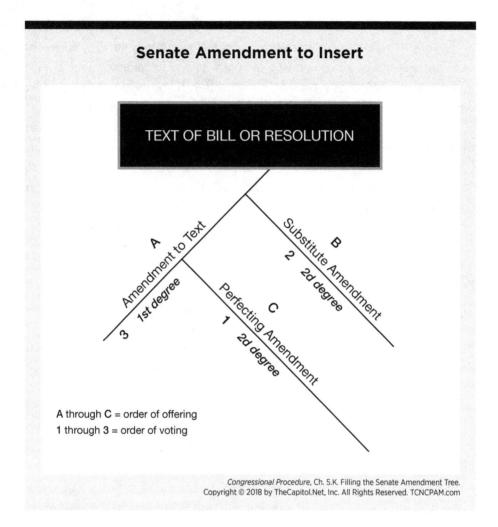

Senate Amendment to Insert

TEXT OF BILL OR RESOLUTION

A
Amendment to Text
3 1st degree

Substitute Amendment
2 2d degree
B

Perfecting Amendment
1 2d degree
C

A through C = order of offering
1 through 3 = order of voting

"Filling the amendment tree" describes purposely offering a sufficient series of amendments one after the other to occupy each branch of the tree. Once this occurs, no further amendments are in order unless and until an amendment is disposed of by the Senate. The amendments occupying the tree may be disposed of if the Senate votes to adopt or defeat the amendment or the amendment is tabled, killing it. Amendments can also be withdrawn or removed by a point of order sustained by the presiding officer.

In theory, any member of the Senate could fill the tree by offering a series of amendments designed to occupy all of the branches. As a practical matter, due to the majority leader's "right of prior recognition" it is only the majority leader who can be assured of being repeatedly recognized by the presiding

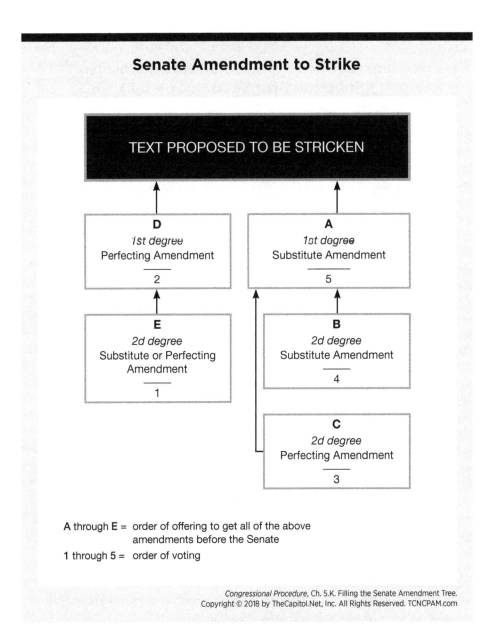

Senate Amendment to Strike

TEXT PROPOSED TO BE STRICKEN

D	A
1st degree	*1st degree*
Perfecting Amendment	Substitute Amendment
2	5

E	B
2d degree	*2d degree*
Substitute or Perfecting Amendment	Substitute Amendment
1	4

C
2d degree
Perfecting Amendment
3

A through **E** = order of offering to get all of the above amendments before the Senate

1 through **5** = order of voting

Congressional Procedure, Ch. 5.K. Filling the Senate Amendment Tree.
Copyright © 2018 by TheCapitol.Net, Inc. All Rights Reserved. TCNCPAM.com

officer and holding the floor to offer the sufficient number of amendments to fill the tree. This is because when a senator has offered an amendment, he or she loses his or her right to the floor. Only the majority leader can be certain of being recognized again immediately to offer another amendment.

When wielded by the majority leader, this can be a powerful tool to deny the minority the ability to offer any or few amendments. On occasion, a majori-

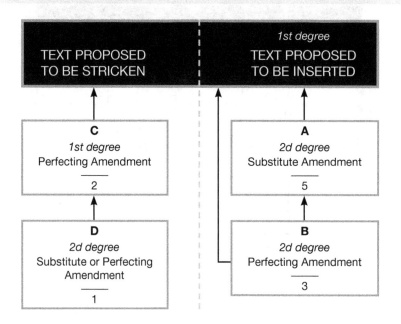

Senate Amendment to Strike and Insert (Substitute for Section of a Bill)

		1st degree
TEXT PROPOSED TO BE STRICKEN		TEXT PROPOSED TO BE INSERTED

C
1st degree
Perfecting Amendment
—
2

A
2d degree
Substitute Amendment
—
5

D
2d degree
Substitute or Perfecting Amendment
—
1

B
2d degree
Perfecting Amendment
—
3

A through D = order of offering to get all of the above amendments before the Senate

1 through 4 = order of voting

ty leader will fill the tree as a way of completely controlling the flow and timing of amendments, allowing only those he or she approves. By asking unanimous consent to temporarily set aside the amendment on the outermost branch of the tree, the majority leader may permit approved amendments to be considered. In this way the majority leader becomes the gatekeeper.

When filling the tree is combined with the filing of a cloture motion, the leader can attempt to both cut off debate and limit amendments on the measure.

The ability to offer amendments is one of the pillars of the protection of minority rights in the Senate. For this reason, filling the tree discourages

Senate Amendment to Strike and Insert (Substitute for Bill)

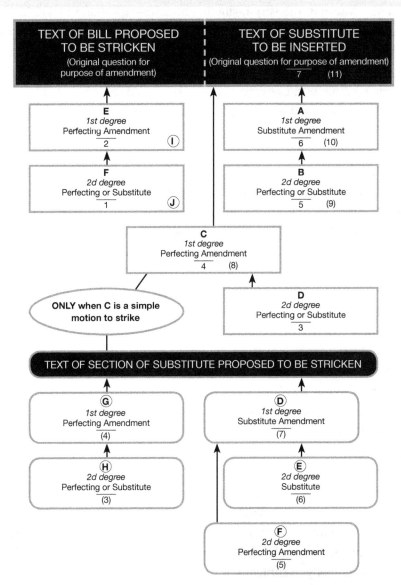

A through J = order of offering to have all amendments pending at the same time

1 through 11 = order of voting

Circled and parenthetical material apply only when **C** is a motion to strike

debate, compromise, and bipartisan negotiation. Filling the amendment tree frustrates the minority, who might in response launch a filibuster on the measure and cease cooperation, leading to gridlock on the floor.

At times, the minority acts first in response to the suspicion that the majority will file cloture at the very beginning of deliberation on the legislation. In such circumstances, the minority has on occasion filibustered the motion to proceed to the bill, holding it hostage, and then demanding the right to offer their amendments when the bill is taken up. Like the chicken-and-egg dilemma, it can be difficult for observers and participants to know where the resultant gridlock began. Often both sides feel aggrieved by the tactics being used by the opposing party.

The late Senator Arlen Specter (D-PA), who was elected to the Senate in 1980 as a Republican and switched to the Democratic party in 2009, was a leading critic of majority leaders of both parties' increasing use of filling the amendment tree. In 2007, the Senate was enduring gridlock over a proposal to block President George W. Bush's plans to send additional troops to fight in the Iraq War. The Republican minority, convinced that majority Democrats would fill the tree and preclude amendments, launched a filibuster on the motion to proceed. Specter, speaking on the Senate floor, declared, "… what is happening today is charges are being leveled on all sides. There has been a lot of finger pointing with most of the Democrats saying the Republicans are obstructing a vote … and Republicans saying … the reason we are doing it is so this procedural device may not be used … to 'fill the tree'."

Speaking about the floor tactics later, Specter expressed the hope that "there would be a truce," but doubted this would happen because the procedural rule "has been used by both sides … when it suits the partisan advantage of one party or the other …," which, he concluded, "is not consistent with sound policy and the public interest."

On another occasion, complaining about then-Majority Leader Harry Reid's (D-NV) use of filling the amendment tree to block Republican amendments on a bill to control climate change, Specter declared, "The American people live under the illusion that we have a United States Senate. The facts show that the Senate is realistically dysfunctional."

In the past, filling the amendment tree was used sparingly, usually as a way to temporarily block amendments to encourage or force the minority leader to negotiate with the majority leader on a time agreement to limit amendments to the measure.

According to a Congressional Research Service study[3] between 1985 and 2015, no leader filled the amendment tree more than Democrat Reid (D-NV), who served as Senate majority leader from 2007 to 2015, who filled the tree ninety-five times.

In 2013, the Senate adopted a standing order, which has the force of a Senate rule, for the 113th Congress only, that sought to protect the minority's ability to offer at least two amendments at the beginning of consideration of a measure. In the face of continued battles over Senate procedures, the standing order has not been renewed in succeeding Congresses.

>>> *See also* related CRS Reports and links on **TCNCPAM.com**.

L. Calendar Days and Legislative Days

Several Senate rules include a period of days when an action may occur. Some specify "calendar days." For example, Senate Rule XIII governing motions to reconsider reads, "When a question has been decided by the Senate, any senator voting with the prevailing side or who has not voted may, on *the same day or on either of the next two days of actual session* thereafter, move a reconsideration ... ." (emphasis added) By precedent, the Senate interprets that language to mean a calendar day, which is a normal twenty-four hour period (*see* Chapter 8.J.).

Other rules refer specifically to or have been construed to mean a "legislative day." For example, Senate Rule VIII, which details the "order of business," states, "All motions made during the first two hours of a *new legislative day* to proceed to the consideration of any matter shall be determined without debate ... ." A legislative day starts when the Senate convenes after an adjournment and continues until the Senate next adjourns. This means that a legislative day can last for a number of calendar days or even weeks or months if the Senate ends one or more successive daily sessions by recessing rather than adjourning.

Because the Senate rules (IV, VII, and VIII) provide for a number of burdensome procedures at the outset of each legislative day, the majority leader frequently, before adjournment, requests unanimous consent to dispense with

---

3. Christopher M. Davis, Congressional Research Service Memorandum, "Instances in Which Opportunities for Floor Amendment Were Limited by the Senate Majority Leader or His Designee Filling or Partially Filling the Amendment Tree: 1985–2015," July 29, 2015, accessed March 9, 2018, https://www.dpcc.senate.gov/files/documents/TreesBy Instance07292015.pdf

those procedures for the next legislative day. Without that consent, the majority leader may seek to "recess" the Senate rather than adjourning, thus keeping the Senate in the same legislative day. For example, then-Majority Leader Robert Byrd (D-WV) kept the Senate in one very long legislative day from January 3 to June 12 in 1980.

Historically, some proponents of changing the Senate rules to eliminate or curtail filibusters have adopted the view, referred to as the "constitutional option," that the Senate has the constitutional right to end debate to change its rules by simple majority at the outset of each session on the first legislative day. The Senate, which considers itself a "continuing body" and therefore does not adopt its rules at the beginning of each Congress (*see* Chapter 1.G.), has never accepted the first-day argument.

However, at the outset of the 112th Congress on January 3, 2011, because the proponents of the constitutional option feared that adjourning until January 25, after the Martin Luther King holiday, would prejudice their chance to prevail, the majority leader, Harry Reid (D-NV), agreed to recess the Senate. Under the Senate rules, by recessing rather than adjourning, the Senate remained in the same legislative day as distinguished from a calendar day. This meant that when it returned, the Senate would remain in its "first legislative day," thereby leaving open the question for the Senate of whether to change its rules by exercising the constitutional option. The *Washington Post* called it [recessing rather than adjourning] "a parliamentary trick to leave the chamber in a state of suspended animation." ("Senate in long recess as leaders seek to rein in Democrats' filibuster rebellion," by Paul Kane, the *Washington Post*, January 22, 2011.)

》》》 *See also* related CRS Reports and links on **TCNCPAM.com**.

M. Voting

The Senate conducts votes by three methods, roll call (often referred to as "the yeas and nays"), voice, and division. (Senate Rule XII.)

Any senator may request the yeas and nays. If the request is seconded by a sufficient number of senators, one-fifth of a quorum, at least eleven senators, the presiding officer will state that "the yeas and nays are ordered." When the debate on the matter is concluded, the roll is called. A roll call vote is generally limited to fifteen minutes, although an additional five-minute grace period is customary and the vote may be held open for a longer period, at the discretion of the majority leader, to accommodate senators having difficulty getting to the floor on time. When many votes are scheduled in a "stack," the period for voting is often reduced by unanimous consent to ten minutes. An example is the often extensive list of consecutive roll call votes, known as a "vote-a-rama," which occurs at the end of debate on a budget resolution or reconciliation bill (*see* Chapter 7.C. and Chapter 7.D.).

A voice vote occurs when no roll call is demanded. Often, when unanimous consent is sought, the presiding officer declares, "without objection (the matter) is agreed to." If the voice vote is actually carried out, the presiding officer will ask for those in favor to say "aye" and those opposed "nay." The presiding officer will announce the judgment based on the loudness of each side's vote, stating tentatively, for example, that "the ayes appear to have it … the ayes do have it and the [question] is agreed to." At the point indicated by the ellipses, a senator may ask for a recorded vote if not satisfied that the presiding officer has judged correctly. This seldom occurs.

Finally, on rare occasions, a division or "standing vote" will be demanded by a senator or requested by the presiding officer. Senators on each side of the question are asked to stand and be counted. On a division vote, no record is made of how individual senators voted.

>>> *See also* related CRS Reports and links on **TCNCPAM.com**.

N. Final Passage

When all amendments have been disposed of, the measure is "engrossed" and "read for the third time (by title)." (Senate Rule XIV)

Following the vote on passage, as with an amendment or motion, a senator on the prevailing side makes a motion to reconsider (Senate Rules XIII, XV, and XXII) and normally this is immediately tabled by voice vote. Occasionally a cloture vote to end debate and move to the vote on final passage is close, but does not succeed. The majority leader, to preserve the ability to try again on cloture at a later time, will "enter" a motion to reconsider. The motion is placed on a special calendar and may be brought up at a future time by unanimous consent or a motion to proceed to it. In an action that often confuses many observers of the Senate, the majority leader at the end of a cloture vote that narrowly failed will change his or her vote from in favor of cloture to against. Because a senator must be on the prevailing side in order to be eligible to enter the motion to reconsider, the majority leader will switch sides.

Once a measure has been passed by the Senate, the enrollment clerk will send the measure to the Government Publishing Office to be officially printed. Certified by the Secretary of the Senate, this is called the "engrossed bill or an engrossed Senate amendment to a House-originated bill."

Engrossed bills and amendments are "messaged" to the House of Representatives.

If the measure passed by the Senate was a measure previously passed by the House and the text remained identical to the House passed measure, it is "enrolled (printed on parchment paper)," signed by the Speaker and the president of the Senate (sometimes the president *pro tempore* or another senator authorized by the Senate) and sent to the president.

>>> *See also* related CRS Reports and links on **TCNCPAM.com**.

O. Review Questions

>>> How are votes conducted in the Senate?

>>> What is a legislative day? Why is it important?

>>> What is required to invoke cloture and end debate on a rules change?

>>> What is meant by "filling the amendment tree?" Who is likely the only senator that can accomplish this?

>>> As a general rule, are amendments in the Senate required to be germane? What are some circumstances in which amendments are required to be germane?

>>> Why are senators more inclined than House members to seek cosponsors on the other side of the aisle?

>>> Did the nuclear option change the cloture rule, Rule XXII?

>>> What is the evidence that the filibuster has seen increased use in recent years?

>>> What is the largest number of amendments that may be pending in the Senate at the same time?

>>> What is meant when the Senate is referred to as a continuing body?

Chapter 6
Resolving Differences between the House and Senate

A. Introduction

For any legislation to become law, under the Constitution, Article 1 Section 7, both the House and the Senate must pass the same measure. The text of the bill or joint resolution must be identical. Only then is it sent to the president for signature or veto.

The House of Representatives is ruled by its majority. The Senate protects its minority. The House has 435 members and rigid rules. The Senate has 100 members and rules and practices that are more malleable in daily practice. The House, with two-year terms for its members, is often buffeted by waves of public opinion. The Senate with six-year terms is more insulated. The House, in many cases, moves comparatively quickly. The Senate is generally slow moving, even glacial at times. (*See* **CongressByTheNumbers.com**.)

This reflects the design of the framers of the Constitution.

So, how do these bodies come together to approve identical text? Having passed sometimes very different versions of legislation, how do they get a bill or resolution to the president?

Legislating in Congress involves negotiation, compromise, moderation, and civility. The process of resolving differences between the chambers is no different. While the Congress of recent decades has made legislative compromise seemingly unreachable at times, the Constitution and the rules of the House and Senate compel the chambers to reach accommodation, at least in some circumstances.

This is often very difficult and complex. When both the House and Senate chambers share the same majority party, even if the president is also of the same party, it still may not be simple. Differing policy views and politics between the chambers or with the president can derail the effort. In the 111th Congress, the Democratic House was able to pass a cap-and-trade bill in 2009 to address climate change. While the Senate majority leader tried for much of the next year, no legislation was passed. Democratic senators from the Midwest were particularly concerned about potential economic impacts, given their states' reliance on coal-burning power plants.

But when the chambers are run by different parties, it is even more challenging, sometimes insurmountable. A Republican House passed some form of a repeal of Obamacare, for example, more than fifty times between 2011 and 2014. The Democratic-controlled Senate never took the bills up.

》》》 *See also* related CRS Reports and links on **TCNCPAM.com**.

B. Resolving Differences

One chamber must pass the product of the other, or they must agree on language added or subtracted. Either way, in the end, the Senate must consider a House measure or the House must consider a Senate measure.

When the first chamber to act passes a measure, it "messages" an "engrossed" copy of the legislation to the other body. In the second chamber, the measure may be "held at the desk" or referred to the appropriate committee.

The easiest case is if the House passes legislation without amendment sent to it by the Senate, simply adopting the Senate measure. Alternatively, it may be the Senate voting to pass without amendment the language of a House-passed bill or joint resolution sent to it.

This process usually occurs on measures that are not controversial. When the same party controls both chambers, the House and Senate leadership may take this as the course of least resistance. For example, the passage of the Affordable Care Act (the bulk of Obamacare), one of the most controversial bills of recent decades, was ultimately passed in this fashion. The Democrats at the time controlled both the House and the Senate. The substance of the bill was first passed by the Senate at 7:00 a.m. on Christmas morning in 2009, by a 60 to 39, party-line vote, by adding its language to a minor, unrelated, House-passed bill. The House passed without amendment the Senate-amended House bill on March 21 of the following year and sent it to President Barack Obama, who signed the bill into law on March 23.

Even with control of both chambers, including a sixty-vote filibuster-proof majority in the Senate, the Democratic leadership knew that the minority in the Senate could make use of a conference committee or amendments between the chambers extremely difficult. As a result they ultimately opted for House acceptance of the Senate bill (*see* Chapter 6.D.).

If the chamber that received the legislation does not pass the identical language, it may pass the measure with an amendment or amendments. Sometimes this is a complete substitute. For example, if the House sends the Senate legislation on a matter, but the Senate has been working on a different version, the Senate will hold the House bill at the desk[1] and will vote to amend it.

---

1. Technically, it takes unanimous consent to hold a measure at the desk. As a practical matter, many measures at the desk are there due to a "blind hold," an informal agreement between the respective party secretaries.

If the differences between the House and Senate legislation cannot be resolved by "amendments between the houses" (*see* Chapter 6.C.), they can attempt to work out differences by creating a "conference committee," a temporary committee made up of House and Senate members (*see* Chapter 6.D.). If the conference committee is able to reach agreement on language acceptable to the conferees from each chamber, the conference committee issues a conference report (*see* Chapter 6.E.) which is sent to each chamber and must be passed by each chamber (no amendments are in order) before going to the president's desk.

》》》 *See also* related CRS Reports and links on **TCNCPAM.com**.

C. Amendments between the Chambers

When a measure is messaged from one chamber to the other and the second chamber amends the legislation, it is returned to the body that originally passed it.

The originating chamber then may accept the amendment. In this case, both chambers having passed the bill or resolution in identical form, it is sent to the president.

In the House, the floor manager of the legislation could ask the House to "concur" in the Senate amendment. Similarly, in the Senate the manager might ask unanimous consent to concur in the House amendment. In either case, if approved, the bill or resolution would then be sent to the president's desk.

However, the originating chamber has the opportunity to further amend the legislation and send it back to the other chamber. For example, the House may concur in a Senate amendment with a further amendment. If this is agreed to, normally by unanimous consent, the House-passed measure with the "House amendment to the Senate amendment to the House bill" is returned to the Senate.

In much the same way, the Senate can concur in a House amendment with a further Senate amendment. However, in the Senate, although the motion to proceed to the House amendment to the Senate measure is nondebatable, the actual consideration of the House amendment to which the Senate has concurred, or concurred with a further amendment, is debatable and could be subject to filibuster. Therefore, if unanimous consent cannot be obtained (it usually is at this point), the option of agreeing to a conference committee must then be considered.

This process of amending and further amending can be continued back-and-forth only two times per side. However, if progress is being made and success seems near, the Senate can permit additional rounds of amendments by unanimous consent and the House can do so with a special rule from the Rules Committee.

Colloquially, this back-and-forth series of amendments is known as "ping ponging" the bill.

If at some point in this amending process either body decides not to act on the legislation sent to it by the other chamber, the leadership may decide to seek a conference with the other chamber. Otherwise, the legislation may die if neither chamber is willing to relent. The process of going to conference with the other chamber is a three step process in either chamber (*see* Chapter 6.D.).

》》 *See also* related CRS Reports and links on **TCNCPAM.com**.

D. Conference Committee

A conference committee is a temporary ad hoc committee made up of members of the House and senators. A conference cannot be held unless and until both chambers formally agree to form a conference committee.

Conference committees exist to draft a compromise bill that both chambers can accept. Conference committees have played such a significant role in the final shaping of major legislation that they have sometimes been referred to as the "third house of Congress."

Convening a conference requires three steps in each chamber.

The first step is to formally disagree with the version sent to it by the other chamber and insist on its own measure. Usually, it is the chamber that first approved the measure that acts first, but the second chamber upon passing its version may "insist on its amendments" and request a conference.

Step two is to request a conference. And the third and final step toward convening a conference committee is the appointment of conferees by the presiding officer. The conference is formed only if the second chamber insists on its amendment, accepts the request for a conference, and appoints its conferees.

In the Senate each of these three steps is carried out by debatable motion. Since debatable matters in the Senate are generally subject to filibuster, there can sometimes be a problem getting the measure to conference if a significant number of senators (forty-one to oppose cloture) are sufficiently opposed to the legislation that they do not want a conference committee to be convened.

Until 2013, the possibility existed that a determined group of senators (or potentially even one) could create an enormous obstacle by filibustering each of the three motions necessary to form a conference committee, thereby making the process time-consuming and perhaps insurmountable.

For example, in 2009, the Democratic majority in the House passed the Affordable Care Act (Obamacare). The Democratic Senate subsequently passed a similar bill, on a party-line vote, which contained several provisions that the House was unwilling to agree to. These had been added to attract the final three Democrats needed to overcome a Republican filibuster. The potential for the considerable delay a filibuster would cause and the narrow margin for error to overcome such filibusters, even though there were sixty Democrats in the Senate, weighed heavily in the Democrats' decision not to seek a conference.

In 2013, the Senate made a change to the standing rules of the Senate allowing the three necessary motions to get to conference to be made in "a single, non-divisible motion," thus reducing the potential number of filibusters from three to one. Also in that rules change, the possible debate time allowed after cloture was invoked on this motion was reduced from thirty hours to only two hours. (Senate Rule XXVIII.)

When a conference is convened conferees are named by each chamber. In the House, the Speaker, under House Rule I, appoints conferees. In the Senate, the presiding officer is typically given the authority by unanimous consent to name conferees (formally, "managers on the part of the Senate.") These decisions in both bodies are generally made through consultation with the committee chair and the party leadership. Usually senior members of the committees of jurisdiction are appointed, but there is wide discretion. Sometimes more junior members are included and possibly even members who do not sit on the committee of jurisdiction, and perhaps representation from the leadership.

The number of conferees from each chamber can range widely. However, since conference committee decisions are made by the majority of each delegation as opposed to a majority vote of all conferees, the relative size of House and Senate delegations plays no significant role and each chamber can decide to name any number of conferees it chooses.

A motion to instruct conferees can be made in the House, but such a motion, if adopted, expresses the view of the body. The motion is not binding. Motions to instruct are rare in the Senate. Such a motion is debatable with a filibuster possible in the Senate and is subject to amendment.

Conference committee meetings are open to the public, unless conferees vote to close them. As described in a CRS report by Elizabeth Rybicki, "There are almost no rules governing procedure in conference. Conferences are negotiating forums, and the two chambers allow conferees to decide for themselves how best to conduct the negotiations." ("Conference Committee and Related Procedures: An Introduction," CRS Report 96-708.)

While conference committees have wide latitude as to how they conduct their negotiations, they are limited in "scope" by the rules of both chambers. That is, they may not consider language not passed by either chamber, nor new spending provisions (whether specific discretionary appropriations or mandatory spending) not in either the House-passed or the Senate-passed version. Such new material is sometimes referred to as "airdropped" into the conference report.

If members of the House believe that the conference has exceeded its authority by including provisions outside the scope, a point of order may be made in the House. These are rare, and to preclude them, the House Rules Committee may adopt a special rule for the conference report that waives all points of order.

In the Senate, under Rule XXVIII, a point of order can also be made if the conference report exceeds the scope of the conference. The point of order can be waived by a three-fifths vote of senators chosen and sworn (usually sixty). The Senate overruled such a point of order in 1996 that, in effect, negated the rule by precedent. Therefore no "out of scope" rule applied until the Senate reinstated the application of the rule at the start of the 107th Congress five years later.

Some conferences are more formal than others. Actual formal meetings of the conference committees can be few, even just one. Informal closed meetings, particularly of the majority members, in some cases can resolve the differences and present the conference with a fait accompli.

For example, in 2003, the Republican-controlled Congress wrote the final Medicare Prescription Drug bill (P.L. 108-173) by abandoning the traditional formalities of a conference committee, excluding most Democrats, including Minority Leader Tom Daschle (D-SD), a major Democratic leader on the bill, and House Ways and Means Committee Chair Charlie Rangel (D-NY).

Since that time, the pattern of excluding the minority when the same party holds the majority in the both chambers has, in turn, made it more likely that senators in the minority party will block the process of going to conference by threatened or actual filibusters.

Often informal "pre-conferences" are held, usually by the House and Senate committee staff to work out differences in advance as a way of facilitating the work of the formal conference if one is held. On occasion, pre-conferencing can begin even before the second chamber has completed action on the bill.

An example is the landmark Alaska National Interest Lands Conservation Act (ANILCA) passed in 1980 (P.L. 96-847). The House passed a version of the bill in May 1979. The following year, 1980, the Senate Energy Committee reported its version. On the Senate floor, Senator Paul Tsongas (D-MA) was successful in a test vote demonstrating the votes for a complete substitute for the bill favored by environmental groups. Alaska's senior Senator Ted Stevens (R-AK) launched a filibuster. Majority Leader Robert Byrd (D-WV) pulled the bill from the floor and instructed the principals to attempt to negotiate a compromise. Energy Committee Chair Scoop Jackson (D-WA), Tsongas, and Stevens launched a negotiation that lasted for months, later expanded into essentially an informal conference with the House Interior Committee led by Chair Mo Udall (D-AZ). The product of the informal conference passed the Senate in August and was accepted by the House and signed into law in December 1980, by President Carter just weeks before leaving office. No formal conference ever occurred.

In the era of partisan polarization, in both the House and Senate, the leadership frequently bypasses formation of conference committees altogether. Fewer conferences have been occurring. Particularly when both chambers are controlled by the same party, the House and Senate leadership seek to avoid a full-scale conference to both reduce minority party involvement in the decisions and to reduce the opportunities for minority obstruction.

The polarization has led to more powerful central leadership in both chambers and those leaders are more likely to want to keep control of the process of resolving differences and negotiating bicameral agreements.

Professor Steven S. Smith wrote in *The Senate Syndrome*, "As the partisan divisions continued to deepen … party leaders were expected to play a more central role in the process of reconciling House-Senate difference. A natural corollary of more leadership involvement was less exclusive reliance on the committee leaders and the formal conference process … ." Smith reports that conference committees' participation in measures enacted into law fell from

13 percent in the 103rd Congress (1993–1994) to only 2 percent in the 110th Congress and 3 percent in the 111th Congress ending in 2010.[2] That pattern has largely continued.

>>> *See also* related CRS Reports and links on **TCNCPAM.com**.

E. Conference Reports

When consideration by the conference committee is complete, it will recommend that either the House recede from all or certain of its amendments or that the Senate recede from all or certain of its amendments, or both. Rarely will a conference committee report the inability to reach an agreement.

A majority of both House and Senate delegations to the conference is necessary to agree to a conference report to be sent to each chamber.

Once the conference committee has reached agreement, its recommendations in the form of a conference report, and an accompanying "joint statement of managers," which explains the decisions made by and the intent of the conferees, is prepared. Conferees must indicate their approval by signing both the conference report and the joint statement of managers.

Typically, the conference report will go first to the chamber that agreed to the conference rather than to the chamber that requested the conference.

The conference report is not open to further amendment. In the first chamber to consider the conference, a member can move to recommit the bill to the conference committee. But once the first chamber has passed the conference report, the conference committee is dissolved and the second chamber to act can no longer recommit the bill to the conference because it no longer exists.

In both the Senate and the House, a conference report is a privileged matter. In the House this means that once the official papers are received the conference report can be taken up at almost any time. In the Senate this means that the motion to proceed to a conference report is not debatable and cannot be filibustered. The conference report itself is subject to filibuster once the Senate is debating it. Like all legislative filibusters, ending debate requires invoking cloture with a three-fifths vote.

If the conference report is rejected by either chamber, the other body is notified. A new conference may or may not be sought.

---

2. Smith, Steven S. *The Senate Syndrome: The Evolution of Procedural Warfare in the Modern U.S. Senate.* Norman: University of Oklahoma Press, 2014.

When both chambers have reached final agreement, an "enrolled" copy of the bill or resolution will be prepared. This is the final official copy. The measure is printed on parchment and certified by the Secretary of the Senate or the Clerk of the House, depending on which body first passed it. The bill or resolution is then signed by the vice president and the Speaker of the House.

The measure is then delivered to the president for his signature or veto.

>>> *See also* related CRS Reports and links on **TCNCPAM.com**.

F. Failure to Take Up a Measure

One of the most rancorous disagreements between the chambers often occurs when one body simply turns a blind eye to legislation sent over from the other body.

This brings to mind the probably apocryphal story of George Washington explaining the need for the Senate to Thomas Jefferson (*see* Chapter 1.A.). Washington pointed out that Jefferson was pouring the hot tea from his cup and sipping it from the saucer. He compared this to the role of the Senate cooling the legislation driven by popular passions.

Overwhelmingly, in the current context, it is the "hot tea" in Washington's words from the House pouring into the Senate saucer, not to cool as in the famous analogy, but perhaps to congeal.

Especially when the chambers are run by different parties, the prolific House peppers the Senate with legislation and much of that legislation simply dies in the Senate.

As mentioned above, from 2011 to 2014, the Republican House voted repeal of Obamacare repeatedly—more than fifty times. The Democratic Senate did not respond.

Then-Senate Minority Leader Mitch McConnell (R-KY), late in 2014, complained, "The House passed over 300 pieces of legislation, many of them on a bipartisan basis, and nothing was done with them in the Senate."

But the differences between the bodies and their rules assure that even when the same party controls both the House and the Senate, the House will send many bills to the Senate that will not be taken up. The leverage afforded the minority party and individual senators of both parties can slow down the pace of House bills in the Senate and frequently block them entirely.

Phillip Bump, of The Fix blog at the *Washington Post*, using data from GovTrack, looked at the numbers in 2014. He discovered that there were nearly 200 or more House bills left unaddressed by the Senate in every single Congress over the past forty years.

Interestingly, the largest pile-up of House legislation over all that time was in the 110th Congress (2007–2008) when more than 700 bills passed by then-new Democratic Speaker Nancy Pelosi's (D-CA) Democratic House died in the Senate headed by Democratic Majority Leader Harry Reid (D-NV). Frustrated by criticism at the time, Reid remarked that he wished that like the Speaker, he could rule with an "iron fist."

It should also be noted that a smaller number of bills passed by the Senate are left unaddressed in the House.[3]

A good example involves the politically complicated subject of immigration reform. In both 2006 and 2013, the Senate passed a bipartisan comprehensive immigration reform bill. In 2006, the Senate voted 62 to 36 for the Comprehensive Immigration Act. Speaker Dennis Hastert (R-IL) refused to bring the Senate bill to the House floor. In 2013, the Senate voted 68 to 32 to pass the Border Security, Economic Opportunity, and Immigration Modernization Act. This time it was Speaker John Boehner (R-OH) who refused to allow the House to consider the Senate bill. In each case, the president strongly supported the legislation (President George W. Bush in 2006 and President Barack Obama in 2013) to no avail.

At times, the knowledge that the minority in the Senate will prevent a particular bill from advancing in the Senate can be a spur to the passage of legislation in the House, because it amounts to a free pass. Members can vote for legislation without the risk of being held accountable for negative outcomes. This may partially explain the ability of congressional Republicans to call for, and in the House, to adopt repeal of the Affordable Care Act repeatedly. When they gained control of both chambers in 2015, they were unable to repeat that feat even though the procedure they were using (budget reconciliation) precluded a filibuster in the Senate.

>>> *See also* related CRS Reports and links on **TCNCPAM.com**.

---

3. Philip Bump, "Yes, the Senate is ignoring hundreds of bills passed by the GOP House. But it's always that way," the *Washington Post*, August 8, 2014, accessed March 9, 2018, https://www.washingtonpost.com/news/the-fix/wp/2014/08/08/yes-the-senate-is-ignoring-hundreds-of-bills-passed-by-the-gop-house-but-its-always-that-way/. Bump notes that his data source was govtrack.us.

G. The President

When a measure has been approved by the House and Senate, an enrolled copy is transmitted to the president. Article I, Section 7 of the Constitution grants the president ten days, not counting Sundays, to act on a measure once it has been presented to him or her. The president may sign the bill or joint resolution, making it law. Alternatively, the president may allow the legislation to become law without his signature, by allowing the ten-day period to elapse.

If the president wishes to disapprove the measure, he or she may veto it and return the legislation to the House or Senate depending on which body originated the measure; it is returned without his or her approval, together with objections in writing, normally referred to as a "veto message."

A veto by the president may be overridden and the measure enacted "the objections of the president to the contrary notwithstanding." Overriding a presidential veto requires a two-thirds vote of members voting, a quorum having been established, in each chamber of the Congress. If Congress overrides the measure with the necessary two-thirds votes, it is not returned to the president. The override is certified by the Clerk of the House and the Secretary of the Senate and the bill is sent to the National Archives and the bill becomes law.

If either chamber fails to provide the two-thirds necessary to approve the vetoed measure, the veto is sustained and the measure does not become law.

The president has an alternative course to disapprove a measure, frequently called a "pocket veto." If the Congress adjourns during the ten-day period in which the president must sign the measure, it does not become law and is not returned to the Congress. Such a veto cannot be overridden. The transmittal of the congressionally enacted bill to the president by the enrolling clerk can be within hours or delayed for weeks. On occasion, this timing may be related to preventing the president from pocket-vetoing a bill or resolution by avoiding a period of adjournment. Both the House and the Senate have also, on rare occasion, designated the Clerk of the House or the Secretary of the Senate to receive a vetoed bill from the president, in an effort to block the use of a pocket veto.

Vetoes are very difficult to override. In the history of Congress from 1789 through early 2018, presidents have exercised their veto power 2,574 times (1,066 of these were pocket vetoes). Of these, 111 were overridden by the Congress, a mere 4 percent of all vetoes.

Nonetheless, all presidents, with the exception of President John Kennedy and Lyndon Johnson, have had bills they have vetoed overridden. One prominent veto override occurred in 1986 when the Senate voted 78 to 21 to override President Ronald Reagan's veto of sanctions against the apartheid government in South Africa (the House had previously overridden the bill). The bill therefore became law. In 1996, a near-override occurred when the House voted 286 to 129 to override President Bill Clinton's veto of the bill to ban late-term abortions. However, in this case, the veto stood when the Senate failed by two votes to override, 58 to 40.

Because vetoes are so difficult to override, the threat of a veto from the president usually plays a powerful role in the course of legislation through the Congress. In most circumstances, the Congress will attempt to take steps to avoid a presidential veto by modifying offending language. On rare occasions, however, the Congress welcomes the battle.

When the president vetoes a bill, the Congress need not and sometimes does not act. This is usually an indication that the president has the votes to sustain the veto in at least one of the two chambers. Even if one chamber votes to override, the other may decline to take it up.

One form of veto that presidents don't have is the "line-item" veto. The line-item veto would permit the president to reject individual items within a bill rather than be required to accept or reject the entire legislation. Governors of most states are able to exercise some form of a line-item veto. Presidents of both parties for more than a century have supported some form of line-item veto.

For many in Congress, the line-item veto is seen as an abdication of its Constitutional role as a check and balance to the president (*see* Chapter 7.O.).

Congress has for a number of years relied upon larger bills with an array of provisions. This is particularly true in the appropriations process where omnibus appropriations bills (*see* Chapter 7.H.) that fund many departments and agencies of the government in one huge bill have become almost routine in recent years. Such bills frustrate presidents because they cannot isolate and veto the parts of the bill that they oppose, sometimes forcing them to sign a bill even though they believe it to be seriously flawed.

In 1996, Congress actually enacted a version of the line-item veto that President Clinton signed into law. Line Item Veto Act of 1996 (P.L. 104-130). Clinton used that new power to strike eighty-two items from eleven different laws. Congress overrode the particular line-item veto twenty-eight times.

In 1998, the Supreme Court in *Clinton v. New York City*, 524 U.S. 417 (1998), struck down the line-item veto by a 6 to 3 vote, declaring it unconstitutional. Justice John Paul Stevens, writing for the majority of the Court declared, "… this act gives the president the unilateral power to change the text of duly enacted statute." He wrote that line-item vetoes of this sort are "the functional equivalent of partial repeals of acts of Congress."

》》》 *See also* related CRS Reports and links on **TCNCPAM.com**.

H. Review Questions

》》》 Is there a problem if House conferees outnumber Senate conferees on a particular conference committee?

》》》 What are the two types of presidential vetoes? How may each be overridden?

》》》 Why did the Senate in 2013 provide that the three necessary motions to get to a conference could be combined into one indivisible motion?

》》》 What are the two ways used to reconcile the House and Senate versions of a measure? What are the advantages of each?

》》》 Why are conference committees used less often in recent Congresses?

》》》 What is a pocket veto?

》》》 Explain what is generally meant by the "scope of Congress." If a senator believes the scope has been violated in a conference report, what is the remedy available?

》》》 Why do presidents favor a line-item veto?

Chapter 7
The Congressional Budget and Other Special Cases

A. Introduction

There are a number of variations in the general legislative process in Congress that come into play in very significant ways.

For example, Article I of the Constitution imposes great responsibility on Congress for the shaping of legislation controlling taxes and other revenues (Article I, Section 7), spending of funds, and borrowing to meet deficits (Article I, Section 8). This is often referred to as "the power of the purse."

The legislative tools that Congress employs include the budget process, the authorization process, and the appropriations process. Each has a separate function, but they are interrelated and often confused by observers of Congress.

It may be useful to think of these in terms of kitchen-table finances. The **budget** is like a personal budget—your plan for how much money you expect to be earning, how much money you will spend, and how you will spend it.

Authorizations may be thought of as decisions you might make that impact your budget, such as signing an apartment lease, buying an automobile, purchasing a home, or even having a child.

Appropriations are like payments you actually make under your budget, like paying the rent, utility bills, or buying groceries. You might have budgeted $300 for groceries, but ended up spending $350. Your appropriation is $350.

If you spend more than you bring in, you must borrow the difference. If you spend less, you have a surplus and may be able to invest it or save for a child's education.

Some of the tools, most notably the budget process, have by law been given special expedited (often called fast-track) procedures to facilitate more efficient progress through Congress and to the president's desk.

While fast-track procedures affect both the House and the Senate by imposing time limits on debate, the impact is greatest in the Senate, where debate is otherwise generally unlimited. In fact, in some circumstances, the majority has used fast-track procedures as a loophole in the normal Senate rules to circumvent unlimited debate, for example, the filibuster in the Senate.

Fast-track procedures have been granted to other types of legislation as well, in trade legislation, treaty enforcement, military base closure legislation, and resolutions regarding the president's ability to commit U.S. armed forces into hostilities.

》》》 *See also The Federal Budget Process*, **FederalBudgetProcess.com**, and related CRS Reports and links on **TCNCPAM.com**.

B. 1974 Budget Act

The Congressional Budget and Impoundment Control Act of 1974 (P.L. 93-344, as amended, 2 U.S.C. §§ 601–688) was enacted on July 12, 1974, and signed by President Richard Nixon. Beginning with the Budget and Accounting Act of 1921, the budgeting process was dominated by the executive branch because the 1921 law gave the president a formal role in the development of the federal budget for the first time. It required that the president submit an annual budget request to Congress prior to its consideration of appropriations and revenue legislation. That Act also created the Bureau of the Budget (later reorganized as the Office of Management and Budget (OMB) in 1971).

Prior to 1974, Congress made its appropriations decisions on individual spending bills and revenue decisions on individual tax bills without systematic consideration of how the overall budget was affected. Bills were passed and signed into law, and it was not until the end of the federal fiscal year (September 30) that the size of the deficit or surplus became clear.

For much of the history of the United States the overall budget and certainly the deficits (except for World War II) or surpluses were small enough that the system seemed to work. However, for a number of years leading up to the passage of the Budget Act, it began to become evident, particularly as annual deficits grew in the early 1970s, that a more comprehensively planned and reasoned approach to budgetary decisions was necessary.

In 1974, the political will and the opportunity came together. Two important contributing factors led to the passage of the Congressional Budget and Impoundment Act. First, President Nixon was refusing to spend approximately $12 billion in funding (around $60 billion in 2018 dollars) that had been appropriated by Congress using a procedure called impoundment (*see* Section 7.O.).

Virtually every prior president throughout U.S. history had impounded funds. However, in those cases the amounts involved were minimal, congressional appropriators were generally consulted, and there were good reasons for declining to spend the funds, for example, a program that was no longer needed. Nixon's impoundments were not small, were not agreed to by Congress, and his reasons were controversial. Nixon declared that it was the "constitutional right for the President of the United States to impound funds." He pledged, "I will not spend money if the Congress overspends ... ."

Many in Congress saw impoundment as presidential usurpation of Congress's control of the purse strings. As this confrontation wore on, it provided some of the impetus for Congress to act. But perhaps most importantly, President Nixon's political standing was weak and he was absorbed by the Watergate crisis, so Congress was able to overcome his objections. The Watergate scandal led to his resignation a month later in August 1974.

The Congressional Budget and Impoundment Control Act was overwhelmingly adopted by the House (401 to 6) and unanimously (95 to 0) in the Senate in June 1974. The Act provided a means for Congress to coordinate and enhance its control over the annual budget and it reduced the ability of presidents to impound funds. Among other things, the Act created the Congressional Budget Office (CBO) to provide independent budget analysis to Congress, ending the executive branch's near domination of budgetary information. Congress would no longer be dependent on the executive branch Office of Management and Budget, which is within the Executive Office of the President.

Among the major assumptions at the time of the enactment of the law was that the new budget process would be largely bipartisan. The battles over appropriations, entitlement programs, and tax legislation could take place within an agreed-upon budgetary framework. Also, it was thought that deficits would be reduced by the new procedures since Congress would be required to explicitly vote on them.

Both of these assumptions turned out to be wrong. Almost without exception, when the annual budget resolution comes to the Senate floor, the vote is close to straight party line. Because the expedited procedures under which the resolution is considered reduces the leverage of the minority in the Senate, the majority can bypass the minority and adopt its budget proposal. It is similar in the House. The process envisioned as a way to temper partisanship has instead contributed to the acceleration and broadening of partisan polarization in the Congress.

Second, the budget process has not effectively restrained annual deficits. As we will see, at times budget procedures (*see* Chapter 7.D.) are used to adopt proposals that greatly increase the deficit.

The provisions of the Act that created legislative procedures were enacted under the rulemaking authority of Congress. As such, these provisions of the Budget Act are similar to House and Senate rules, in that either chamber is able to amend those provisions that affect its operations without the concurrence of the other chamber and without the enactment of a law. As Senate Parliamentarian Emeritus Alan Frumin has pointed out, if these were technically rules in the Senate, it would take a two-thirds vote to invoke cloture to change them.

One unusual provision in the Budget Act that applies to both consideration of the Congressional Budget Resolution (*see* Chapter 8.C.) and reconciliation bills (*see* Chapter 8.D.) in the Senate is that although time for debate is limited (fifty hours on the Budget Resolution and twenty hours on reconciliation), there is no limit on the number of amendments that can be offered. This creates a situation in which a large stack of amendments are voted on after all debate has expired. This process, known as a "vote-a-rama," often takes many hours, sometimes two days.

⟫⟫ *See also* related CRS Reports and links on **TCNCPAM.com**.

C. The Congressional Budget Resolution

The heart of the process created by the Budget Act is the requirement that Congress pass a concurrent resolution each year known as the Congressional Budget Resolution. This required budget resolution is privileged for consideration and adoption, that is, it can't be filibustered. As a concurrent resolution (numbered as H. Con. Res. xx or S. Con. Res. xx), it must be adopted in identical form by both chambers, but it is not sent to the president and does not become law. It creates a binding budget "blueprint" that Congress is expected to follow throughout as it makes its spending and revenue decisions. It should be noted that when Congress binds itself, it may also unbind itself at the end of the day.

The president is required by law to submit a comprehensive budget request to Congress on or after the first Monday in January (31 U.S.C. § 1105), but no later than the first Monday in February. The president's budget request is a detailed line-by-line proposal for all federal programs and is accompanied by multiple volumes of historical tables, charts, legislative and policy proposals, and supporting documents. The budget also includes estimated receipts, expenditures, and proposed appropriations for the following five fiscal years, although some presidents have submitted ten-year budgets.

Once the president has developed a budget request and presented it to Congress, the congressional budget process begins. The law requires that this be done on or before the first Monday in February, although that date often slips. Budget decisions are made on the basis of the federal fiscal year; since 1974, the federal fiscal year begins on October 1 and ends on September 30. The law sets forth a timetable for each procedural step along the way to the adoption of the budget resolution. From "The Budget Reconciliation Process: Timing of Legislative Action," CRS Report RL30458:

"An explicit requirement that Congress complete action on any necessary reconciliation measure was established in Section 310(f) of the 1974 Congressional Budget Act by Section 201(b) (at 99 Stat. 1040) of the 1985 Balanced Budget Act. Section 13210(2) of the Budget Enforcement Act of 1990 (Title XIII of P.L. 101-508) deleted this requirement from Section 310(f) but left unchanged the reference to the deadline in the general timetable set forth in Section 300."

The Senate Budget Committee must report the budget resolution by April 1. The law contains no similar deadline for the House Budget Committee. There are consequences if the Senate Budget Committee fails to meet this deadline. Specifically, should that deadline pass, budget resolutions submitted by individual senators are considered referred to and discharged from the Budget Committee and placed on the Senate calendar. Under these conditions, such individual budget resolutions are privileged for consideration.

The law stipulates that the budget resolution must be adopted by Congress by April 15. However, budget resolutions have rarely been completed by this date and at least nine times since 1974 no resolution was adopted.

Procedures related to the timetable established by the Budget Act are enforced in both chambers by points of order. In the House, these may be waived by a special rule (*see* Chapter 4.D.). In the Senate, points of order may be waived by simple majority vote with the exception of a prohibition against the Senate acting on any appropriations measures until the Appropriations Committee has established the spending caps for each of its subcommittees (called sub-allocations) that requires a three-fifths vote. The Act requires that the budget resolution establish budget "aggregates" and spending levels for each broad "functional category" of the budget (for example, national defense, energy, health, natural resources and environment, and Medicare). In total, there are currently twenty-one such functions.

The budget aggregates required are:
- total revenues (and the amount by which the total is to be changed by legislative action);
- total new budget authority and outlays;
- the deficit or surplus; and
- the debt limit.

The budget resolution does not allocate funds among specific programs. However, it is common in floor debate (and sometimes in the Budget Committee report) to detail "assumptions" underlying the totals for budget functions. These assumptions are not binding.

Members when speaking about proposed amendments to the budget resolution, however, will frequently give the impression that such assumptions are, in fact, substantive changes affecting specific line items in the budget. For example, an amendment to increase the Education, Training, Employment, and Social Services function by $200 million, may be referred to by its supporters as a $200 million increase in "special education." This is the assumption of the sponsors, but the additional funding may ultimately be spent in an appropriation on some other purpose within the budget function.

>>> *See also The Federal Budget Process,* **FederalBudgetProcess.com**, and related CRS Reports and links on **TCNCPAM.com**.

D. Reconciliation Bills

The 1974 Budget law also set up a second, optional procedure known as "budget reconciliation." There are two steps to the implementation of the budget reconciliation process. The first is the inclusion in the budget resolution of "reconciliation instructions." Second, legislation, known as a "reconciliation bill," is enacted to change laws affecting spending or revenue.

The reconciliation instructions are used to require both House and Senate committees to report changes in current law regarding revenues and entitlement spending. These instructions include a dollar amount for an increase or reduction by the legislation to be reported pursuant to those instructions. How the substance of the proposed legislation is to accomplish those instructions is left to the committee of jurisdiction receiving the instructions in the budget resolution.

If more than one committee receives reconciliation instructions, the recommendations reported by those committees are assembled by the House and Senate Budget Committees into one bill. Neither the House nor the Senate Budget Committee, under the Congressional Budget and Impoundment Control Act of 1974, can amend the recommendations submitted to it.

Although reconciliation bills under the Congressional Budget and Impoundment Control Act of 1974 are handled with expedited procedures in both the House and the Senate, it is in the Senate where the most dramatic procedural effects of reconciliation, and consequently the most controversial impacts, occur.

Debate in the Senate on reconciliation measures is limited to twenty hours, and, as a result, filibusters are not possible. Cloture is therefore not necessary to end debate and consequently only a simple majority, not the supermajority three-fifths (normally sixty votes), is needed to end the debate and pass the bill. Also, unlike normal Senate rules, the Congressional Budget and Impoundment Control Act of 1974 requires that all amendments considered on a reconciliation bill be germane. (Germaneness is a requirement that an amendment be closely related to the precise subject of the text it proposes to amend.) (*See* Chapter 5.J.)

In another departure from Senate rules, when reconciliation is used for its legitimate deficit-reduction purpose, there is the general requirement imposed that all amendments, to be in order, must not cause a committee to fail to meet its reconciliation instruction. Unless a committee has recommended savings in excess of its instruction, this means that amendments must be deficit-neutral. Therefore, amendments that increase spending must be offset by language reducing spending by a like amount or raising the necessary revenues. Likewise, amendments that might have the effect of reducing revenue must be offset by revenue increases of a like amount or direct spending cuts matching the revenue loss, typically referred to as mandatory or entitlement spending.

The House is not impacted in the same way because it legislates under a special rule reported by the Rules Committee. On reconciliation, the special rule generally expedites the process by limiting debate, amendments and other action, but this is not outside of the House's normal procedures.

The expectation of the drafters of the reconciliation process was that it would be used to make minor adjustments in spending and tax bills passed earlier in the year to bring them in line with the budget resolution. The aggressive use of reconciliation as a way to work around the Senate filibuster rules to pass major sweeping legislation was not contemplated in 1974.

Beginning in 1981, Congress began using reconciliation bills in a significant way to implement policies laid out in the budget resolution. In 1996, the Clinton administration used the process to push welfare reform through the Congress. In 2003, George W. Bush used reconciliation to pass major tax cuts, with Vice President Cheney casting the deciding vote, 51 to 50. Measures like these, which served to increase the deficit or enact major nonbudgetary provisions, were also not envisioned by the authors of the congressional budget process in 1974.

The principal attraction of using the budget process in this way is the effect of circumventing the filibuster in the Senate. Because debate is limited on a reconciliation bill under the Congressional Budget and Impoundment Control Act of 1974, a filibuster is precluded and the reconciliation bill can be passed with a simple majority. This enables the majority to act on major legislation without input from the minority.

》》》 *See also The Federal Budget Process*, **FederalBudgetProcess.com**, and related CRS Reports and links on **TCNCPAM.com**.

E. The "Byrd Rule"

By 1985, it had become clear that the reconciliation process created in the Congressional Budget and Impoundment Control Act of 1974 was being increasingly used to circumvent the regular rules of the Senate, particularly the filibuster. At the urging of Minority Leader Robert Byrd (D-WV), the Senate acted to limit nonbudgetary matters in reconciliation bills by creating a new point of order commonly referred to as the "Byrd Rule." (2 U.S.C. § 644, Extraneous matter in reconciliation legislation.) Senator Byrd, who had been one of the authors of the reconciliation provisions in the 1974 Act, declared:

> "It was never foreseen that the Budget Reform Act would be used in that way. So if the budget reform process is going to be preserved, and more importantly if we are going to preserve the deliberative process in this U.S. Senate—which is the outstanding, unique element with respect to the U.S. Senate, action must be taken now to stop this abuse of the budget process."

The Byrd Rule basically prohibits provisions that do not have an impact on the budget. Byrd's concerns were shared by other senators and his 1985 amendment was adopted 96 to 0.

The Byrd rule has been extended and modified a number of times. In 1990, it was enacted as a permanent part of the Congressional Budget Act (CBA). It is now Section 313 of that law (2 USC § 644).

In 2001, Byrd explained, "Reconciliation is a nonfilibusterable 'bear trap' that should be used very sparingly and, I believe, only for the purposes of fiscal restraint. That was the intention in the beginning. … [R]econciliation should be used only for reducing deficits or for increasing surpluses … ."

The Byrd Rule has a significant impact because an effort to waive the rule requires a three-fifths vote of all senators (sixty votes in the absence of vacancies). If a point of order under the Byrd Rule is sustained, the offending provision is struck from the bill or, if made against an amendment, the amendment falls. In this way, if a provision is found to violate the Byrd Rule and the rule is not waived, the advantage gained by use of the reconciliation process (the circumvention of the supermajority requirement under cloture) is negated.

The rule is quite complex. However, it can be characterized as prohibiting "extraneous matter" from reconciliation bills. The Byrd Rule provides a six-part definition of extraneous matter; a provision:

1. that does not produce a change in spending or revenues;
2. recommended by a committee that produces a spending increase or revenue reduction while that committee is not in compliance with its reconciliation instruction;
3. outside of the jurisdiction of the committee that produced it;
4. that produces a change in spending or revenues that is merely incidental to the nonbudgetary parts of the provision;
5. that would increase the deficit for a year beyond the budget period covered by the reconciliation bill; and
6. that recommends changes in Social Security.

While the problem of restricting extraneous material in reconciliation is acute in the Senate because of the availability of the filibuster under the normal Senate rules, the House sometimes addresses extraneous matters by including a prohibition in a special rule.

The leadership, typically the majority party, supporting the reconciliation bill and senators hoping to amend the bill will generally meet with the Senate parliamentarian to learn in advance whether legislative language will pass muster with the Byrd Rule. These extensive and multiple sessions are referred to as "Byrd baths."

A Byrd Rule point of order has an unusual effect in that it strikes individual provisions from a bill that continues to be considered. At times this feature of the Byrd Rule has been a barrier, intended at least by Senator Byrd, to the use of reconciliation for major sweeping authorizing legislation like the Affordable Care Act in 2010 or the efforts to fully repeal it in 2017. Early in the consideration of Obamacare, some Democrats advocated the use of the reconciliation process to pass the bill in order to lower the threshold from sixty to a simple majority (fifty-one if all senators are voting). However, the Democratic leadership, based on strong advice from the Senate parliamentarian and Senator Byrd himself, knew that the legislation contained many nonbudgetary items needed to set up an entirely new health insurance system. It was pointed out that the likely effect of many successful Republican Byrd Rule points of order knocking multiple provisions out of the bill would be a law that looked like "Swiss cheese," legislation full of holes.

It is a widely held misconception that the reconciliation process was used to enact Obamacare. The Affordable Care Act (ACA) was adopted in the Senate under regular rules with sixty Democratic votes (to invoke cloture under Rule XXII) overcoming a filibuster. In the end, a targeted reconciliation bill, the Health Care and Education Reconciliation Act of 2010, carefully scrubbed to ascertain compliance with the Byrd Rule, was used to strike several budgetary provisions from the ACA to make it more acceptable to the House.

>>> *See also The Federal Budget Process*, **FederalBudgetProcess.com**, and related CRS Reports and links on **TCNCPAM.com**.

F. PAYGO

In 1990, concern about the long-term impact of mandatory (entitlement) spending or tax cuts prompted Congress to enact a new budget rule popularly called "PAYGO" or pay-as-you-go. These "pay-as-you-go" (PAYGO) processes and limits on discretionary spending were established under the Budget Enforcement Act of 1990 (Title XIII of P.L. 101-508).

The statutory Pay-As-You-Go Act of 2010 (P.L. 111-139 2 U.S.C. §§ 931–939), was enacted in statute under the Budget Enforcement Act of 1990. PAYGO requires that increases in mandatory spending, because they have ongoing impacts on the deficit in future years, must be offset by either reductions in mandatory spending elsewhere in the budget or, alternatively, by increases in taxes. Similarly, tax cuts projected to reduce revenue in future years are required to be "paid for" by increases in other taxes or reductions in entitlement spending.

The 1990 PAYGO provision was "sunsetted," or ended, at the end of FY2002. Although it was replaced by a series of House and Senate rules that were less effective (confusingly also referred to as PAYGO), statutory PAYGO rules were reestablished in 2010; this version of PAYGO was enacted on a permanent basis.

Under the new PAYGO rules, the budgetary effects of mandatory spending and tax provisions enacted into law are tracked on a rolling five-year and ten-year basis monitored by the Office of Management and Budget. At the end of the year if the scorecards for either of these periods show the effect would be an increase in the deficit, the president must issue a "sequestration" order. This would require an "across-the-board" cut in mandatory spending programs (only those not exempted by previous law).

Some programs are exempt from PAYGO sequestration: Social Security, unemployment insurance, Medicaid, and other social safety net programs such as the Supplemental Nutrition Assistance Program (SNAP), referred to by some as "food stamps," are exempt, which increases the severity of the impact of sequestration on programs that are not exempt. Another major exemption is that "emergency spending" is not included. This explains, in part, why some administrations have used emergency supplemental bills to finance wars. Also, PAYGO does not affect deficit increases arising from changes in mandatory spending or revenues that are projected to occur under existing law.

Finally, sequestration under PAYGO has on several occasions been avoided simply by Congress enacting a law instructing OMB to ignore increases in the deficit for that year.

>>> *See also The Federal Budget Process*, **FederalBudgetProcess.com**, and related CRS Reports and links on **TCNCPAM.com**.

G. Authorizations

An authorization is a law that establishes a program or agency and the terms and conditions under which it operates. Authorizations enable and set upper limits on the enactment of appropriations for that program or agency. It is an appropriations act that actually provides the funding (*see* Chapter 7.H.). Senate Rule XVI and House Rule XXI each require that any appropriation, with certain exceptions, may not be considered unless an authorization for that appropriation has been enacted and signed into law.

Authorization bills describe what an agency is permitted to or required to do. Authorization bills may also restrict or prohibit actions by an agency. They typically authorize appropriations ceilings that are higher than what the relevant appropriations committee ultimately provides for an agency or program. One way to think of this is that authorizations are like a glass and appropriations are the milk that fills that glass.

Authorization bills can also establish programs under which recipients who meet certain qualifications and criteria are able to receive funds. These are referred to as mandatory spending programs and sometimes as "entitlement" programs. Entitlement refers to the fact that such programs create a requirement to provide the benefits to individuals who qualify under that law. Examples are Medicare, Social Security, and some veterans' benefits.

Except for these entitlement programs, authorization bills do not have direct budgetary impacts, with some exceptions of small programs that are mandatory, not subject to annual appropriations, but which are not entitlement programs. Authorization bills merely provide the authority for discretionary spending through appropriations bills under the jurisdiction of the House and Senate Appropriations Committees. Most appropriations are made on an annual basis. (*See* Chapter 7.H., Appropriations.)

Authorization bills may be permanent or temporary for one or more years. Authorization bills that expire require reauthorization. Sometimes politically sensitive programs within a particular authorization can lead Congress to neglect the necessary reauthorization. For example, State Department programs are authorized annually under the Foreign Relations Authorization Act. The programs were reauthorized in 2002 and, although the Act expired two years later, it was reauthorized in December 2016, when the Department of State Authorities Act became law. From 2002 through 2016, Congress avoided working through the many thorny foreign policy issues that would arise in this authorization. By contrast, the National Defense Authorization bill for the Department of Defense has been enacted into law every year since 1961.

Although appropriations require prior authorization under House and Senate rules, there are frequent examples of unauthorized appropriations, especially in the Senate. Often the appropriations bill in question merely waives the applicable requirement.

Rules also prohibit legislating on an appropriations bill; legislating refers to language that changes or repeals existing law. However, if points of order are not raised against offending provisions and they become law, there is no legal bar against such provisions.

>>> *See also The Federal Budget Process,* **FederalBudgetProcess.com**, and related CRS Reports and links on **TCNCPAM.com**.

H. Appropriations

Appropriations bills allow the federal government to spend money. When passed by Congress and signed by the president, appropriations acts are laws that allow federal agencies to incur obligations and the federal treasury to spend funds. Article I, Section 9 of the Constitution states: "No Money shall be drawn from the Treasury, but in Consequence of Appropriations made by Law ... ."

The founders saw this as a limitation of executive power. James Madison explained in *The Federalist* No. 58: "The House of Representatives cannot only refuse, but they alone can propose the supplies requisite for the support of the government. They, in a word, hold the purse ... . This power over the purse may, in fact, be regarded as the most complete and effectual weapon with which any constitution can arm the immediate representatives of the people, for obtaining a redress of every grievance, and for carrying into effect every just and salutary measure." This limitation lies at the heart of the principle of separation of powers.

The practice from the very first session of Congress has been to provide most appropriations for no more than a single year, necessitating an annual process.

The president is required by law (The Budget and Accounting Act of 1921, (P.L. 67-13)) to submit a budget request to the Congress no later than the first Monday in February (*see* Chapter 7.C.). As part of that submission, the executive branch provides extensive information assembled by the Office of Management and Budget in support of the budgetary proposals the president is making.

The Congress considers twelve appropriations bills, each in a separate subcommittee of the House and Senate Appropriations Committees. In the 115th Congress, the subcommittees are:

- Agriculture, Rural Development, Food and Drug Administration, and Related Agencies
- Commerce, Justice, Science, and Related Agencies
- Defense
- Energy and Water Development, and Related Agencies
- Financial Services and General Government
- Homeland Security
- Interior, Environment, and Related Agencies
- Labor, Health and Human Services, Education, and Related Agencies
- Legislative Branch
- Military Construction, Veterans' Affairs, and Related Agencies
- State, Foreign Operations, and Related Programs
- Transportation, Housing and Urban Development, and Related Agencies

There are three types of appropriations bills considered by the Congress.

Regular appropriations bills provide funding to agencies for the next fiscal year, which runs from October 1 to September 30.

Supplemental appropriations bills provide additional funding during the year when regular appropriations are insufficient. One common reason for a supplemental appropriation is to fund recovery from natural disasters. Some administrations have also requested supplemental appropriations to fund military actions. For example, much of the funding for the wars in Iraq and Afghanistan during the Bush administration was funded through supplemental appropriations.

Continuing resolutions are joint resolutions often referred to as CRs. CRs are frequently used to provide funding for agencies when the normal regular appropriations bills for those agencies have not been enacted into law by the beginning of the fiscal year. CRs often extend the funding at the same level as the last regular appropriations for the agencies affected. Other times they may increase or reduce funding. For example, CRs have been passed based on adopting the lower amount provided in a House-passed or Senate-passed regular appropriations bill. CRs are in effect for a fixed period of time. In recent years, it has often been necessary to enact multiple CRs, often providing the necessary appropriations in place of regular appropriations. Some of these stopgap measures are for a short period of time, a matter of days, while negotiations are being conducted in Congress in an effort to pass the regular appropriations bills. At other times, the period is much longer, weeks or months, and in some years, a CR has been necessary to provide funding for the entire fiscal year.

In some years, Congress, having failed to enact some or all of the regular appropriations bills, has instead opted to combine two or more appropriations into one piece of legislation. These are referred to as "omnibus" appropriations bills. These are often considered late in the calendar year before Congress adjourns and when time is limited. As a result, rank-and-file members often complain they have insufficient time to study these massive bills. Some members who otherwise might support the provisions contained in an omnibus bill feel compelled to vote against it in opposition to the procedure. One senator called these bills a "giant ball of wax," referring to the huge size of the bill and the fact other legislation which might not succeed on a stand-alone basis is attached by the leadership to the omnibus. Smaller omnibus bills with just a few regular appropriations bills combined are sometimes labeled "minibus" bills.

The origination clause of the Constitution, Article I, Section 7, reads, "All Bills for raising Revenue shall originate in the House of Representatives." The House has traditionally viewed this as requiring not only that tax bills originate in that body, but all spending bills as well. Although the Senate has never accepted this interpretation, it typically permits the House to go first. This is because the House enforces its position through the "blue slip" process (*see* Chapter 1.B.), rejecting any spending bill that may have originated in the Senate.

Before the House or Senate Appropriations Committees act on an appropriations bill, extensive hearings will be held in the relevant subcommittee and that subcommittee will have marked up the bill. These markups are guided by spending allocations provided under the budget resolution (*see* Chapter 7.C.). The Appropriations Committee in each chamber receives a single allocation set out in the statement of managers that accompanies the conference report on the budget resolution, known as the "302(a) allocation." The Appropriations Committee (chair) divides that amount into twelve separate allocations, one for each of its subcommittees. These are known as the "302(b) sub-allocations."

In both the House and the Senate, appropriations bills are prepared and marked up in the appropriate subcommittee. The full committee may mark the bill up further, but usually the work of the subcommittee is influential and oftentimes little or no change will occur at the full committee level.

In the House, appropriations bills are privileged (*see* Chapter 4.E.). Although as a privileged matter appropriations bills do not require a special rule, typically appropriations bills do come to the floor under a special rule, that is, a rule that waives points of order against appropriating funds for programs not previously authorized.

》》》 *See also The Federal Budget Process*, **FederalBudgetProcess.com**, and related CRS Reports and links on **TCNCPAM.com**.

I. Government Shutdown

When the necessary appropriations are not enacted into law by the end of the fiscal year or by the expiration of a continuing resolution, government agencies that have not been funded must cease operations. Shutdowns are required and governed under the Antideficiency Act, originally enacted in 1884. The Antideficiency Act (P.L. 97-258, 31 U.S.C. § 1341) prohibits federal agencies from obligating or expending federal funds without or in excess of an appropriation. Exceptions are carved out for "essential" government functions such as the military, federal law enforcement, the courts, and the continued functioning of Congress itself.

Government shutdowns in recent years have been a consequence of disagreements between the president and the opposition party in the Congress. It has become routine for Congress to fail to complete the necessary twelve appropriations bills (*see* Chapter 7.H.) by the end of the fiscal year. The last time all twelve appropriations bills became law prior to the beginning of the next fiscal year was in 1996. This has frequently emboldened both parties to use the impending upheaval of a government shutdown as powerful leverage in appropriations negotiations. As in a game of "chicken," each side expects the other to give way. This creates the danger of a government shutdown that neither party intends, however, sometimes one party believes it is in their interest.

In December, 1995, a showdown between President Bill Clinton and congressional Republicans led to the shutdown of the government for twenty-one days. During the Obama administration, a stalemate between the president and congressional Republicans led to a sixteen-day closure. In 2018, during the Trump administration, the government was shut down for three days in January. This was a notable occurrence because the president's party controlled the Congress, unlike prior shutdowns. There were nineteen government shutdowns between 1976 and 2018.

》》》 *See also The Federal Budget Process*, **FederalBudgetProcess.com**, and related CRS Reports and links on **TCNCPAM.com**.

J. Debt Ceiling

Another familiar game of "chicken" between the president and Congress are the periodic battles over the raising of the "debt ceiling." The debt ceiling is a statutory limit (31 U.S.C. § 3101) on the amount that the government can borrow to finance the national debt. The ceiling has existed in law since 1918.

When the limit is reached, additional borrowing cannot occur, which would eventually lead the federal government to default on its debts. This has never occurred in American history. U.S. Treasury Bonds are considered among the safest investments by private borrowers and foreign governments alike. Defaulting on these obligations would raise the cost of borrowing for the government, severely impact the U.S. economy, and likely create upheaval in the world's financial markets.

Both parties have treated the lifting of the debt ceiling as a political football. Since public understanding of the debt limit is limited, it has been easy for politicians to suggest that lifting the debt ceiling is a way of increasing debt. However, the debt in question is typically already obligated and it's more a question of the government's ability to meet its debts.

The opposition party to the president, by threatening an imminent default, attempts to gain concessions. For example, in 2011, the House Republicans refused to cooperate in the lifting of the ceiling unless President Obama would agree to significant cuts in federal spending. The 2011 debt-limit episode was resolved on August 2, 2011, when President Obama signed the Budget Control Act of 2011 (BCA) (P.L. 112-25). The BCA included provisions aimed at deficit reduction and allowing the debt limit to rise in three stages, the latter two subject to congressional disapproval. Once the BCA was enacted, a presidential certification triggered a $400 billion increase. A second certification led to a $500 billion increase on September 22, 2011, and a third, $1,200 billion increase took place on January 28, 2012.

While the crisis was averted, the near-miss involved led to a downgrade of the nation's credit rating. In August 2011, Standard & Poor's, one of the nation's largest credit rating agencies, stripped the United States of its AAA status. S&P declared, "The political brinksmanship of recent months highlights what we see as America's governance and policymaking becoming less stable, less effective, and less predictable than what we previously believed. The statutory debt ceiling and the threat of default have become political bargaining chips in the debate over fiscal policy."

Federal debt again reached its limit on December 31, 2012 (112th Congress), when Democrats controlled the Senate. Extraordinary measures were again used to allow payment of government obligations until February 4, 2013, when H.R. 325, which suspended the debt limit until May 19, 2013, was signed into law (P.L. 113-3). On that date, extraordinary measures were reset, which would have lasted until October 17, 2013, according to Treasury estimates issued in late September 2013. On October 16, 2013, enactment of a continuing resolution (H.R. 2775; P.L. 113-46) resolved a funding lapse and suspended the debt limit through February 7, 2014. On February 15, 2014, a measure to suspend the debt limit (S. 540; P.L. 113-83) through March 15, 2015, was enacted. Once that debt-limit suspension lapsed after March 15, 2015, the limit was reset at $18.1 trillion. On November 2, 2015, the Bipartisan Budget Act of 2015 (BBA2015; H.R. 1314; P.L. 114-74) was enacted, which suspended the debt limit through March 15, 2017, and relaxed some discretionary spending limits.

Nonetheless, one simple fact is clear. No matter the political storm over the debt limit, the ceiling has always been lifted when necessary; the limit has been raised over eighty times from 1960 to 2017.

≫ *See also The Federal Budget Process*, **FederalBudgetProcess.com**, and related CRS Reports and links on **TCNCPAM.com**.

K. Earmarks

One of the controversial aspects of the appropriations process has been the practice, and subsequent banning, of certain targeted expenditures known as "earmarks."

Definitions of what is meant by earmark vary. Even the Congressional Research Service (CRS) has had difficulty developing an all-inclusive and effective definition. OMB used a definition that characterized any expenditure of funds on a specific project not requested by the president as an earmark. Viewed through the lens of checks and balances, this is clearly an executive branch-centric view of earmarks. Presidents frequently embed earmarks in their budget requests.

An earmark is a provision in an appropriations bill, or under some circumstances authorization bill, or a tax expenditure contained in a revenue bill focused on a specific program or project requested by a member or members of Congress or in the president's budget request. Earmarks typically benefit a single entity or category of recipient. For example, a provision that increases spending for a light rail grant program might not be an earmark, but a provision that requires only an airport exactly seven miles from the center of a city will receive 20 percent of the light rail funding would likely be labeled an earmark.

Although earmarks became controversial for a number of reasons, one was the concern about unnecessary spending during a period of large federal deficits. Most earmarks, however, targeted a portion of an existing appropriation prioritizing the specified use, but not increasing the deficit. In reality, earmarks at their peak accounted for about 1 percent of the budget.

Often, these earmarks were not contained in the legislative language, but in committee reports or statements of managers accompanying conference reports.

For example, in 2005, when there was controversy over a $223 million earmark included in a highway bill to fund the construction of a bridge in Alaska from Ketchikan to a nearby island that had only about fifty residents, and the Ketchikan airport. This was labeled the "bridge to nowhere."

From 2007–2010, both the House and the Senate responded to concerns about earmarks with rules increasing transparency. These rules were in response to the concern about abuses in the approving of earmarks, such as putting them into bills at the last moment.

For example, Senate Rule XLIV adopted in 2007 requires that any "congressionally directed spending item, limited tax benefit, and limited tariff benefit [earmarks], if any, in [a] bill or joint resolution, or in [a] committee report accompanying the bill or joint resolution" be identified through "lists, charts, or other similar means including the name of each Senator who submitted a request to the committee for each item so identified." Also, Senate Rule XLIV requires that this information be "available on a publicly accessible congressional website in a searchable format at least 48 hours before such vote."

In 2011, a ban on earmarks was imposed by the House and Senate party caucuses. Neither chamber has adopted a rule banning earmarks.

However, some contend that banning earmarks removes decision-making from elected members of Congress and shifts it to bureaucrats in the executive branch. The ban had the effect of taking a relatively public process, at least after the reforms, and made it less transparent. Some refer to "phonemarks" and "lettermarks" to characterize the ability of appropriations committee members and others to deal directly with federal agencies to target funding to programs and projects they favor. This is particularly effective for the members of appropriations subcommittees that control the budget of the agency in question. Another negative impact has been the dismantling of a tool historically used by leadership to negotiate, bargain, and put together support for legislation. Some cite the earmark ban as removing a process that often enhanced and encouraged bipartisanship.

》》 *See also The Federal Budget Process*, **FederalBudgetProcess.com**, and related CRS Reports and links on **TCNCPAM.com**.

L. Other Fast-Track Legislation

In an effort to avoid potential filibusters and the burdens of cloture, 161 separate expedited procedures, also known as "fast-track procedures," have been included in legislation adopted by Congress since 1969.[1]

A few expedited procedures, in addition to the budget resolution and reconciliation bills (*see* Chapter 7.C. and Chapter 7.D.), are of particular significance: joint resolutions under the War Powers Resolution (P.L. 93-148) (*see* Chapter 7.N.); trade implementation fast-track provisions based on the Trade Act of 1974; the Congressional Review Act (*see* Chapter 7.M.); and resolutions of disapproval authorized under legislation creating Defense Base Closure and Realignment Commissions (BRAC) in 1988, 1991, 1993, 1995, and 2005. Under the procedures designed for BRAC, the entire package of closures of unneeded facilities recommended to Congress by the commission go into effect unless disapproved by the Congress.

》》 *See also The Federal Budget Process*, **FederalBudgetProcess.com**, and related CRS Reports and links on **TCNCPAM.com**.

M. Congressional Review Act

Given the complexity of implementing many laws and regulations, Congress regularly delegates rule-making authority to the president, to the executive branch, and to independent agencies. However, Congress has the ability to oversee such delegated authority through oversight, appropriations, and the Congressional Review Act (P.L. 104-121, 5 U.S.C. §§ 801–808), passed in 1996, which provides for a period of time to consider and potentially overturn a rule issued by a federal agency before it takes effect.

Under the Congressional Review Act, agencies submit a report to Congress laying out the details of a new rule. Any member of the House or Senate may introduce a joint resolution of disapproval of any final agency rule. Congress then considers the joint resolution to disapprove the rule under expedited procedures that provide for a sixty-day window in which the Congress may act, and that limits debate on that joint resolution, thus eliminating the possibility of a filibuster in the Senate. This means that only a simple majority is needed in both chambers to pass a joint resolution of disapproval.

---

1. Molly E. Reynolds, *Exceptions to the Rules: The Politics of Filibuster Limitations in the U.S. Senate* (Washington, D.C.: Brookings Institution Press, 2017) 185.

If both the House and the Senate pass a resolution of disapproval, it may be signed or vetoed by the president. If a resolution of disapproval is enacted by Congress and signed by the president or if a presidential veto of the resolution is overridden, the rule is voided and cannot be reemployed in "substantially the same form" unless Congress has enacted a new law authorizing the rule.

If the sixty-day window for action under the Congressional Review Act does not expire prior to *sine die* adjournment, a new sixty-day clock is available to the new Congress. This provision can be especially significant following a presidential election when the presidency changes hands.

During President Trump's first year in office in 2017, the Congressional Review Act was used extensively by the Republican majority in Congress. Fifteen separate rules promulgated by the Obama administration and independent agencies were disapproved. Since its adoption in 1996, the Congressional Review Act was successfully used to reject a rule only one other time, in 2001, during President George W. Bush's administration.

》》》 *See also* related CRS Reports and links on **TCNCPAM.com**.

N. The War Powers Resolution

The framers of the Constitution, consistent with their design of checks and balances, divided the war-making powers between the Congress and the president.

In Article I, Section 8, Congress is given the power "to declare war," the responsibility "to raise and support armies," and "to provide and maintain a navy."

Article II, Section 2 of the Constitution states that "the president shall be commander in chief of the army and the navy."

The shared responsibilities for sending the U.S. military into hostile circumstances have given rise to tensions from time to time between the president and Congress. In the nation's history, Congress has declared war on only five occasions, and not since World War II in 1941 (individual declarations of war against countries in World War I in 1917 and World War II in 1941 and 1942 increase the technical number of declarations passed by Congress to eleven). Presidents have submitted more than 120 reports to Congress pursuant to the War Powers Resolution

To declare war, Congress must pass a joint resolution. This joint resolution is subject to the rules and procedures in both chambers, including the potential for filibuster in the Senate (no senator voted against any of the eleven declarations of war referred to above).

U.S. military forces have been involved in combat situations on numerous occasions without a declaration of war. For example, the longest war in the nation's history, the Afghanistan War, which began in 2001, involved as many as 100,000 U.S troops at one point and cost the lives of nearly 2,400 American military personnel. It was not authorized by a declaration of war.

The Vietnam War was escalated by President John Kennedy from 1961 to 1963 and President Lyndon Johnson from 1963 to 1969. Public opposition to the war in Vietnam increased substantially from 1963 through 1972, while the war continued under President Richard Nixon from 1969 until U.S. forces were withdrawn from Vietnam in 1975. In response to the growing public opposition, Congress, in 1973, enacted the War Powers Resolution (P.L. 93-148), sometimes referred to as the War Powers Act, over the veto of President Richard Nixon. The War Powers Resolution was intended to establish clear procedures for the president and the Congress to follow in situations that might lead to the involvement of U.S. forces in hostilities abroad.

The War Powers Resolution requires that the president report to Congress, within forty-eight hours, the use of U.S. armed forces in hostilities or in situations where imminent involvement in hostilities is clearly indicated by the circumstances. Further, the War Powers Resolution requires that the president withdraw those forces from hostilities within sixty days, plus an additional thirty days if the president certifies to Congress that the safety of the troops "requires the continued use of such armed forces in the course of bringing about a prompt removal of such forces." The law states that the deadline applies in the absence of "a declaration of war or specific statutory authorization" and can be enforced by the Congress by passage of a joint resolution.

Every president since the adoption of the Act, beginning with Nixon, has asserted that the War Powers Resolution is unconstitutional. They assert it is legislative branch interference with the president's authority as commander in chief.

Since 1975, presidents have submitted numerous reports under the War Powers Resolution, usually asserting that they are doing so "consistent with" the law. The implied distinction is that the action is not taken "pursuant to" the War Powers Resolution.

One notable example was the joint resolution for the "Authorization for the Use of Military Force" (P.L. 107-40) passed by the Congress in the wake of the September 11, 2001, terror attacks at the World Trade Center and the Pentagon. S.J. Res. 23 was signed into law on September 18, 2001. This Joint Resolution did not invoke the War Powers Resolution. However, reports to Congress mandated by S.J. Res. 23 have been submitted *"consistent with"* the War Powers Resolution. That joint resolution, since 2001, has been used at least thirty-seven times in fourteen different nations.[2]

The extraordinary expedited procedures contained in the War Powers Resolution are designed to facilitate Congress making a judgment about the authorization of the commitment of the U.S. military within the sixty- to ninety-day deadline imposed by the War Powers Resolution.

The "fast-track" provisions include the introduction of a joint resolution and its referral to committee, the committee reporting to the floor or being automatically discharged from its consideration after twenty-four days, floor consideration and a vote required within three days, and further consideration in conference committee, if necessary. The unusual fast-track procedures can empower any one senator (or member of the House) to force a vote on a joint resolution restricting the president's ability to commit the armed forces. These unprecedented fast-track provisions have come to be called, by some, the "rocket docket."

》》 *See also* related CRS Reports and links on **TCNCPAM.com**.

O. Impoundment and Rescissions

The Congressional Budget and Impoundment Control Act of 1974 (P.L. 93-344, 31 U.S.C. § 1105) reformed procedures for the impoundment of appropriated funds by the president (*see* Chapter 7.B.). An impoundment is the withholding (or delay), usually by the president, of funds provided for in appropriations. A federal agency can also impound funds by failing to spend the appropriations allocated to it for a given fiscal year.

The Budget and Impoundment Act divides impoundment into "deferrals," delays in the use of funds, and "rescissions," which are requests by the president that Congress cancel an appropriation.

A rescission requires that the president submit a specific request to the

---

2. Matthew Weed. "Presidential References to the 2001 Authorization for Use of Military Force in Publicly Available Executive Actions and Reports to Congress." Congressional Research Service Memorandum, May 11, 2016.

Congress. More than one rescission can be listed in a request. Congress has a period of forty-five days of "continuous session," during which it may approve the rescission(s) in whole or in part. If Congress fails to act, the president is compelled to spend the funds for the purpose for which it was appropriated.

A deferral also requires a specific request to Congress from the president. Deferrals are limited to purposes listed by the Antideficiency Act, for example, providing for contingencies or achieving savings through greater efficiency. The president cannot defer funding for policy reasons (for example, to cut overall federal spending or because of opposition to a particular program).

》》 *See also* related CRS Reports and links on **TCNCPAM.com**.

P. Line-Item Veto

Presidents of both parties have for many years sought authority to veto particular items contained in appropriations and tax bills (*see* Chapter 6.G.). Proponents argued that this would allow a president to eliminate wasteful "pork-barrel" spending and tax loopholes without being required to veto an entire bill that they might otherwise support in order to get at the offending provisions.

In 1996, the Line Item Veto Act (P.L. 104-130) was enacted on a bipartisan vote. President Clinton supported it and it was a part of the "Contract with America" that Speaker Newt Gingrich (R-GA) had used in the 1994 midterm elections to elect Republican majorities in the House and Senate. Under the Line Item Veto Act, presidential proposals would take effect unless overturned by legislative action.

The Act authorized the president to identify, at enactment, individual items in legislation that he proposed should not go into effect. Congress had to respond within a limited period of time by enacting a law if it wanted to disapprove the president's proposals. Otherwise, the president's proposals would take effect.

In 1997 and 1998, President Clinton used the line-item veto power to strike eighty-two provisions from eleven different laws in just eighteen months.

Senators Robert Byrd (D-WV), Carl Levin (D-MI), and Daniel Patrick Moynihan (D-NY) opposed the law and immediately challenged it in federal courts. In 1997, the Supreme Court ruled that the senators lacked legal standing to bring the case. However, the senators joined a subsequent case in 1998 through amicus curiae briefs. In a 6 to 3 decision, in June 1998, the Supreme

Court in *Clinton v. City of New York*, 524 U.S. 417 (1998), ruled the Line Item Veto Act unconstitutional.

In the years since the 1998 ruling, presidents have continued to ask for some form of line-item veto that might pass constitutional muster. There have been various proposals for "enhanced rescission" authority, under which the president could propose rescissions under expedited procedures that Congress would be forced to act on. However, no such legislation has been enacted.

⟫⟫ *See also* related CRS Reports and links on **TCNCPAM.com**.

Q. Review Questions

⟫⟫ Explain why presidents with majorities in both chambers might prefer the use of reconciliation bills to enact major legislative agenda items.

⟫⟫ Why do presidents of both parties favor the line-item veto?

⟫⟫ What are rescissions and deferrals?

⟫⟫ What is the main objective of the War Powers Resolution?

⟫⟫ What is an "earmark"?

⟫⟫ What is meant by "expedited procedures" in the Congress? Give two examples of legislation that contain expedited procedures.

⟫⟫ What is the "debt ceiling" and why is it often controversial?

⟫⟫ When has the Congressional Review Act been used extensively since its passage in 1996?

⟫⟫ Compare and contrast the appropriations process and the authorization process. How do these relate to the budget resolution?

⟫⟫ What is the purpose of PAYGO?

Chapter 8
Additional Congressional Responsibilities and Procedures

A. Introduction

In addition to legislative powers granted in Article I, Congress has a number of other obligations under the Constitution. Some of the most important are actually contained in Article II, which creates the executive branch. Article II, Section 1 conveys to the president the power to nominate "with the Advice and Consent of the Senate" ambassadors, judges, and executive branch officials (*see* Chapter 8.B.). The president is also empowered by the Constitution to appoint executive branch officials and judges in Congress's absence (*see* Chapter 8.C.).

Article II, Section 1 gives the president the "power, by and with the Advice and Consent of the Senate, to make treaties, provided two thirds of the Senators present concur" (*see* Chapter 8.D.).

The responsibilities to concur in the ratification of treaties and particularly the obligation to participate in the appointment of federal judges have been at the center of considerable political debate in recent years.

Two other activities of importance discussed in this chapter are the congressional role in oversight of both the performance of the executive branch and the private sector in carrying out the laws, and the related congressional responsibility to investigate matters where abuse of power, scandal, wrongdoing, or malfeasance are charged (*see* Chapter 8.E.).

One tool used by Congress to maintain control while at the same time delegating responsibilities to the executive is the legislative veto. The Supreme Court has held the mechanism in most of its forms unconstitutional, but Congress has continued to use legislative vetoes (*see* Chapter 8.I.).

Article III gives the Congress important duties with respect to the judiciary, including establishing courts other than the Supreme Court (*see* Chapter 8.Q.) and determining the jurisdiction of all federal courts (with the exception of limiting the Supreme Court's original jurisdiction).

This chapter also discusses the responsibility given to the House to impeach a president, when warranted, and the power to remove that president by trial in the Senate (*see* Chapter 8.G.). Congress is also provided an important role should removal of the president pursuant to the Twenty-fifth Amendment be undertaken (*see* Chapter 8.H.).

The Constitution grants Congress important responsibilities in the counting and certification of electoral ballots in presidential elections and the authorization of Congress to legislate regarding the line of succession to the presidency. The procedures to be followed in the event of a presidential vacancy are established both by constitutional provisions and succession laws passed by Congress and signed by the president (*see* Chapter 8.O. and Chapter 8.P.).

Article I, Section 5, which allows both the House and the Senate to write their own rules, and is a provision of crucial importance to the independence of the Congress, further enhances that independence by assuring that only the House and the Senate may deny a seat to a representative-elect or a senator-elect, respectively. Also, only the House and the Senate are empowered to remove a member from their body. There is no other way to deny a member or member-elect their seat in the Congress (*see* Chapter 8.N.).

Article V places Congress at the heart of the process of amending the Constitution. This far-reaching power, shared with the states, does not involve a role for the president (*see* Chapter 8.R.).

Several important elements of congressional procedure are discussed in this chapter, including the differences between congressional recesses and adjournments (*see* Chapter 8.J.).

Rulings by the presiding officer and successful appeals to such rulings play a key role in both chambers, but particularly in the Senate, where the body is more likely to overturn its presiding officer. A recent example was the use of the "nuclear option" in the Senate to change the precedents related to cloture votes on executive branch and judicial nominations (*see* Chapter 5.I. and Chapter 8.B.).

Finally, this chapter explains the practice of permitting senators to speak on any subject during a period called "morning business" and a procedure in the House, known as "special orders," allowing members to make short speeches after the House has completed its legislative business for the day (*see* Chapter 8.K. and Chapter 8.L.).

》》》 *See also* related CRS Reports and links on **TCNCPAM.com.**

B. Nominations

The Constitution provides for shared power between the president and the Senate with respect to nominations to high executive offices (including the cabinet) and to all federal judicial nominations. Congress may determine whether lower-level executive nominations require Senate confirmation.

There are more than 1,200 executive branch positions that currently require Senate confirmation, including department heads (such as secretaries, deputy secretaries, under secretaries, and general counsels), leaders of independent agencies (such as administrators and deputy administrators), and members of boards and commissions (such as commissioners). Presidential appointments of U.S. attorneys and U.S. marshals must also be confirmed by the Senate. Promotions of military officers are also confirmed by the Senate, most routinely.

Every four years, following presidential elections, the Senate and the House alternate in publishing a book-length listing of politically appointed positions entitled *Policy and Supporting Positions* (printed by the Government Publishing Office), more popularly known as the "Plum Book." The Plum Book is named for its original cover color (although appreciated for the double meaning).

The Senate alone, with stability in mind, was chosen by the framers to share the power to appoint judges and executive branch officials with the president. James Madison wrote at the Constitutional Convention in 1787, "... the Senate is to consist in its proceeding with more coolness ... and with more wisdom, than the popular branch." In fact, the word "senate" derives from the Latin "senatus," meaning an assembly of wise old men.

French political theorist Alexis de Tocqueville in his classic work, *Democracy in America*, observed, "In the exercise of the executive power the President of the United States is constantly subject to a jealous scrutiny. He may make, but he cannot conclude, a treaty; he may designate, but he cannot appoint, a public officer."

The process of confirming presidential nominations begins in the committee of jurisdiction over the agency involved: for example, all ambassadors and the Secretary of State would be considered in the Senate Foreign Relations Committee, the Attorney General in the Judiciary Committee, and the Secretary of Defense in the Armed Services Committee.

Hearings are held to evaluate the qualifications of the nominees. Typically the nominee and others, supporting or opposing the nomination, may testify. Often senators will use these opportunities to extract promises to take certain actions, if confirmed, from the nominees. Commonly, chairs or other members of the committee will seek a commitment during the hearings that the nominee, if confirmed, will agree to testify before the committee when requested to do so. This hearing process plays an important role in facilitating congressional oversight of the executive branch. Nominations may be reported favorably, unfavorably, or without recommendation to the full Senate by a simple majority vote of the committee. Senate Rule XXVI, 7.(a) requires that a physical majority of the committee be present when this recommendation is made and that a majority of those present approve the recommendation.

Hearings by the Senate Judiciary Committee are held to consider the qualifications and temperament of judicial nominations made by the president. Judicial nominations also require a simple majority vote to be reported to the full Senate. Like executive branch nominations, they may be reported favorably, unfavorably, or without recommendation. They may also be simply ignored at this stage. Some judicial nominations in recent years have languished with or without hearings for years, mostly at the will of the Judiciary Committee chair.

A recent example was the handling by the Senate majority Republicans of President Obama's nomination of Merrick Garland to be a Supreme Court justice. Within hours of the news of the death of Supreme Court Justice Antonin Scalia on February 13, 2016, Majority Leader Mitch McConnell (R-KY) vowed that the Senate would not take up any nomination that the president might make, stating, "The American people should have a voice in the selection of their next Supreme Court Justice. Therefore, this vacancy should not be filled until we have a new president."

President Obama ignored the majority leader's advice that he make no nomination, and on March 16, he nominated Merrick Garland, the chief judge of the D.C. Circuit Court of Appeals, to fill the Scalia seat.

Backed by the Senate majority and Judiciary Committee Chair Chuck Grassley (R-IA), the majority leader successfully stonewalled the Garland nomination. After Donald Trump was elected president in November and took office in January he nominated Neil Gorsuch to the Supreme Court.

Democrats, believing the failure to consider President Obama's nominee was unprecedented, launched a filibuster of the Gorsuch nomination. With only fifty-two Republican senators at the time, it was unlikely that the sixty votes necessary for cloture could be reached. Majority Leader McConnell eventually used the same parliamentary tactic that his Democratic predecessor Harry Reid (D-NV) had used to create a Senate precedent reinterpreting the language of Rule XXII as requiring only a simple majority to end debate by invoking cloture, extending its effect to Supreme Court nominees. This was the so-called nuclear option (*see* Chapter 5.I.).

Supreme Court confirmation hearings have become major public events and can be quite contentious. In recent decades, hearings for Supreme Court nominees have garnered intense national interest and often live television coverage.

Once hearings are concluded, the committee of jurisdiction votes to report the nomination to the full Senate, favorably, unfavorably, or without a recommendation. The committee may also choose not to act on a nomination.

A nomination reported to the Senate is placed on the executive calendar (*see* Chapter 5.C.). The Senate considers nominations in executive session as opposed to legislative session. The Senate proceeds to executive session by motion or unanimous consent to take up nominations or treaties on the Executive Calendar. By precedent, the motion to proceed to executive session to consider a specified nomination, wherever it may be among the nominations listed on the calendar, is not debatable. Routine nominations may be called up *en bloc* and confirmed by unanimous consent.

Nominations that have not been acted upon when the Senate adjourns or recesses for more than thirty days or, when it adjourns *sine die*, are returned to the president.

When a nomination is called up, the presiding officer poses the question, "Will the Senate advise and consent to this nomination?" The nomination is confirmed by simple majority vote, a quorum being present.

For much of its history, filibusters of nominations in the Senate were rare. In more recent years, as the level of partisanship in the body has increased, it is not uncommon for the opposition party to the president to oppose some of his nominations. If the president's party is in the majority in the Senate, the minority not infrequently employs a filibuster or threat of a filibuster to delay a nomination. Filibusters of Supreme Court nominations remain comparatively rare. Cloture has been sought only five times, including the nomination of Neil Gorsuch. Before Gorsuch, cloture votes were required only on the nominations of Abe Fortas in 1968 (at least in part due to ethics problems that later caused Fortas to resign from the Court), twice on William Rehnquist (when he was confirmed as an associate justice and again when elevated to chief justice) in 1971 and 1986, and Samuel Alito in 2006.

Supreme Court nominations are of particularly high profile and the mere possibility of a filibuster being employed often has some effect on the president's nomination decision in the first place. Presidents anticipated, because of the supermajority (sixty vote) requirement to invoke cloture, that their nominee would likely require some votes from the minority party (or votes from the opposition if the president's party were in the minority). This may have and often appears to have had the effect of presidents avoiding some nominees. The same applies to circuit court and district court nominees, but often in a less publicized fashion.

This changed beginning in 2013 when Senate Majority Leader Harry Reid (D-NV) employed the parliamentary tactic that has been called the "nuclear option" (*see* Chapter 5.H. and Chapter 5.I.). The majority, at the time Democrats, was successful in establishing the precedent that the words of Senate Rule XXII—ending debate requires a vote of "three-fifths of the Senators duly chosen and sworn"—was to be understood to require only a simple majority on all executive branch nominees and all judicial nominees below the level of the Supreme Court.

In 2017, Republican Majority Leader Mitch McConnell (R-KY) executed the same parliamentary tactic to extend the precedent to cloture on Supreme Court nominees. This brought the Democratic filibuster of the nomination of Neil Gorsuch to the Supreme Court to a halt.

The changes in the Senate's interpretation of the number of votes needed to invoke cloture means that a president, if his party is in the majority in the Senate, will only require the support of his own party to confirm judicial nominees to lifetime appointments on the federal courts. As former Senator Richard Lugar (R-IN) observed, "If nominating and confirming judges becomes a purely partisan affair, it will be far more likely that judges subjected to such proceedings will feel less inclined to uphold strict norms of impartiality and non-partisanship" (*see* Chapter 5.H. and Chapter 5.I.).

》》 *See also* related CRS Reports and links on **TCNCPAM.com**.

C. Recess Appointments

The president is able to make temporary appointments during a recess of the Senate without the advice and consent of the Senate. Article II, Section 2 of the Constitution provides that "[t]he President shall have Power to fill up all Vacancies that may happen during the Recess of the Senate, by granting Commissions which shall expire at the End of their next Session."

This clause was included in the Constitution by the Framers to ensure that government agencies could continue to function during periods when Congress was not in session and therefore the Senate was unavailable to confirm presidential nominees. In earlier periods, Congresses sometimes met for only a few months each year and recesses could be quite extended. Also, travel to and from the capital was slow and less reliable.

The power to make recess appointments has been used by presidents throughout American history at times to circumvent advice and consent by the

Senate. This occurs typically for political reasons when a nominee is controversial and may be blocked in the Senate.

Presidents since George Washington have made recess appointments. According to the Congressional Research Service Report R42329, President Ronald Reagan made 243 recess appointments during his eight years in office (1981–1989). President George H. W. Bush (1989–1993) made seventy-seven recess appointments, President Bill Clinton (1993–2001) made 139, and President George W. Bush (2001–2009) made 171. President Obama (2009–2017) made thirty-two, reflecting the increased use of pro forma sessions (discussed below).

The use of the Recess Appointments Clause is subject to controversy when it is used to place judges on the federal bench. In our history, although only three justices have been named to the Supreme Court via recess appointments, more than 300 judges have been placed in the lower federal courts in this manner.

A recess held within a congressional session is referred to as an "intrasession recess" and the period between the *sine die* adjournment of one session and the convening of the next session is referred to as an "intersession recess." Presidents have made recess appointments during each.

While the interpretation of the Recess Appointments Clause and its use has been controversial throughout its history, during the last years of the George W. Bush administration, Senate Majority Leader Harry Reid (D-NV) in 2007 pioneered the use of "pro forma sessions." Pro forma sessions are sessions in which little or no business occurs in either chamber, but it's the Senate that is relevant here. The presiding officer gavels the body into session and typically immediately gavels the session to a close, in most cases in less than a minute. Usually, only one senator is present.

A 1993 Department of Justice memo argued that the president could make a recess appointment during any recess of more than three days. Therefore, Reid argued, by holding a pro forma session of the Senate every three days, the Senate would technically not be in recess. Since the Senate was not in recess, no recess appointment could be made by the president.

When the Republicans regained control of the Senate and were interested in blocking recess appointments by President Obama, Majority Leader Mitch McConnell (R-KY) adopted the Reid pro forma session strategy.

President Obama, in 2012, during an intrasession recess, made recess appointments of three members to the National Labor Relations Board and a director for the Consumer Financial Protection Bureau, a new agency created by the Dodd-Frank Wall Street Reform and Consumer Protection Act (P.L. 111-203), ignoring the fact that the Senate was holding pro forma sessions.

Obama made the argument that "the President may determine that pro forma sessions at which no business is to be conducted do not interrupt a Senate recess for the purposes of the Recess Appointments Clause." The Republicans took issue with Obama's interpretation.

In 2014, the battle reached the Supreme Court in *National Labor Relations Board v. Noel Canning*, No. 12-1281 (573 U.S. ___, 2014). In its 9-to-0 decision, the Court held that President Obama exceeded his constitutional authority by making the appointments. Justice Stephen Breyer wrote for the Court, "We conclude that we cannot ignore these pro forma sessions …. Thus we conclude that the president lacked the power to make the recess appointments … ." The Court expanded the number of days required to trigger qualification as a recess under the Recess Appointment Clause from three to ten.

Finally, Breyer wrote, "For purposes of the Recess Appointments Clause, the Senate is in session when it says that it is … ."

On some occasions the Senate has been forced into pro forma sessions by the House of Representatives. The Constitution, Article I, Section 5, stipulates that neither chamber may recess for more than three days without the approval of the other. By withholding its approval for the necessary concurrent resolution to allow the Senate to adjourn, the House assures that the Senate will conduct at least pro forma sessions. Therefore, the House, if controlled by the opposition party even if the Senate is not, can prevent recess appointments by the president.

〉〉〉 *See also* related CRS Reports and links on **TCNCPAM.com**.

D. Treaties

Another form of executive business in the Senate is treaties. The president negotiates treaties with other nations. A treaty may be bilateral, with one other nation like the two Panama Canal Treaties signed in 1977 (with Panama), or multilateral, like the North Atlantic Treaty (which established NATO) signed in 1949 with eleven other founding nations.

Once the president has negotiated and signed a treaty, it is submitted to the Senate. The president performs the formal act of ratification of treaties, but only after the Senate has, pursuant to Article II, Section 2 of the Constitution, advised and consented to such ratification. This consent requires that "two thirds of the Senators present concur." (*See* Senate Rule XXX.)

When a treaty is submitted to the Senate, it is referred to the Senate Foreign Relations Committee. The committee generally holds hearings, receiving testimony from the administration, other outside experts, opponents of the treaty, and its proponents.

The Foreign Relations Committee may decide to take no action on the treaty. The committee may report the treaty to the full Senate favorably, unfavorably, or without recommendation, at which time it is placed on the Senate's Executive Calendar. The committee generally also submits a written report, known as an executive report.

The Foreign Relations Committee also reports a recommended resolution of ratification, in the form of a Senate Resolution, which is the actual document conveying the Senate's advice and consent. The resolution of ratification may include committee-recommended conditions: proposed amendment to the actual text of the treaty, or proposed reservations, declarations, or understandings that would not change the text of the treaty but would qualify the sentiment of the Senate in advising and consenting to ratification.

Likewise, the actual text of a treaty may be amended on the floor of the Senate, and when consideration of the text of the treaty has been concluded on the Senate floor, the resolution of ratification may also be amended on the floor by the inclusion of reservations.

Reservations are formal declarations that modify the effect of one or more of the provisions of the treaty. The Senate sometimes also includes other additions to the resolution of ratification called "understandings," "interpretations," or "declarations" that do not modify the force of the treaty but are intended to further clarify its meaning. Each of these matters requires only a simple majority for adoption.

- **Reservations** are "specific qualifications or stipulations which change U.S. obligations without necessarily changing treaty language."
- **Understandings** are "interpretive statements that clarify or elaborate the provisions of the treaty but do not alter its language."
- **Declarations** are "statements of the Senate's position, opinion or intentions on matters relating to issues raised by the treaty, but not to its specific provisions."

"Treaties and Other International Agreements: The Role of the United States Senate," S. Prt. 106-71 (January 2001).

Once consideration of both the treaty and the resolution of ratification are completed, and the treaty is reported by the committee, the treaty is placed on the Executive Calendar. The motion to proceed to the executive calendar to consider a treaty is not subject to debate and therefore can easily be resolved by unanimous consent or simple majority vote.

When all debate has ended and there are no additional proposed treaty amendments to consider, the Senate begins consideration of the "resolution of ratification." Once the Senate is considering the resolution of ratification, no further amendments to the treaty itself are in order except by unanimous consent. However, "reservations" to the treaty are only in order during the Senate's consideration of the resolution of ratification. Additional or modified understandings, declarations, statements, or provisos may be added on the Senate floor at this stage of consideration.

Under the Constitution, Article II, Section 2, adoption of the resolution of ratification requires a two-thirds vote of those present, a quorum being present.

Treaties, unlike legislation and nominations, remain before the Senate from Congress to Congress, once submitted by the president. An extreme example of this was the Genocide Convention that was submitted to the Senate by President Harry Truman in 1949. The Senate in 1986, thirty-seven years later, finally agreed to its ratification. Senator William Proxmire (D-WI) began speaking in support of ratification of the Genocide Treaty in 1967. He pledged to speak virtually every day the Senate was in session. He made more than 3,000 speeches on the Senate floor in support and persisted for nineteen years. Senator Proxmire finally succeeded when the Senate voted 93 to 1 to consent to the treaty on February 19, 1986.

When the Senate consents to the ratification of a treaty and it is formally ratified by the president, it becomes the supreme law of the land, like laws passed by Congress and provisions of the Constitution.

Treaties submitted to the Senate are secret under Senate Rule XXIX. The Senate must act to remove the injunction of secrecy. In most cases, this occurs by unanimous consent at the time the treaty is referred to the Committee on Foreign Relations.

》》》 *See also* related CRS Reports and links on **TCNCPAM.com**.

E. Congressional Oversight

Congressional oversight plays a fundamental role in the checks and balances envisioned by the Constitution, by enabling Congress to review actions taken by other parts of the federal government. Oversight responsibilities are implicit in the Constitution and have been a central undertaking of the Congress since its early beginnings.

The words of James Madison in *The Federalist* No. 51 are frequently cited as the most eloquent statement of the need for Congress to assure that the federal government remains in check. Madison wrote: "If men were angels, no government would be necessary. If angels governed men, neither external nor internal controls on government would be necessary. In framing a government which is to be administered by men over men, the great difficulty lies in this: you must first enable the government to control the governed; and in the next place, oblige it to control itself."

Many members and those who study Congress have recognized the imperative that if democracy is to work properly, legislative control and the review of administrative action are necessary to provide that control. Oversight is conducted by Congress largely through its committees and subcommittees.

Although the Constitution does not explicitly lay out the power of Congress to oversee and investigate, the Supreme Court in *McGrain v. Daugherty*, 273 U.S. 135 (1927), ruled that congressional investigations have a legislative purpose and are authorized by the Constitution's "Necessary and Proper" clause (also known as the "Elastic" clause) that gives Congress in Article I, Section 8, the power to "make all laws which shall be necessary and proper for carrying into execution the foregoing powers, and all other powers vested by this Constitution in the government of the United States."

The Supreme Court in the 8-to-0 *McGrain* decision held that "the power of inquiry—with process to enforce it—is an essential and appropriate auxiliary to the legislative function."

Congressional oversight has routinely examined both the public and private sectors. Today, the federal bureaucracy is made up of about 2 million civilian federal employees working in approximately 440 federal agencies. Overseeing the execution and evaluating the performance of laws passed by Congress by the federal bureaucracy is an ever-increasing task. Woodrow Wilson in *Congressional Government* wrote, "Quite as important as legislation is vigilant oversight of administration ... ." He wrote, "The argument is not only that a discussed and interrogated administration is the only pure and efficient administration, but more than that, the only really self-governing people is that people which discusses and interrogates its administration."

Private-sector wrongdoing is also subject to congressional oversight. Past investigations have included examining such matters as the collapse of Enron, the Deepwater Horizon oil spill, pricing abuses by pharmaceutical companies, and consumer ripoffs by financial institutions. Those inquiries have examined not only whether current laws are working, but also whether new laws or tougher agency enforcement actions are needed.

When scandals, disasters, or wrongdoing have occurred, Congress has often undertaken the responsibility for oversight to get the facts. The exercise of that fact-finding responsibility has, at times, had profound impacts on the course of public policy.

One of the watersheds in bringing congressional oversight into sharper focus was the establishment in 1946 of the Joint Committee on the Organization of Congress, known as the LaFollette-Monroney Committee. That committee, charged with "enabling [the Congress] to better meet its responsibilities under the Constitution," shaped the Legislative Reorganization Act of 1946, which was signed into law by President Harry Truman. Truman had pioneered the modernization of congressional oversight as the chair of the Special Committee to Investigate the National Defense Program, known as the Truman Committee. Then-Senator Truman investigated waste and corruption by contractors and defense agencies during World War II, and his committee is credited with being one of the most effective oversight efforts in congressional history, saving millions of taxpayer dollars.

The Legislative Reorganization Act of 1946, among a range of other committee reforms like reducing the number of committees in the Senate from thirty-three to fifteen and in the House from forty-eight to nineteen, directly addressed congressional oversight. Section 136 made the oversight responsibilities of standing congressional committees explicit.

The Act stated that, "To assist the Congress in appraising the administration of the laws and in developing such amendments or related legislation as it may deem necessary, each standing committee of the Senate and the House *shall exercise continuous watchfulness* of the execution by administrative agencies concerned of any laws, the subject matter of which is within the jurisdiction of such committee ... ." (Emphasis added.)

The authority granted to each standing committee for this function included the ability to issue subpoenas and to open investigations on matters within their jurisdiction on their own. The practice prior to the 1946 Act had been to create a special committee to investigate individual policy problems as they arose.

Both the House and Senate rules now authorize standing committees to conduct oversight investigations. House Rule X provides a general charge of oversight responsibility to the House Committee on Oversight and Governmental Reform. Rule X further mandates, "Each standing committee ... shall review and study on a continuing basis the application, administration, and execution of all laws within its legislative jurisdiction." In the Senate, Rule XXVI contains virtually the same language regarding standing committees, charging them with oversight responsibilities on a "continuing basis."

Another important oversight mechanism available to Congress is the Government Accountability Office (GAO) that was created as the General Accounting Office in the legislative branch by the 1921 Budget and Accounting Act. In the years after World War II, GAO's mission shifted from accounting matters to broad investigations and evaluations of federal programs. In recent years, congressional committees, congressional leadership, and individual members of Congress have increasingly sought GAO assistance. As a nonpartisan agency, its audits and reports give added credibility to congressional oversight, uncovering inefficiencies, waste, fraud, and wrongdoing.

Congress also enlists the assistance of the Inspectors General (IG) in the agencies of the federal government. In approximately seventy federal agencies, IGs head permanent, nonpartisan and independent offices charged with overseeing the efficient and effective operation of those agencies. Established by the Inspector General Act of 1978 (P.L. 95-452), IGs are required to report to Congress every six months on their activities. They are unique in the executive branch in that they report directly to Congress as well as to the head of their home agency. Their findings and reports are not reviewed by or filtered through their agency, an important element of their ability to be independent. In the event of discovery of egregious abuses within a federal agency, the IG is required to immediately notify the agency head and then the Congress within seven days. Cabinet-level departments and some other large agencies have IGs who are appointed by the president with the advice and consent of the Senate. The IG Act includes among its principal purposes "keeping ... the Congress fully and currently informed about problems and deficiencies relating to the administration of ... programs and operations and the necessity for and progress of corrective action."

Legal tools available to committees conducting oversight or investigations include subpoena powers, deposition authority, grants of congressional immunity (sometimes used to gain testimony of witnesses who have asserted their Fifth Amendment rights not to incriminate themselves), and the potential to hold witnesses in contempt of Congress for failing to provide requested information. Whether provided through public testimony under oath or statements made in more private settings, and whether sworn or unsworn, federal law prohibits making false statements to Congress (18 U.S. Code § 1001).

One Senate oversight subcommittee of note has played an historic role in the evolution of congressional oversight: the Senate Permanent Subcommittee on Investigations (PSI) within the Homeland Security and Governmental Affairs Committee. That committee had its roots in the Truman Committee and later notoriously served as the authority and forum for Senator Joseph McCarthy's (R-WI) investigations into alleged "Communist infiltration of the U.S. government." When his closed sessions were made public after fifty years and showed Senator McCarthy berating and badgering witnesses, then-Chair Senator Carl Levin (D-MI) and Ranking Member Senator Susan Collins (R-ME) wrote that "These hearings are a part of our national past that we can neither afford to forget nor permit to reoccur." Because the subcommittee, or PSI, as it is known, did not forget, it has distinguished itself by meeting high standards for conducting fact-based, bipartisan, professional oversight. In recent years, it has become known for conducting high-quality, bipartisan investigations on a broad range of issues such as money laundering, Oil-for Food at the UN, offshore tax abuses, unfair credit card practices, health care fraud, and tax avoidance, to mention just a few.

The conduct of bipartisan, fact-based oversight is described well by former PSI Staff Director Linda Gustitus in an oral history conducted by the Senate Historical Office in 2012. She observed that, "If a committee does oversight well, and not many do ... the job ... is to gather the facts ... so that the members don't disagree on the facts." There are two ways Congress gets information: people and documents. People don't need to be under oath—it's against the law to lie to the federal government, including Congress, whether under oath or not (False Statements Accountability Act of 1996, P.L. 104-292). Gathering the right documents and interviewing the right people is critical to getting the facts. "Then the members can disagree about the interpretations of the facts ... they can have different views on the facts, but the purpose of the oversight subcommittee, of the staff and the work, is to make sure that the committee gets the facts."[1]

In recent years, the fact-finding responsibility of congressional oversight has often been driven by partisan investigations and hearings. Some committees when controlled by the opposition party have sought to gain political leverage over the president through burdensome oversight. In other instances, where committees are controlled by the president's own party, necessary oversight has too often given way to simply supporting the president's policies and political efforts.

One area of congressional oversight that raises special issues involves the intelligence community of the United States because of the secrecy and national security demands that must be weighed against transparency and accountability norms in an open and democratic system.[2]

To address those issues, the Senate created the Select Committee on Intelligence (SSCI) in 1976 and the House created the Permanent Select Committee on Intelligence (HPSCI) in 1977. The committees grew out of recommendations made by the "Church Committee," formally the Senate Select Committee to Study Governmental Operations with Respect to Intelligence Activities, which published its final report in April 1976, and the Pike Committee in the House that was chaired by Representative Otis Pike (D-NY).

The select intelligence committees do not have exclusive jurisdiction over issues involving the intelligence community; oversight can also be exercised in both chambers by the Armed Services Committee, the Appropriations Committee, the Foreign Relations Committee (Foreign Affairs in the House), and the Judiciary Committee.

Committees with broad, overlapping jurisdictions are common in Congress; while critics deplore the duplication, others value the ability of more than one committee to examine a problem. In the intelligence context, because many of the intelligence committee hearings and analyses are shielded from the public, attendance and involvement in the work of the select committee by

---

1. "Linda Gustitus: Staff Director, Subcommittee on Oversight of Government Management and of the Permanent Subcommittee on Investigations, and Chief of Staff, Senator Carl Levin, 1979–2003," Oral History Interviews, September 24 to December 10, 2012, Senate Historical Office, Washington, D.C.

2. The author, as Special Assistant to the Majority Leader for National Security Affairs, served as Senator Mitchell's primary liaison to the Senate Intelligence Committee and the intelligence community, 1989–1994.

members other than the chair and vice chair has been a fairly consistent problem, making the ability of other committees to examine intelligence issues an ongoing benefit.

Events have from time to time laid bare weaknesses in the existing oversight structure. For example, the Iran-Contra Affair and the attack on September 11, 2001, disclosed flawed intelligence activities and analyses that had been kept from Congress and the public. The Select Iran-Contra Committee report and the report of the 9/11 Commission both included recommendations for strengthening intelligence oversight by Congress, but most have never been carried out.

A potential step that has met with surprising resistance in both chambers would be to give the existing "select" committees status as standing committees. Also, eliminating the current term limits on members of the committees could strengthen the depth of experience and enhance continuity. The argument against doing so has been the desire to consistently add "new blood" to the committees, which otherwise may develop an excessively close working relationship with the intelligence organizations and could become reluctant to criticize them. Also, the current rotation broadens member understanding and awareness on intelligence matters.

>>> *See also* related CRS Reports and links on **TCNCPAM.com**.

F. Investigations

Congressional oversight can take many forms with various levels of intensity. The most intense form of congressional oversight is conducting a lengthy and detailed investigation. Some congressional investigations have achieved a high public profile—Teapot Dome, Iran-Contra[3], Watergate, Whitewater, terrorist attack at Benghazi, and Russia investigations.

Although more adversarial, investigations share much with other oversight functions. The ultimate goal is to improve Congress's ability to carry out its legislative role in addressing matters of public policy in both the private and public sectors by assessing the executive branch's implementation of current laws, exposing private-sector abuses, and determining whether new laws are needed.

---

3. The author served as Senator George Mitchell's "Designated Liaison" to the Iran-Contra Committee in 1987 and helped to draft the "Report of the Committees Investigating the Iran-Contra Affair."

Because witnesses in an investigatory context may be less forthcoming, they may be subjected to subpoenas compelling them to provide documents or testimony, brought in for lengthy interviews, placed under oath, or perhaps brought before the committee in a public hearing.

Witnesses subject to committee inquiries, of course, retain their constitutional rights, including the Fifth Amendment protection against self-incrimination.

In the Iran-Contra investigation, the House and Senate each appointed their own investigative committee and the two committees conducted their investigations separately, but by agreement of the two committees their public hearings and the final report on the Iran-Contra matter were carried out jointly.

For investigations by the Congress to be credible and influence public policy, they must exhibit something beyond reflexive party loyalty.

》》》 *See also* related CRS Reports and links on **TCNCPAM.com**.

G. Impeachment and Trial

Article I, Section 2 of the Constitution grants to the House the authority to decide whether to impeach the president or other executive-branch officials or judges sitting on any of the three levels of federal courts. Impeachment in the House is similar to indictment. Impeachment of the president, vice president and other federal officers (including judges) requires a simple majority vote in the House, a quorum having been established. Impeachment may be initiated by any Member of the House of Representatives by submitting a House resolution. The resolution is referred to the House Judiciary Committee. Individual "articles of impeachment" are voted on and there may be a number of them reported by the Judiciary Committee. All that is required to impeach the official is for any one of the articles of impeachment to be passed by simple majority.

The Senate, under Article I, Section 3, possesses the "sole Power to try all Impeachments." It is the Senate that determines whether to convict and remove from office any impeached official. House "managers" are appointed to argue the case before the Senate. Conviction requires a two-thirds vote of senators present, a quorum being present. When the president is tried, the chief justice of the United States is required by the Constitution to preside in the Senate. (The vice president or president *pro tempore* presides over other impeachment trials.)

Former Senate Parliamentarian Robert Dove told a story about Chief Justice Rehnquist presiding over the impeachment trial of Bill Clinton. Bob Dove had invited his father, who was proudly sitting in the visitors' gallery overlooking the Senate floor as his son sat in his designated seat on the podium. At some point in the proceedings the chief justice, like normal Senate presiding officers, needed the advice of the parliamentarian on Senate procedural matters. The chief justice leaned down over the desk and in a voice that could be heard in the galleries, asked Dove, "What the hell do I do now?"

Alexander Hamilton wrote in *The Federalist* No. 65, "Where else than in the Senate could have been found a tribunal sufficiently dignified, or sufficiently independent? What other body would be likely to feel confidence enough in its own situation, to preserve, unawed and uninfluenced, the necessary impartiality between an individual accused, and the representatives of the people, his accusers?"

The language of Article II, Section 4 states: "The President, Vice President and all civil officers of the United States, shall be removed from office on impeachment for, and conviction of, treason, bribery, or other high crimes and misdemeanors."

Much debate has focused on the words *"high crimes and misdemeanors"* since its meaning in a legal context is not clear. In the final analysis, impeachment and trial in the Congress is a political process, not a legal one.

The House has impeached nineteen individuals, including six since 1986 (prior to 1986, there had not been an impeachment for fifty years). Only eight officials, all federal judges, have been convicted by the Senate in its history. Only one Supreme Court Justice has been impeached, Samuel Chase in 1804. Chase was acquitted by the Senate on all eight articles of impeachment.

The House has impeached two presidents, Andrew Johnson in 1868, over his firing of Secretary of War Edwin Stanton, and Bill Clinton in 1998, over alleged perjury before a grand jury and obstruction of justice. Both presidents were acquitted by the Senate. President Andrew Johnson came close to removal. The Senate voted 35 to 19 to remove him, one vote short of the necessary two-thirds (there were only fifty-four senators at the time). President Clinton was acquitted on both articles of impeachment brought against him by the House with fifty-five votes for acquittal and forty-five for conviction on the perjury charge, and fifty votes for acquittal and fifty votes for conviction on the obstruction of justice charge.

President Richard Nixon was seriously threatened with impeachment during the Watergate scandal. The House vote to give formal authority to the Judiciary Committee to consider impeachment of Nixon passed 410 to 4. In July 1974, the House Judiciary Committee reported three articles of impeachment against Nixon: obstruction of justice, abuse of power and contempt of Congress, by a bipartisan majority. Seven of the Committee's seventeen Republicans voted for the abuse of power article. Two additional articles were proposed, but defeated.

On August 8, 1974, a small group of Congress members headed by Senator Barry Goldwater went to the White House to warn the president that if he did not resign from office, the House was about to impeach and it was very likely the Senate would remove him from office. The next day, August 9, 1974, Nixon resigned before the House could impeach him. President Gerald Ford who rose to the presidency when Nixon resigned, pardoned Nixon for any wrongdoing.

>>> *See also* related CRS Reports and links on **TCNCPAM.com.**

H. Twenty-fifth Amendment

The Twenty-fifth Amendment was ratified in 1967 in the wake of President Kennedy's assassination. It was designed to clarify procedures for the replacement of a president or vice president upon death, disability, or removal from office.

The amendment was invoked several times during the Watergate era in the 1970s. Congressman Gerald Ford (R-MI) was named to replace Vice President Spiro Agnew, who resigned in the face of corruption and tax-evasion charges. Less than a year later, in August 1974, when Richard Nixon resigned the presidency, Ford became president. He named Nelson Rockefeller to fill the vacant vice presidency.

When a nominee is chosen by the president to assume the office of vice president, that appointment must be confirmed by a majority vote of both the House of Representatives and the Senate.

The Congress could also play a critical role should the vice president and a majority of the cabinet, acting under Section 4 of the Twenty-fifth Amendment, declare the president unable to discharge his powers and duties. If the president were to resist that declaration by asserting that he or she were capable of discharging the duties, the president would resume the powers and duties as president unless by a two-thirds vote of each chamber, Congress determines the president is unable to do so.

Congress under the Constitution has always had the power to remove a president through impeachment and conviction. The Twenty-fifth Amendment is meant to provide a way for the vice president, the cabinet, and the Congress to remove a president temporarily or permanently under dire circumstances when the president is ill or otherwise incapacitated. This section has never been invoked to remove a president.

》》》 *See also* related CRS Reports and links on **TCNCPAM.com**.

I. Legislative Veto

Legislative vetoes are a device whereby the Congress delegates authority to the executive branch, but retains the right to disapprove an action taken pursuant to that authority. This has historically taken the form of a two-chamber veto, a one-chamber veto, or a committee veto. None of these devices is submitted to the president for his signature or veto.

The Supreme Court ruled in 1983 in *INS v. Chada*, 462 U.S. 919 (1983), that the legislative veto is unconstitutional. The Court held that the legislative veto violated the Presentment Clause of the Constitution (Article I, Section 7, Clauses 2 and 3) because it did not require action by the president. Also, one-chamber vetoes and committee vetoes failed to meet the constitutional requirement that legislation must be passed by both chambers with identical text.

Although the Court views these mechanisms as unconstitutional and Congress has removed them from several statutes, the legislative veto has not disappeared. Now, typically, legislative vetoes are designed as committee vetoes and are mostly agreements worked out between the executive and legislative branches.

In some instances, statutes have included a legislative veto provision in the form of a joint resolution of disapproval. Unlike the two-chamber veto that requires a concurrent resolution that is not presented to the president, a joint resolution of disapproval requires passage by both chambers and the signature of the president and presumably meets the requirements of the Presentment Clause.

》》》 *See also* related CRS Reports and links on **TCNCPAM.com**.

J. Recess and Adjournment

In the Senate, the distinction between recessing at the end of the day and adjourning is very significant.

An adjournment motion is the formal action to end the session for the day in either the House or the Senate. The adjournment motion may establish the day or time certain that the House or Senate will next convene. When the Senate or House adjourns for the final time for a congressional session for the year, it adjourns *sine die.*

By contrast, a recess in the Senate or House is generally a temporary interruption in Senate or House business, occurring on occasion within the same day. The Senate also at times recesses rather than adjourning at the end of the day.

Somewhat confusingly, the term "recess" is used to refer to periods in which the House or Senate is adjourned pursuant to a concurrent resolution either within or between sessions of Congress. Such periods within a congressional session are referred to as an "intrasession recess." When the House and Senate have adjourned *sine die* at the end of a congressional session, the period until the bodies next convene is referred to as an "intersession recess" (*See* Chapter 8.C.).

The Speaker is authorized to declare recesses in the House. Often recesses are declared in the House "at the call of the chair."

The Senate frequently recesses at the end of the day. The House adjourns at the end of the day.

Whether the Senate recesses or adjourns at the end of the day determines, for example, "legislative days" and "calendar days." (*See* Chapter 5.K.) A calendar day for the purposes of the Senate is understood to be a twenty-four-hour period. However, a legislative day ends when the Senate adjourns.

The Senate majority leader sometimes chooses to recess in order to avoid triggering a number of burdensome requirements (*see* Chapter 8.J.) that the Senate Rules (Rules V, VII, and XIV) require at the outset of a new legislative day. When the majority leader wishes the Senate to adjourn, he typically seeks unanimous consent to waive these requirements for the next legislative day.

If the majority leader is unable to obtain the necessary unanimous consent, he may simply choose to recess the Senate. Therefore, a legislative day may continue for days or weeks.

Senator Robert Byrd (D-WV), when he served as majority leader, made it a frequent practice to recess rather than adjourn. In 1980, Senator Byrd repeatedly recessed the Senate, keeping it in one long legislative day from January 3 to June 12. During the Senate's deliberations on June 12, Senator Byrd asked unanimous consent that the Senate adjourn for two seconds, thus ending the legislative day. After the adjournment, the Senate immediately reconvened and at the end of the calendar day, Senator Byrd once again recessed the Senate.

The two-second adjournment was necessitated by the implications of adjournments and recess. Majority Leader Byrd was trying to have the Senate proceed to the Legal Services Corporation bill. He attempted to do so by unanimous consent. However, Senator James McClure (R-ID) objected. The next step for the majority leader would be to move that the Senate proceed to the matter. However, Senate Rules require that any bill placed on the calendar lay over for one *legislative* day. Because the Senate had been recessing since the first day of session for the year, January 3, the Senate was still in the *same* legislative day. Therefore, to turn the page on the calendar in order to make the Legal Services Corporation bill eligible to be proceeded to, Senator Byrd needed to adjourn, thus the two-second adjournment. The added advantage was that under Senate Rule VIII, "All motions made during the first two hours of a new legislative day to proceed to the consideration of any matter shall be determined without debate." Therefore, the possibility of a filibuster on the motion to proceed to the bill was foreclosed, and the motion to proceed would be adopted provided the majority leader had the support of at least a simple majority of senators. At the end of that session later in the (calendar) day, he once again recessed the Senate.

It should be noted that the Constitution provides in Article I, Section 5 that "Neither House, during the session of Congress, shall, without the consent of the other, adjourn for more than three days … ." This provision is sometimes used by one chamber or the other to gain leverage over the other. One example already mentioned (*see* Chapter 8.C.), is the use of this constitutional requirement by the House, if controlled by the opposition party, even if the Senate is not, to deny permission for the Senate to recess or adjourn for more than three days. This prevents recess appointments by the president. There are also times when one chamber or the other threatens to adjourn in order to leave the other chamber with a "take-it-or-leave-it" proposition on passing a particular version of a bill. (*See* Chapter 5.C., Recess Appointments.)

》》》 *See also* related CRS Reports and links on **TCNCPAM.com.**

K. Senate Morning Business

When the Senate adjourns, upon reconvening, under the rules, a number of requirements arise (*see* Chapter 8.J.) on the new legislative day. The first two hours at the outset of a new legislative day are called the "morning hour." (Rule VII.)

The term morning hour is often confused, even by some senators, with "morning business." Morning business is a period *within* the morning hour intended to be used to conduct a number of routine tasks, such as introducing bills and resolutions, receiving presidential messages and messages from the House, filing committee reports, and other actions.

In order to keep the Senate operating smoothly and to avoid time-consuming routine actions at the outset of each new legislative day, the majority leader or his designee will seek unanimous consent at some earlier time to dispose of some of the requirements and to move others to a more convenient time. For example, the majority leader may say:

"I ask unanimous consent that when the Senate completes its business today, it adjourn until the hour of 10 a.m. on Friday, [date]. I further ask unanimous consent that on Friday, immediately following the prayer, the Journal of proceedings be approved to date, the morning hour be deemed expired, the time for the two leaders be reserved for their use later in the day, and the Senate then begin a period for morning business, with Senators permitted to speak for up to five minutes each."

Such unanimous consent agreements have become a common part of each session and the resultant "period of morning business" is thought of as a block of time during the Senate day when senators may go to the floor and speak briefly on any matter they choose. Sometimes unanimous consent is sought for a senator to consume a longer block of time in morning business. In recent years, both parties have on occasion organized members of their caucus to come to the floor together or in sequence to speak on a particular subject they want to highlight. Therefore, while morning business has become a common term in the Senate parlance, the "morning hour" is more arcane.

》》》 *See also* related CRS Reports and links on **TCNCPAM.com**.

L. House Special Orders

Somewhat like morning business speeches in the Senate, members of the House are usually able to make speeches, known as "special orders," at the end of the day after the House has completed all legislative business. Members reserve special orders in advance through their party's leadership. Because the House Rules limit debate in both the House of Representatives and the Committee of the Whole House, special orders play an even more important role in that chamber than do morning business speeches in the Senate. Special orders provide a rare opportunity for House members to speak on nongermane subjects and sometimes at length, with a sixty-minute limit. Most special order speeches are less than five minutes.

Both morning business in the Senate and special orders in the House have gained in importance since the onset of television coverage by C-SPAN. Television coverage of the House began in 1979 and of the Senate in 1986.

Special orders have evolved as a unanimous consent practice of the House. Recognition for special orders is the prerogative of the Speaker.

House Rules place the broadcast of proceedings under the exclusive control of the Speaker (House Rule V: Broadcasting the House). Interestingly, today both the House and Senate prohibit cameras from panning the floor to avoid showing the chambers empty or senators or House members appearing inattentive.

》》 *See also* related CRS Reports and links on **TCNCPAM.com**.

M. Rulings and Appeals of Rulings of the Chair

An important feature of the Senate is that when the presiding officer rules on a point of order that has been raised or when an appeal of that ruling is successful a new precedent is established. These precedents have the full force and effect of a Senate rule.

Senate Rule XX states that a "question of order may be raised at any stage of the proceedings, except when the Senate is voting or ascertaining the presence of a quorum, and, unless submitted to the Senate, shall be decided by the Presiding Officer without debate, subject to an appeal to the Senate."

Rulings on these matters invariably follow the advice of the Senate parliamentarian, a professional, nonpartisan official.

A prominent example was the ruling by the chair against the so-called "nuclear option." (*See* Chapter 5.I.) The nuclear option was an unprecedented interpretation of the language of Senate Rule XXII resulting from two points of order, first made in 2013 by Majority Leader Harry Reid (D-NV), and the second made in 2017 by Majority Leader Mitch McConnell (R-KY). The Senate parliamentarian appropriately in each case advised the presiding officer to rule that the point of order was "not well taken." In each case, the presiding officer accepted the parliamentarian's recommendation and ruled against the majority leader's point of order. The ruling in each case was appealed by the majority leader and their majority answered the question, "Shall the decision of the Chair stand as the judgment of the Senate?" in the negative. The overturning of these rulings thus established new precedents in the Senate regarding filibusters on nominations by the president (*see* Chapter 5.I. and Chapter 8.B.).

The Senate decided that the meaning of the words "three-fifths of the senators duly chosen and sworn" in Senate Rule XXII is "a simple majority."

>>> *See also* related CRS Reports and links on **TCNCPAM.com**.

N. Expelling a Member or Denying a Seat to a Member-Elect

Article I, Section 5 of the Constitution states: "Each House shall be the Judge of the Elections, Returns and Qualifications of its own Members ... ." Under this provision, the Senate may decline to seat a senator-elect and the House may refuse to seat a representative-elect by a simple majority vote.

This step may be taken if the chamber finds that the member-elect fails to meet the qualifications for office in that body set out in the Constitution, age (twenty-five for the House and thirty for the Senate), U.S. citizenship (seven years for the House, nine years for the Senate), and residence in the state from which he or she is elected. Each chamber may also find defects in the election itself that may lead to the denial of that seat to the member-elect.

This constitutional right to exclude a member-elect was narrowly defined by the Supreme Court in 1969, in *Powell v. McCormack*, 395 U.S. 486 (1969). The case arose in 1967, when the House voted 307 to 116 to exclude Congressman Adam Clayton Powell (D-NY) from being seated in the 90th Congress. The House found that Powell had engaged in deceptive and possibly illegal actions surrounding his prior service as chair of the House Committee on Education and Labor in a preceding Congress.

The 7-to-1 decision in *Powell v. McCormack* held that the House could not exclude a duly elected member unless he failed to meet the constitutional requirements of age, citizenship, or residence. Chief Justice Earl Warren wrote for the Court, "Congress is limited to the standing qualifications described in the Constitution."

Prior to the *Powell* case many constitutional scholars and numerous members of Congress over its history believed that the right to deny a seat extended to "qualifications" more broadly defined to include such considerations as violations of law and moral fitness to serve in the body.

Article I, Section 5 also states: "Each house may… punish its Members for disorderly behavior, and, with the concurrence of two-thirds, expel a Member." Each chamber may execute these disciplinary powers without the concurrence of the other chamber and has wide authority regarding the grounds and procedure for expelling a member. Other punishments short of expulsion, such as censure or reprimand, may also be imposed by the body.

The grounds for expulsion are much broader than exclusion. As a practical matter, either body may choose whatever grounds it deems appropriate to expel a member by a two-thirds vote. For example, the House may expel a Member for "conduct reflecting discredit on the House."

Although the power to expel is robust, it has been employed rarely. Lesser punishments have been somewhat more common, at least in the House. Since 1789 the Senate has censured nine senators, the most prominent one Joseph McCarthy (R-WI) in 1954. The most recent censures were Thomas J. Dodd (D-CT) in 1967, Herman E. Talmadge (D-GA) in 1979, and David F. Durenberger (R-MN) in 1990. Twenty-three Members of the House have been censured (the most recent Charles B. Rangel (D-NY) in 2010) and another ten reprimanded.

The Senate in its history has only expelled fifteen senators. Fourteen of those were for treason or supporting the rebellion during the Civil War. No senator has been expelled since 1862. Only five Members of the House have been expelled, the first three for disloyalty during the Civil War. More recently, Congressman Michael Myers (D-PA) was expelled in 1980 after conviction for bribery in the FBI's sting operation known as ABSCAM. In 2002, Congressman James Traficant (D-OH) was expelled after conviction for bribery and obstruction of justice.

In more recent times, when the likelihood of expulsion seemed imminent, senators have resigned rather than suffering expulsion. Senator Robert Packwood (R-OR) in 1995, accused of sexual harassment by twenty women, resigned when it became clear that expulsion was certain. New Jersey Senator Harrison Williams (D-NJ), also caught in the FBI's ABSCAM sting operation, was convicted of bribery and conspiracy. He was the first senator convicted of a crime since 1906. He did not resign until eight days after the floor debate in the Senate had begun on the resolution to expel him. When expulsion seemed a certainty, he stepped down.

These issues of exclusion and expulsion and the differences in grounds and how they might be employed arose prominently in the public debate in 2017, when a candidate for the Senate in Alabama, Roy Moore, was accused of sexual misconduct by nine women, including a girl who was fourteen years old at the time. Moore was defeated in a special election. However, Majority Leader Mitch McConnell (R-KY) made clear the intention to seek expulsion from the Senate if Moore was elected.

An issue widely discussed with respect to this case is whether the Senate and its Ethics Committee would have jurisdiction over an incident that occurred before a member took office. This question arose in 2007 in the case of Senator David Vitter (R-LA) who admitted to having committed a "very serious sin" when his solicitation of prostitutes came to light. The occurrences happened prior to the senator's election to the Senate. The Senate Ethics Committee dismissed the case on the grounds that the behavior had occurred prior to Vitter's election, did not involve criminal charges or involve improper use of his public office. The committee did state, however, that "… based upon these specific grounds, the committee has determined that it should *not further exercise its jurisdiction over this matter at this time.*" (Emphasis added). This appears to at least leave open the question of whether the Vitter precedent would preclude future Ethics Committee investigations into cases in which the alleged offense occurred prior to election.

The powers of exclusion and expulsion given to each chamber are the only ways that a representative or a senator may be removed from or denied office. For example, there is no provision for recall of federally elected officials by the electorate or by state legislatures. Even the judiciary is not given the constitutional power to remove a member of Congress. The very first federal officer impeached by the House of Representatives was Senator William Blount, in 1797. However, the Senate declined to accept that he could be impeached, and voted to expel him on its own authority.

⟩⟩⟩ *See also* related CRS Reports and links on **TCNCPAM.com**.

O. Presidential Election

There are no special elections for the presidency. Presidential elections occur every four years. Congress has an important role to play in the selection of the president and vice president.

Article II, Section 1 of the Constitution, as modified by the Twelfth Amendment, establishes Congress's role in the Electoral College system. Under these constitutional provisions and federal law, Congress, in joint session on January 6 (or another date set by Congress) following a presidential election, receives and counts electoral ballots, and the election of the president and vice president is announced. Congress is empowered to resolve objections regarding the electoral ballots at that time.

In order to be elected president or vice president by the Electoral College, a candidate must receive a majority, and not merely a plurality, of the electoral ballots (currently 270 of 538). The Twelfth Amendment, as modified by the Twentieth Amendment, provides the procedures to be followed in the event that no candidate for president or vice president attains a majority of the electoral ballots. In the case of the president, the House of Representatives chooses the president from among the three candidates with the largest numbers of electoral ballots; each state delegation casts a single vote. A majority of states is needed for election. In the case of the vice presidential candidate, the Senate must choose between the two candidates with the largest number of electoral ballots; each senator has one vote, and a majority of votes is needed for election.

These provisions could lead to a strange outcome. For example, for much of the spring and summer of 1992 in the presidential election campaign, polls showed incumbent President George H.W. Bush and Independent challenger Ross Perot trading the lead. Democrat Bill Clinton, for most of that period, was polling as a distant third. (Clinton was elected president in November 1992.) If the election had turned out the way it looked in June with Bush and Perot in the mid-thirties and Clinton mired in the mid-twenties, there would very likely be no candidate with a majority. The presidential election would have been determined in the House of Representatives from among the three highest electoral vote-getters, Bush, Perot, and Clinton. If the Democratic House nonetheless elected Clinton, the Democratic candidate, Clinton's vice presidential running mate, Al Gore, would not have been available since he would have been the third-place candidate; the Senate would have been required to select either Republican Dan Quayle or the Independent candidate, Perot's running mate, Admiral James Stockwell, to serve as Clinton's vice president.

》》 *See also* related CRS Reports and links on **TCNCPAM.com**.

P. Presidential Succession

Article II, Section 1 of the Constitution, modified by the Twenty-fifth Amendment, specifies that the "vice president shall become president" upon the president's death, resignation or removal from office. This has occurred eight times in American history. It is left to Congress, however, to determine the order of succession to the presidency should both the president and vice president be dead or removed from office.

The Twenty-fifth Amendment also provides for the filling of a vacancy in the vice presidency (*see* Chapter 8.H.). Prior to the ratification of the Twenty-fifth Amendment, although seven vice presidents had died in office and one resigned, leaving a vacancy, there was no provision for filling the office. The nation had been fortunate that although it has been without a vice president in office for a total of nearly thirty-eight years in our history, no president died or resigned during those periods. After President Kennedy's assassination in 1963, Lyndon Johnson became president, leaving the office of vice president vacant for more than a year. This spurred the Congress to address the situation. The Twenty-fifth Amendment was passed by Congress in 1965 and ratified by the states in 1967. The Twenty-fifth Amendment also establishes procedures should the president become incapacitated (*see* Chapter 1.B. and Chapter 8.H.).

The current Presidential Succession Act, 3 U.S.C. § 19, provides that the Speaker of the House of Representatives, the president *pro tempore* of the Senate, and duly-confirmed cabinet officers, in order of the creation of their departments, would be eligible to act as president. This is the third iteration of succession laws. The first was passed by the Second Congress, the Succession Act of 1792, which provided for the president *pro tempore* of the Senate and the Speaker of the House of Representatives, in that order, to assume the presidency. This first succession law also provided for a special election for the presidency. No such special election has ever occurred in U.S. history.

The Presidential Succession Act of 1886 was enacted in reaction to the death of President James Garfield during a period when there was neither a president *pro tempore* nor a Speaker of the House in place. The new law removed the congressional constitutional officers and placed the cabinet officers in the line of succession after the vice president.

The Presidential Succession Act of 1947, the present law, returned the constitutional officers to the line of succession although in the reverse order with the Speaker of the House of Representatives first. The cabinet officers then follow beginning with the Secretary of State. The Act has a little noticed provision, called "bumping rights," that provide if a cabinet officer is serving as acting president, that individual can be replaced at any time by the Speaker or the president *pro tempore*.

》》》 *See also* related CRS Reports and links on **TCNCPAM.com**.

Q. The Courts

The Constitution created the Supreme Court, the highest court in the land, but left it to Congress to establish by law whatever additional lower courts it deemed necessary. Article III, Section 1 states: "The judicial Power of the United States, shall be vested in one Supreme Court, and in such inferior courts as the Congress may from time to time ordain and establish."

In addition, Congress by law determines the Supreme Court's budget, the pay of justices and even its jurisdiction (with the exception of original jurisdiction under the Constitution). Congress also determines these factors for lower courts that it has created, including the federal district courts and the circuit courts of appeal. The president appoints judges to these courts, including the Supreme Court, for life, with the advice and consent of the Senate (*see* Chapter 8.B.).

The Constitution left the decision of how many justices sit on the Supreme Court to Congress. Currently, there are nine. Originally, the Judiciary Act of 1789 set the number of justices at six. Eighteen years later, it was raised to seven. The number first reached nine in 1837 and rose to ten in 1863, its largest size in U.S. history.

The current size of the court has been stable (with occasional vacancies) at nine since 1869. President Franklin Roosevelt in 1937 proposed to Congress a court reform bill that would have enlarged the Supreme Court to as many as fifteen. Thought to be motivated by FDR's desire for a Court more friendly to his New Deal legislation, the plan came to be known as "court packing" and was rejected by the Senate, 70 to 22.

In 2016, the size of the Court was again widely discussed. Following the death of Justice Antonin Scalia, during the period of nearly a year in which the Senate majority led by Majority Leader Mitch McConnell (R-KY) refused to consider President Obama's nominee to the Court, the Supreme Court had only eight members. This meant that tie votes were possible and 4-to-4 votes would uphold lower-court decisions, but create no precedent. A number of such ties did occur including a high-profile decision having the effect of blocking President Obama's immigration policy authorized by executive action allowing approximately 5 million undocumented immigrants to stay in the United States legally. Senator Ted Cruz (R-TX) even argued for the possibility of reducing the Court's size by leaving it at eight.

>>> *See also* related CRS Reports and links on **TCNCPAM.com**.

R. Amending the Constitution

We began discussion of congressional procedure, in Chapter 1, with a discussion of the relationship between the Congress and the Constitution. We end it with the procedures for amending the Constitution.

Article V of the Constitution states: "The Congress, whenever two thirds of both Houses shall deem it necessary, shall propose Amendments to this Constitution ... which ... shall be valid to all Intents and Purposes, as Part of this Constitution, when ratified by the Legislatures of three fourths of the several States ... ."

In many ways, Article V is a powerful statement of the expectations for Congress by the framers of the Constitution. It is Congress, the people's branch, ratified by the vote of state legislatures, which is entrusted with the great responsibility of safeguarding the Constitution by holding the keys to its modification. An alternative method of conventions called by the states is also included in Article V, but has never been used. The president and the judicial branch are not involved in the amendment process.

In the years since 1789, the Constitution has been amended twenty-seven times, only seventeen since the Bill of Rights, the first ten amendments, were ratified together in 1791. Seven amendments adopted by Congress and transmitted to the states have failed. Since the Eighteenth Amendment (Prohibition), with one exception (the repeal of Prohibition), joint resolutions proposing constitutional amendments contain a stated time-limit for ratification. Without such a provision, there is no limit to the time elapsed before a sufficient number of states might ratify an amendment. The most recent amendment took more than 202 years. The Twenty-seventh Amendment requiring that changes in congressional salary not take effect until after the next congressional election was one of the twelve amendments originally proposed by James Madison for inclusion in the Bill of Rights. It was adopted in 1789 by the 1st Congress but was not ratified by the requisite number of states until Michigan ratified it in 1992.

The joint resolution proposing the amendment known as the Equal Rights Amendment, passed by Congress in 1972, contained a time limit of seven years. In 1978, the Congress voted to extend the limit until 1982. At the deadline only thirty-five states had ratified, thirty-eight were necessary to meet the three-fourths requirement. Even today, proponents of the amendment have introduced the so-called "three state solution," a joint resolution that would again extend the deadline allowing time for additional states to ratify.

The process laid out in Article V has never changed. All amendments to the Constitution that have been adopted have been proposed by Congress. All but the Twenty-first Amendment, which repealed the Eighteenth Amendment (Prohibition), were ratified by state legislatures. The Twenty-first Amendment was ratified in 1933 by the vote of state conventions of three-fourths of the states.

Constitutional amendments may be proposed by any member of Congress. Constitutional amendments are introduced in the form of a joint resolution, although unlike other joint resolutions, they do not require the president's signature to take effect. A joint resolution may be introduced in the House (H.J. Res.) or Senate (S.J. Res.). Joint resolutions proposing to amend the Constitution are referred to the House and Senate Judiciary Committees.

If reported by the committee to either the House or the Senate, they are considered under ordinary legislative rules. In the Senate, they are subject to amendment and in the House they may also be amended consistent with House rules.

The Constitution requires a vote of two-thirds of members of each house, present and voting, a quorum being present. Should the House and Senate pass differing versions of the amendment, a conference committee would be needed. Adoption of the conference report would require another two-thirds vote in each chamber.

》》 *See also* related CRS Reports and links on **TCNCPAM.com**.

S. Review Questions

》》 How was sequence of cabinet officers in the line of succession to the presidency determined?

》》 What is the procedure if no candidate for the presidency receives a majority of the electoral votes? What is the process if there is no majority for vice president?

》》 Can a member of the Senate be denied a seat on the grounds that he or she is unfit to serve in the Senate? If not, on what basis may the seat be denied?

》》 How many members of the House must vote to impeach a president? What vote is needed in the Senate to convict? Can members of the federal judiciary be impeached by the House and removed from office by the Senate?

》》 Why would a member of the House of Representatives choose to make a special order speech?

》》 Describe the importance of oversight by the Congress.

》》 What is the president's role in amending the Constitution?

》》 What is the effect if a ruling by the presiding officer of the Senate is overturned upon appeal?

》》 What is the importance of the difference between adjourning and recessing in the Senate?

Chapter 9
Conclusion

The founders intended to place Congress at the heart of our national government. Much of this book has focused on and attempted to explain what is commonly called the "regular order," the normal legislative procedures established by the rules and precedents (*see* Chapter 2.N.). That describes the anatomy and physiology of that heart.

The process of lawmaking has been afflicted by constant cycles of procedural tactics deployed by the majority and the response of obstruction and delay by the minority. Both major political parties have exploited their advantages whether in the majority or the minority with the net effect being an erosion of courtesy, comity, and deliberation. What might be called the "irregular order."

Our politics have become more polarized, political parties have become more closely aligned with ideological beliefs, Congressional leadership has centralized and the parties have moved farther and farther apart. Political scientists document the intensification of that polarization over at least the last thirty to forty years, virtually year by year by year.

Many Democrats would date the origins of this divisiveness back to the tactics of Newt Gingrich (R-GA) and the Republican minority in the House in the early 1990s. Republicans point to the strong-arm tactics of the Democratic majority in the House in the 1980s. Whatever the origins, many now believe the Congress is more polarized than at any time since at least Reconstruction and the Civil War itself. This cannot be healthy for a democracy.

This hyper-partisan polarization has set up in the legislative branch a repeating cycle of action and reaction. Procedure, tradition, and precedent are used for short-term partisan gain, and the victim party strikes back with whatever procedural tool is at hand.

The sources of political information in the media, the mass media, the mainstream, cable news, the Internet, blogs, and social media platforms intensify this process, focusing on and often demanding partisan combat and demanding shortcuts in the legislative process.

This book discusses in detail many of these practices that despite the fact that they fall outside of the regular order and distort the rules and precedents, have come to dominate the proceedings of Congress. Recognizing these is crucial to understanding why Congress is struggling to function as intended.

Both parties have, serving as the congressional majority and as the minority, sought to "weaponize" procedure. A sharp increase in the use of the filibuster by minorities in the Senate (*see* Chapter 5.H.), the use of the nuclear option to advantage the majority (*see* Chapter 5.I.), the exploitation of the thirty hours permitted post-cloture to frustrate the majority's agenda (*see* Chapter 5.H.), increasing numbers of holds to slow progress in the Senate (*see* Chapter 5.D.), the repeated use of reconciliation to avoid the Senate rules (*see* Chapter 7.D.), the filling of the amendment tree by majority leaders in the Senate to block minority amendments (*see* Chapter 5.K.), the use of closed rules in the House to freeze out minority input on legislation (*see* Chapter 4.D.), the bringing of legislation directly to the House and Senate floors, often without committee action (*see* Chapter 2.M.), fewer conference committees and the use of informal negotiations to circumvent the minority party (*see* Chapter 6.D.), and the near-collapse of the appropriations process (*see* Chapter 7.H.) under the weight of partisan warfare is to mention only a few.

We have repeatedly seen a preference for expediency in the service of partisan advantage, exacerbated by a decline in civility and the near-constant vilification of the opposition.

The founders, in Article I, Section 5, empowered the Congress, each chamber, to write its own rules. This was a fundamental protection of the independence of the legislative branch in the system of checks and balances.

Those rules and the procedures they frame, the regular order of the Congress, continue to protect that independence and are crucial to the stability and resilience of the House and Senate in their protection of American freedoms and the rule of law. In *Malinski v. New York*, 324 U.S. 401, 414 (1945), Supreme Court Justice Felix Frankfurter wrote, "The history of American freedom is, in no small measure, the history of procedure."

Democracy is something more than majority rule. It also involves protection of the rights of the minority. Our democratic process operates on the assumption that both parties will come to the table and negotiate in good faith. Congress must negotiate, moderate, and compromise, in other words, "legislate."

Although the root of the problem is excessive partisanship, the abuse of procedure is not itself a partisan issue. It's worth reminding ourselves of Nelson Mandela's admonition, "Where you stand depends on where you sit."

Glossary

(See also **CongressionalGlossary.com**)

References are to chapter and section number (e.g., 3.F. refers to section F. in chapter 3).

Account: Control and reporting unit for budgeting and accounting.

Act: Legislation that has passed both chambers of Congress and signed by the president or passed over his veto, thus becoming law. Also, parliamentary term for a measure that has been passed by one chamber and engrossed. (*See* bills; laws)

Adjourn: Formal motion to end a day's session of a chamber of Congress. (5.L., 8.J.)

Adjourn for More than Three Days: The Constitution, Article I, Section 5, provides that neither chamber may adjourn for more than three days without the approval of the other. Both chambers are required to pass a concurrent resolution. (2.G.)

Adjourn *Sine Die*: Final adjournment of a session of Congress. (2.G., 8.J.)

Adjourn to a Day or Time Certain: Adjournment that fixes the next day and time of meeting for one or both chambers. (8.J.)

Adoption (Adopted): Usual parliamentary term for approval of conference report. (1.C., 1.H., 2.G., 2.H., 3.B., 3.F., 3.H., 4.A., 4.C., 4.G., 5.E., 5.F., 5.J., 7.C., 8.D.)

Advice and Consent: Constitutional role (Article II, Section 2) given to the Senate to confirm nominations (executive branch and judicial) by simple majority and treaties by a two-thirds vote. (8.D., 8.Q.)

Agreed To: Usual parliamentary term for approval of motions, amendments, and simple and concurrent resolutions. (1.C., 3.B., 3.G., 5.D., 5.N., 6.C., 7.B.)

Amendment: Proposal of a member of Congress to alter the text of a measure. (1.G., 3.F., 3.G., 4.D., 4.H., 4.K., 5.I., 5.J., 5.K., 6.B., 6.C., 6.D., 7.B., 7.C., 8.D., 8.R., 9)

Amendment in the Nature of a Substitute: Amendment that seeks to replace the entire text of the underlying measure. The adoption of such an amendment usually precludes any further amendment to that measure. (3.G.)

Amendment Tree: Diagram showing the number and types of amendments to a measure permitted by the chamber. It also shows the relationship among the amendments, their degree or type, and the order in which they may be offered and the order in which they are voted on. *See also* Filling the Amendment Tree. (4.H., 5.J., 5.K., 9)

Amendment Tree (Filling of): Procedure used by the Senate majority leader to offer enough amendments to preclude other senators from offering amendments. This is a tactic sometimes used to exclude amendments by the minority.

Amendments between the Houses: Method for reconciling differences between the two chambers' versions of a measure by passing the measure back and forth between them until both have agreed to identical language; sometimes referred to in the media as the "ping-pong" approach to reconciling differences in legislation. *Contrast to* Conference Committee. (6.B., 6.C.)

Amendments in Disagreement: Provisions in dispute between the two chambers.

Amendments in Technical Disagreement: Amendments agreed to in a conference but not included in the conference report because they may violate the rules of one of the chambers and would open the conference report to a point of order.

Appeal: Member's challenge to a ruling made by the presiding officer or a committee chair. In the Senate, on a point of order, any senator may appeal the ruling made by the presiding officer. (8.B., 8.M.)

Appropriated Entitlement: An entitlement for which budget authority is provided in annual appropriations acts. (7.K.)

Appropriation: Provision of law providing budget authority that permits federal agencies to incur obligations and make payments out of the Treasury. *See* Budget Authority. (7.H.)

Appropriations Bill: Bill that, if enacted as law, gives legal authority to spend or obligate money from the Treasury. *See* Budget Authority. (1.B., 2.N., 3.B., 7.G., 7.H., 7.J., 7.K.)

Authorization: Provision in law that establishes or continues a program or agency and authorizes appropriations for it. (7.A., 7.G.)

Baseline: Projection of future revenues, budget authority, outlays, and other budget amounts under assumed economic conditions and participation rates without a change in current policy.

"Bigger Bite" Amendment: Although an amendment cannot amend previously amended language under House rules, a "bigger bite" amendment can be offered because it changes more of the measure or amendment than the original amendment. (5.J.)

Bill: Measure that becomes law when passed in identical form by both chambers and signed by the president or passed over his veto. Designated as H.R. or S. *See also* Joint Resolution. (2.E.)

Blue-Slip Resolution: House resolution ordering the return to the Senate of a Senate bill or amendment that the House believes violates the constitutional prerogative of the House to originate revenue measures. (1.B., 7.H.)

Blue-Slip (Senate): Informal process imposed by chairs of the Senate Judiciary Committee to access the approval or disapproval by home-state senators of judicial nominees from their states. Different chairs have given differing weight to a blue slip disapproving of a nominee.

Borrowing Authority: Spending authority that permits a federal agency to incur obligations and to make payments for specified purposes out of funds borrowed from the Treasury or the public.

Budget Authority: Authority in law to enter into obligations that normally result in outlays. (7.C.)

Budget Resolution: Concurrent resolution incorporating an agreement by the House and Senate on an overall budget plan; may contain reconciliation instructions. (4.E., 4.K., 5.N., 7.B., 7.C., 7.D.)

By Request: A designation on a measure that appears next to the sponsor's name and indicates that a member has introduced the measure on behalf of the president, an executive agency, or a private individual or organization. (2.B.)

Byrd Rule: Bars the inclusion of extraneous matter in a reconciliation measure considered in the Senate. (7.E.)

Calendar: Printed listing of matters eligible for consideration. House has four calendars. They are the Union Calendar, the House Calendar, the Private Calendar, and the Discharge Calendar. In the Senate, there are two calendars. Bills and resolutions are placed on the Calendar of Business (often referred to simply as the Senate calendar) and treaties, nominations, and related measures are placed on the Executive Calendar. (4.E., 5.L., 8.J.)

Chairman's Mark/Staff Draft/Committee Print: Recommendation by committee (or subcommittee) chair of the measure to be considered in a markup, usually drafted as a bill. (3.E.)

Christmas-Tree Bill: Jargon for a bill containing many amendments (*see* Rider) unrelated to the bill's subjects; frequently an appropriations bill.

Clean Bill: New measure reported by a House committee incorporating all changes made in markup. Measure, with new number, is introduced by the chair and referred to the committee, which then reports that measure. (3.G.)

Closed Rule: Permits general debate for a specified period of time but generally permits no amendments. (4.D., 9)

Cloture: Process by which a filibuster can be ended in the Senate. *See also* Post-Cloture Debate. (1.C., 5.C., 5.E., 5.H.)

Cluster Voting: Allowance for sequential recorded votes on a series of measures or amendments that the House finished debating at an earlier time or on a previous date. The Speaker may reduce the minimum time for the second and subsequent votes in a series of five minutes each. The chair of the Committee of the Whole may reduce the minimum time for the second and subsequent votes in a series to two minutes each.

Colloquy: Discussion between members during floor proceedings, generally to put on the record a mutual understanding about the intent of a provision or amendment. The discussion is usually scripted in advance.

Committee of the Whole: The House in a different parliamentary form. Committee consisting of all members of the House, where measures are considered for amendment. The quorum is one hundred. Members are generally permitted to speak for five minutes. A chair presides in lieu of the Speaker. (2.J., 4.E., 4.G., 4.K.)

Committee Report: Document accompanying a measure reported from a committee. It contains an explanation of the provisions of the measure, arguments for its approval, and other information. (3.G., 3.H.)

Companion Bills: Identical or similar bills introduced in both chambers.

Concur: Agree to an amendment of the other chamber, either as is or with an amendment.

Concurrent Resolution: Used to express the sentiment of both chambers on some matter without making law, or to carry out the administrative business of both chambers. A concurrent resolution does not require presidential approval or become law, but requires passage in identical form by both chambers to take effect between them. Designated as H. Con. Res. or S. Con. Res. (6.C.)

Conferees: Representatives from each chamber who serve on a conference committee; also referred to as managers. (6.D., 6.E.)

Conference Committee: Temporary joint committee created to resolve differences between the chambers on a measure. *Contrast to* Amendment between the Houses. (1.F., 6.B.–6.D., 8.Q., 9)

Conference Report: Document containing a conference committee's agreements and signed by a majority of conferees from each chamber. *See also* Joint Explanatory Statement of Managers. (6.B., 6.E.)

Continuing Appropriations Act: An appropriations act that provides stop-gap funding for agencies that have not received regular appropriations. (Also referred to as a continuing resolution (CR).) (2.N., 7.H.)

Cordon Rule: Senate rule that requires a committee report to show changes the reported measure would make in current law.

Cost Estimate: An estimate of the impact of legislation on revenues, spending, or both, generally as reported by a House or Senate committee or a conference committee; the 1974 Congressional Budget Act requires the Congressional Budget Office to prepare cost estimates on all public bills.

Credit Authority: Authority to incur direct loan obligations or make loan guarantee commitments.

Custody of the Papers: Custody of the engrossed measure and other documents that the two chambers produce as they try to reconcile differences in their versions of a measure. *See* Papers.

Deferral: Action or inaction that temporarily withholds, delays, or effectively precludes the obligation or expenditure of budget authority. (7.O.)

Deficit: Excess of outlays over revenues. (7.B., 7.C., 7.F.)

Degrees of Amendment: Designations that indicate the relationship of an amendment to the text of a measure and of one amendment to another. Amendments are permitted only in two degrees. *See* Amendment Tree. (3.F.)

Direct Spending: Spending controlled outside of annual appropriations acts, and specifically including the Food Stamp (now SNAP) program; also referred to as mandatory spending. *See also* Entitlement Program; *contrast to* Discretionary Spending. (7.D.)

Disagree: To reject an amendment of the other chamber. (6.D.)

Discharge Calendar: A calendar in the House that lists motions to discharge committees that have received 218 signatures. (4.B., 4.E.)

Discharge Petition: Procedure to remove a measure from a committee to which it was referred, to make it available for floor consideration. (3.G.)

Discretionary Spending: Spending provided in, and controlled by, annual appropriations acts. *Contrast to* Direct Spending. (7.F., 7.H., 7.K.)

Division Vote: A vote in which the committee chair or House presiding officer counts those members in favor and those in opposition to a proposition with no record made of how each voted. The chair can either ask for a show of hands or ask members to stand. (4.I., 5.N.)

Earmark: For expenditures, an amount set aside within an appropriations account for a specified purpose, sometimes referred to as "member-directed spending." Some also consider targeted tax provisions intended to affect an individual or small group or specific corporation as earmarks. Also, some view specific projects or programs included in the president's budget request as earmarks. (7.K.)

Electronic Vote: A vote in the House using electronic voting machines. Members insert voting cards into one of the devices located throughout the House chamber. (4.I.)

En Bloc Amendment: Several amendments, affecting more than one place in a measure, offered as a group after obtaining unanimous consent. (8.B.)

Enacting Clause: Phrase at the beginning of a bill that gives it legal force when enacted: "Be it enacted by the Senate and House of Representatives of the United States of America in Congress assembled. . . ."

Engrossed Measure: Official copy of a measure as passed by one chamber, including the text as amended by floor action. Measure is certified by the clerk of the House or the secretary of the Senate. (5.N., 6.B.)

Enrolled Measure: Final official copy of a measure as passed in identical form by both chambers and then printed on parchment. Measure is certified by the chamber of origin and signed by the Speaker of the House and the president *pro tempore* of the Senate before it is sent to the president. (6.E.)

Entitlement Program: Federal program that guarantees specific benefits to individuals, businesses, or units of government that meet eligibility requirements. (7.G.)

Executive Document: A document, usually a treaty, sent by the president to the Senate for its consideration and approval.

Executive Session: Meeting of the Senate devoted to the consideration of treaties or nominations. Also a term used to describe a chamber or committee session closed to the public. (8.B.)

Expenditures: Often a synonym for outlays; a general term to mean spending. (7.C., 7.K.)

Fast-Track Procedures: Procedures that circumvent or speed up all or part of the legislative process. Some rule-making statutes prescribe expedited procedures for certain measures, such as trade agreements. (3.A., 7.A., 7.L., 7.N.)

Federal Funds: All monies collected and spent by the federal government other than those designated as trust funds. (7.J.)

Filibuster: Tactic in the Senate to delay or defeat a measure by unlimited debate and other means. *See* Cloture. (5.H.)

Filling the Amendment Tree: A procedure used generally by majority leaders in the Senate to offer amendments in sequence intended to be pending simultaneously in order to preclude the offering of additional amendments. Used as a tactic to preclude or restrict minority amendments. *See also* Amendment Tree. (5.K.)

First-Degree Amendment: Amendment offered to the text of a measure or a substitute offered to a first-degree amendment. (4.H., 5.J.)

First Reading: Required reading of a bill or joint resolution to a chamber by title after its introduction. (2.M.)

Fiscal Year: The period from October 1 through September 30; fiscal year 2019 began October 1, 2018, and ended September 30, 2019. (7.C.)

Five-Minute Rule: House limit of debate on an amendment offered in the Committee of the Whole to five minutes for its sponsor and five minutes for an opponent. In practice, the Committee of the Whole permits the offering of pro forma amendments, each pro forma amendment allowing five more minutes of debate on an amendment. *See* Pro Forma Amendment. (3.D., 3.F.)

Floor Manager: Member steering legislation through floor debate and the amendment process, usually a committee or subcommittee chair or ranking minority member. (2.J., 5.F., 6.C.)

General Debate: Term for period of time at the beginning of proceedings in the Committee of the Whole to debate a measure. The time is generally divided equally between majority and minority floor managers. (4.D., 5.E.)

Germaneness: Rule in the House requiring that debate and amendments pertain to the same subject as the bill or amendment under consideration. In the Senate, germaneness is not generally required. (3.F., 4.H., 5.H., 5.J.)

Hastert Rule: Informal rule imposed by Republican Speakers requiring support by "a majority of the majority" before bringing a bill to the House floor for a vote. (4.A.)

Hearing: A formal committee session in which oral testimony (and written testimony, for the record) from witnesses is collected and questioning of witnesses by members of Congress occurs. (3.D., 3.E., 3.F., 3.G.)

Hereby Rule: *See* Self-Executing Rule. (4.I.)

Hold: Senator's request to party leadership to delay or withhold floor action on a measure or executive business—understood as a senator's unwillingness to permit action on a measure by unanimous consent. (5.D., 9)

Hopper: Box on the Speaker's dais near the House clerk's desk where members place bills and resolutions to introduce them. (2.J.)

Impoundment: Action or inaction by an executive official that delays or precludes the obligation or expenditure of budget authority. *See* Deferral and Rescission. (7.B., 7.O.)

Insert: Amendment to add new language to a measure or another amendment. (5.K., 5.J.)

Insist: Motion by one chamber to reiterate its previous position during amendments between the chambers. (5.J., 6.D.)

Instruct Conferees: Formal, although not binding, action by one chamber urging its conferees to uphold a particular position in conference. (6.D.)

Intersession Recess: The period between adjournment *sine die* and the reconvening of Congress for the next session, pursuant to a concurrent resolution. *See* Intrasession Recess; *see also* Recess. (8.C., 8.J.)

Intrasession Recess: A period of adjournment pursuant to a concurrent resolution within a session of Congress. *See* Intersession Recess; *see also* Recess. (8.C., 8.J.)

Joint Committee: A committee with membership from both chambers. Joint committees do not have legislative jurisdiction. The Joint Committee on Taxation plays an important role in estimating the budgetary effect of tax legislation. (1.H., 3.B.)

Joint Explanatory Statement of Managers: Statement appended to a conference report explaining the conference agreement and the intent of the conferees. *See also* Conference Report. (6.E.)

Joint Meeting: A ceremonial meeting of both chambers of Congress often to hear addresses from foreign dignitaries. Joint meetings are established by unanimous consent agreements in both chambers. *See also* Joint Session. (2.G.)

Joint Resolution: Similar to a bill, though limited in scope (for example, to change a minor item in existing law). Becomes law when passed in identical form by both chambers and signed by the president. It also is the form of legislation used to consider a constitutional amendment. A constitutional amendment requires a two-thirds vote in each chamber but does not require the president's signature. Designated as H.J. Res. or S.J. Res. *See also* Bill. (2.F.)

Joint Session: A formal session of both chambers of Congress for purposes of hearing an address from the president or to conduct formal business. A joint session requires that both chambers adopt a concurrent resolution establishing the session. *See also* Joint Meeting. (2.G.)

Lame-Duck Session: Session of Congress held after the election for the succeeding Congress. (1.D.)

Law/Public Law/Private Law: Act of Congress signed by the president or passed over his veto. (2.B., 2.C., 2.E.)

Legislative Day: Time a chamber meets after an adjournment until the time it next adjourns. (2.M., 5.L., 8.J.)

Line-Item Veto: A proposed power giving the president the right to veto specific items in an appropriation bill without vetoing the whole measure. (6.G., 7.P.)

Managers: Representatives from a chamber to a conference committee; also called conferees. (6.E., 7.H., 8.G.)

Mandatory Spending: *See* Direct Spending. (7.F.)

Mark: *See* Vehicle.

Markup: Meeting by a committee or subcommittee during which members offer, debate, and vote on amendments to a measure. (3.E., 7.H.)

Minority, Supplemental, and Additional Views: Statements in a committee report presenting individuals' or groups' opinions on the measure.

Modified Closed Rule: Permits general debate for a specified period of time, but limits amendments to those designated in the special rule or the House Rules Committee report accompanying the special rule. May preclude amendments to particular portions of a bill. Also called a structured rule. (4.D.)

Modified Open Rule: Permits general debate for a specified period of time, and allows any member to offer amendments consistent with House rules subject only to an overall time limit on the amendment process and a requirement that amendments be pre-printed in the *Congressional Record*. (4.D.)

Morning Business: In the Senate, routine business transacted at the beginning of the Morning Hour, or by unanimous consent throughout the day. (8.A., 8.K.)

Morning Hour: In the Senate, the first two hours of a session following an adjournment, rather than a recess. (8.K.)

Motion to Instruct: In the process of establishing a conference committee, each house may instruct its conferees to take a particular position. Such instructions are not binding on the conferees. (5.G., 6.D.)

Nomination: Appointment by the president to executive office or judicial office that is subject to Senate confirmation. (8.B.)

Nuclear Option: Parliamentary maneuver to use a point of order and a successful overturning of an appeal to create a precedent for simple majority cloture rather than the three-fifths duly chosen and sworn provided for in Senate Rule XXII. (5.I., 8.A., 8.B., 8.L., 9)

Obligation: Binding agreement by a government agency to pay for goods, products, or services. (7.H., 7.J.)

Official Objectors: House members who screen measures on the Private Calendar. (4.E.)

Official Title: Statement of a measure's subject and purpose, which appears before the enacting clause. *See also* Popular Title.

Omnibus Bill: A measure that combines the provisions related to several disparate subjects into a single measure. Examples include continuing appropriations resolutions that might contain two or more of the twelve annual appropriations bills. (2.N., 7.H.)

Open Rule: Permits general debate for a specified period of time and allows any member to offer an amendment that complies with the standing rules of the House. (4.D.)

Ordered Reported: Committee's formal action of agreeing to report a measure to its chamber.

Original Bill: A measure drafted by a committee and introduced by its chair when the committee reports the measure back to its chamber. It is not referred back to the committee after introduction. (3.G.)

Outlays: Payments to liquidate obligations. (7.C.)

Papers: Documents passed back and forth between the chambers, including the engrossed measure, the amendments, the messages transmitting them, and the conference report. *See also* Custody of the Papers. (6.E.)

Parliamentary Inquiry: Member's question posed on the floor to the presiding officer, or in committee or subcommittee to the chair, about a pending procedural situation.

Pass Over without Prejudice: A request in the House to defer action on a measure called up from the Private Calendar without affecting the measure's position on the calendar. (4.E.)

Passed: Term for approval of bills and joint resolutions. (1.F., 2.A., 2.E., 2.L., 5.J., 5.N., 6.B., 6.D., 6.F.)

PAYGO (Pay-As-You-Go): Process by which direct spending increases or revenue decreases must be offset so that the deficit is not increased or the surplus reduced. A statutory PAYGO requirement was in effect from 1991 through 2002; the House and Senate each have their own PAYGO rules. (7.F.)

Perfecting Amendment: Amendment that alters, but does not completely substitute or replace, language in another amendment. *See* Amendment Tree. (4.H.)

Pocket Veto: Act of the president in withholding approval of a measure after Congress has adjourned. A pocket veto precludes Congress's ability to override the veto. *See* Veto; *see also* Veto Override. (2.E., 6.G.)

Point of Order: Objection to a current proceeding, measure, or amendment because the proposed action violates a rule of the chamber, written precedent, or rule-making statute. (3.F., 4.H., 5.I., 5.K., 6.D., 7.E., 7.M., 8.M.)

Popular Title: The name by which a measure is known. *See also* Official Title.

Post-Cloture Debate: A provision of Senate Rule XXII providing for up to thirty hours' consideration (all activity including debate, votes, and quorum calls) after cloture has been invoked. *See also* Cloture. (5.H., 9)

Postpone: There are two types of motions to postpone: to postpone (indefinitely) kills a proposal, but to postpone to a day certain merely changes the day or time of consideration.

Preamble: Introductory language in a bill preceding the enacting clause. It describes the reasons for and intent of a measure. In a joint resolution, the language appears before the resolving clause. In a concurrent or simple resolution, it appears before the text.

Precedence: Order in which amendments or motions may be offered and acted upon.

Precedent: Previous ruling by a presiding officer that becomes part of the procedures of a chamber. (1.C., 1.G., 2.L., 2.M., 3.F., 4.H., 5.A., 5.B., 5.C., 5.F., 5.H., 5.I., 5.J., 5.K., 5.L., 6.D., 8.A., 8.B., 8.M., 8.N.)

President *pro tempore*: Presiding officer of the Senate in the absence of the vice president, established in the Constitution (Article I, Section 3); usually the majority-party senator with the longest period of continuous service. (1.F., 1.G., 2.E., 2.J., 5.I., 8.G., 8.P.)

Previous Question: Nondebatable House (or House committee) motion, which, when agreed to, cuts off further debate, prevents the offering of additional amendments, and brings the pending matter to an immediate vote. (1.C., 3.F.)

Private Bill: A measure that generally deals with an individual matter, such as a claim against the government, an individual's immigration, or a land title. Private bills are considered in the House via the Private Calendar on the first and third Tuesdays of each month. (2.B., 4.B., 4.E.)

Privilege: Attribute of a motion, measure, report, question, or proposition that gives it priority status for consideration. (4.E., 6.E., 7.H.)

Pro Forma Amendment: Motion whereby a House member secures five minutes to speak on an amendment under debate, without offering a substantive amendment. The member moves to "strike the last word" or "strike the requisite number of words." The motion requires no vote and is deemed automatically withdrawn at the expiration of the five minutes. *See also* Five-Minute Rule. (3.D., 3.F.)

Pro Forma Session: Session of either the House or Senate with little or no business conducted. Pro forma sessions became particularly controversial in the Senate after 2007 when used to prevent the president from making recess appointments. (8.C.)

Proxy Vote: The practice of permitting a member to cast the vote of an absent colleague. Proxy voting is permitted only in Senate committees if committee rules allow them. (3.E.)

Public Debt: Amounts borrowed by the Treasury Department from the public or from another fund or account.

Public Law: Act of Congress that has been signed by the president or passed over his veto. It is designated by the letters *P.L.* and numbers noting the Congress and the numerical sequence in which the measure was signed; for example, P.L. 112-7 was an act of Congress in the 112th Congress and was the seventh measure signed by the president (or passed over his veto) during the 112th Congress.

Queen-of-the-Hill Rule: A special rule that permits votes on a series of amendments, usually complete substitutes for a measure, but directs that the amendment receiving the greatest number of votes is the winning amendment. (4.I.)

Quorum: Minimum number of members required for the transaction of business. (1.C., 1.E., 2.H., 3.E., 3.G., 4.A., 4.F., 4.I., 5.G., 5.H., 5.M., 6.G., 8.B., 8.D., 8.G., 8.M., 8.R.)

Quorum Call: A procedure for determining whether a quorum is present— 218 in the House and 100 in the Committee of the Whole House on the State of the Union; a quorum in the Senate is 51. (2.J., 5.H.)

Ramseyer Rule: House rule that requires a committee report to show changes the reported measure would make in current law.

Ranking Member: The highest-ranking minority member of standing committees. (3.C., 3.D., 8.E.)

Recede: Motion by one chamber to withdraw from its previous position during amendments between the chambers. (6.E.)

Recede and Concur: Motion to withdraw from a position and agree with the other chamber's position.

Recede and Concur with an Amendment: Motion to withdraw from a position and agree, but with a further amendment.

Recess: Temporary interruption or suspension of a committee or chamber meeting. In the House, the Speaker is authorized to declare recesses. In the Senate, the chamber may recess rather than adjourn at the end of the day so as not to trigger a new legislative day. The term is also used to refer to a period in which the House or Senate has adjourned pursuant to a concurrent resolution. *See* Intrasession Recess; *see also* Intersession Recess. (5.L., 8.J.)

Recess Appointment: A temporary presidential appointment, during a recess of the Senate without the advice and consent of the Senate, provided for in Article II, Section 2 of the Constitution. (8.C.)

Recommit: To send a measure back to the committee that reported it. A motion to recommit without instructions kills a measure; a motion to recommit with instructions proposes to amend a measure. In the House, the motion may be offered just before vote on final passage. In the Senate, the motion may be offered at any time before a measure's passage. (4.E., 4.J., 4.K., 6.E.)

Reconciliation: Process by which Congress changes existing laws to conform revenue and spending levels to the limits set in a budget resolution. Limited to twenty hours of debate in the Senate. (7.B., 7.D., 7.E., 9)

Reconciliation Instruction: A provision within a Budget Resolution directing committees to report legislation changing existing law. Such instructions are a precondition to the consideration of a reconciliation bill. (7.D.)

Reconsider: Parliamentary practice that gives a chamber one opportunity to review its action on a motion, amendment, measure, or any other proposition.

Refer: Assignment of a measure to committee. (2.L., 3.G.)

Report/Reported: Formal submission of a measure by a committee to its parent chamber. (3.G.)

Reprogram: Shifting funds from one program to another in the same appropriation account. *Contrast to* Transfer.

Rescission: Cancellation of budget authority previously provided by Congress. (7.O., 7.P.)

Resolution/Simple Resolution: Sentiment of one chamber on an issue, or a measure to carry out the administrative or procedural business of the chamber. Does not become law. Designated as H. Res. or S. Res. (2.H., 3.F., 7.H., 8.D., 8.G.)

Resolution of Inquiry: A simple resolution calling on the president or the head of an executive agency to provide specific information or papers to one or both chambers.

Resolution of Ratification: Senate vehicle for consideration of a treaty. (8.D.)

Resolving Clause: First section of a joint resolution that gives legal force to the measure when enacted: "Resolved by the Senate and House of Representatives of the United States of America in Congress assembled. . . ."

Revenues: Income from individual and corporate income taxes, social insurance taxes, excise taxes, fees, tariffs, and other sources collected under the sovereign powers of the federal government. (4.B., 7.A., 7.C., 7.D., 7.E., 7.F.)

Rider: Colloquialism for an amendment unrelated to the subject matter of the measure to which it was attached. (5.J.)

Rise: In order only in the Committee of the Whole during the amendment stage, it has the effect of terminating or suspending debate on the pending matter. (4.I.)

Rise and Report: Term to refer to the culmination of proceedings in the Committee of the Whole. The Committee of the Whole sends the measure it has been considering back to the House for final disposition. (4.I.)

Roll-Call (Record) Vote: A vote in which members are recorded by name for or against a measure. (5.M.)

Scope of Differences: Limits within which a conference committee is permitted to resolve its disagreement. (6.D.)

Scorekeeping: Process for tracking and reporting on the status of congressional budgetary actions affecting budget authority, revenues, outlays, and the surplus or deficit.

Second: The number of members required to indicate support for an action, such as calling for a vote.

Second-Degree Amendment: An amendment to an amendment. Also called a perfecting amendment. *See* Amendment Tree. (4.H., 5.J.)

Second Reading: Required reading of a bill or joint resolution to a chamber: in the House, in full before floor consideration in the House or Committee of the Whole (usually dispensed with by unanimous consent or special rule); in the Senate, by title only, before referral to a committee. Under Senate Rule XIV, if objection is made to further proceedings on the measure after the second reading, it is placed directly on the calendar. (2.M.)

Self-Executing Rule: If specified, the House's adoption of a special rule may also have the effect of amending or passing the underlying measure. Also called a "hereby" rule. (4.I.)

Seniority System: Preferential treatment given on the basis of length of service in the chamber or on a congressional committee. (3.C.)

Slip Law: First official publication of a law, published in unbound single sheets or pamphlet form.

Special Orders: Speeches in the House that take place after the House has completed its legislative business for the day for periods of up to sixty minutes. (8.A., 8.L.)

Special Rule: A House resolution reported by the Rules Committee that sets the terms for debate, amendment, and votes on a measure. (4.D.)

Stage of Disagreement: Stage at which one chamber formally disagrees with an amendment proposed by the other chamber and insists on its own amendment. A measure generally cannot go to conference until this stage is reached.

Star Print: A reprint of a measure, amendment, or committee report to correct errors in a previous printing. The first page carries a small black star.

Strike: Amendment to delete a portion of a measure or an amendment. (5.K.)

Strike and Insert: Amendment that replaces text in a measure or an amendment. (5.K.)

Strike the Last Word/Strike the Requisite Number of Words: Also called a pro forma amendment. Means of obtaining time to speak on an amendment without actually offering a substantive change. *See* Pro Forma Amendment.

Structured Rule: Another term for a modified closed rule.

Substitute Amendment: Amendment that replaces the entire text of a pending amendment. *See* Amendment Tree. (4.H., 5.J.)

Supplemental Appropriations Act: An appropriations act that provides additional budget authority during the current year when the regular appropriation is insufficient. (7.H.)

Surplus: Excess of revenues over outlays. (7.A., 7.B., 7.C., 7.E.)

Suspension of the Rules: Expeditious procedure for passing noncontroversial measures in the House. Requires a two-thirds vote of those present and voting, after forty minutes of debate, and does not allow floor amendments. (4.F.)

Table/Lay on the Table: Prevents further consideration of a measure, amendment, or motion, thus killing it. (5.H., 5.K., 5.N.)

Tax Expenditure: Loss of revenue attributable to an exemption, deduction, preference, or other exclusion under federal tax law. (7.C., 7.K.)

Teller Vote: A House procedure in which members cast votes by passing through the center aisle of the chamber to be counted. Now used only when the electronic voting system breaks down and for ballot votes.

Third Reading: Required reading of bill or joint resolution to chamber before vote on final passage; usually a pro forma procedural step. (4.K., 5.N.)

Transfer: Shifting funds from one appropriation account to another, as authorized by law. *Contrast to* Reprogram.

Trust Funds: Accounts designated by law as trust funds for receipts and expenditures earmarked for specific purposes.

Unanimous Consent: Refers to the absence of objection by any senator. (1.G., 5.E.)

Unanimous Consent Agreement/Time Limitation Agreement: Device in the Senate to expedite legislation by spelling out the process for considering a proposal. (1.G., 5.E.)

Unprinted Amendment: Senate amendment not printed in the *Congressional Record* before its offering. Unprinted amendments are numbered sequentially through a Congress in the order of their submission.

Vehicle/Legislative Vehicle: Term for legislative measure that is being considered. (2.D., 3.E.)

Veto: Disapproval by the president of a bill or joint resolution (other than a joint resolution proposing a constitutional amendment). *See* Veto Override; *see also* Pocket Veto. (6.G.)

Veto Override: Passage of legislation vetoed by the president may occur by two-thirds recorded voted of each chamber. *See* Veto; *see also* Pocket Veto. (6.G.)

Views and Estimates: Annual report of each House and Senate committee on budgetary matters within its jurisdiction to respective chamber's Budget Committee; submitted in advance of Budget Committees' drafting of a concurrent resolution on the budget.

Voice Vote: A method of voting where members who support a question call out "aye" in unison, after which those opposed answer "no" in unison. The chair decides which position prevails. (4.I., 5.M.)

Waiver Rule: A special rule in the House that waives points of order against a measure or an amendment.

Well: Open space in the front of the House and Senate chambers between members' seats and the podium. Members in the House may speak from lecterns in the well. (2.J.)

Yeas and Nays: A vote in which members respond "aye" or "no" on a question. Their names are called in alphabetical order. (5.M.)

Index

References are to chapter and section number (e.g., 3.F. refers to section F. in chapter 3).

Foley, Tom, 1.F.

Food Stamps (now Supplemental Nutrition Assistance Program (SNAP)), 7.F.

Ford, Gerald, 8.G., 8.H.

Foreign Affairs Committee, House, 3.B., 8.E.

Foreign Relations Authorization Act, 7.G.

Foreign Relations Committee, Senate, 3.B., 3.C., 8.B., 8.D., 8.E.

formal disagreement requiring conference committee to resolve, 6.D.

Fortas, Abe, 8.B.

Frankfurter, Felix, 9

Frumin, Alan, 7.B.

funding, 3.B. *See also* appropriations; budget

G

Garfield, James, 8.P.

Garland, Merrick, 8.B.

general debate, 4.D., 5.E.

Genocide Convention, 8.D.

Gephardt, Richard, 4.I.

Gephardt rule (former House Rule XXVIII), 4.I.

germaneness, 3.F., 4.H., 5.H., 5.J.

Gerry, Elbridge, 1.B.

gerrymandering, 1.E.

Gingrich, Newt, 1.C., 1.F., 3.C., 4.A., 7.P., 9

Goldwater, Barry, 8.G.

Gore, Al, 8.O.

Gorsuch, Neil, 8.B.

Government Accountability Office (GAO) (formerly General Accounting Office), 8.E.

Government Publishing Office, 5.N., 8.B.

government shutdown, 2.N., 4.A., 4.B., 7.I.

GovTrack, 6.F.

Grassley, Chuck, 8.B.

Great Compromise (1787), 1.E.

Gustitus, Linda, 8.E.

H

Hamilton, Alexander: *The Federalist No. 65*, 8.G.

Hastert, Dennis, 4.A., 6.F.

Hastert Rule, 4.A.

Health, Education, Labor, and Pensions Committee, Senate, 3.B.

Health Care and Education Reconciliation Act (2010), 7.E.

hearings in committees, 3.D.
 amendment procedure, 3.F.
 markups, 3.E.
 reporting legislation to floor, 3.G.

Heckler, Margaret, 4.I.

Helms, Jesse, 3.C.

Herbert, A.J., 1.G.

hereby rule (self-executing rule), 4.I.

high crimes and misdemeanors, 8.G.

holds, 5.D., 9

Homeland Security and Governmental Affairs Committee, Senate, 3.B., 8.E.

Homeland Security Committee, House, 3.B.

hopper, 2.J.

hotline, 5.D.

House Calendar, 3.H., 4.B., 4.C.

House Committees. *See specific type of committee*

House of Representatives, 4
 acceptance of Senate bill, 6.B.
 amendments to legislation, 3.F., 4.H.
 clerks, 2.J.
 Constitution and, 1.F.
 debate, 4.G.
 differences with House. *See* resolving differences between chambers
 exclusion/expulsion of members, 8.N.

R

Useful Links

Congress by the Numbers
CongressByTheNumbers.com

Leadership of Congress
CongressLeaders.com

Congressional Schedule
CongressSchedules.com

Congress Seating Charts
CongressSeating.com

Terms and Sessions of Congress
TermsofCongress.com

Senate Classes: Terms of Service
SenateClasses.com

Congressional Glossary
CongressionalGlossary.com

You have 2 cows
YouHave2Cows.com

CPSIA information can be obtained
at www.ICGtesting.com
Printed in the USA
BVHW051934130820
586215BV00004B/59

9 781587 332821